Books by

RICHARD E. FLATHMAN

POLITICAL OBLIGATION   1972
PUBLIC INTEREST   1966

Political
Obligation

STUDIES IN POLITICAL THEORY
Michael Walzer, General Editor

POLITICAL
OBLIGATION

Richard E. Flathman

ATHENEUM

New York

1972

FOR
Nancy, Kristen, Karen, and Jennifer

Acknowledgments

A N AGREEABLE RESULT of writing this book on obligation is that I have acquired and can now discharge the obligations to express my gratitude to the many persons and organizations who have assisted me.

The generosity of the American Philosophical Society and the Committees on Research of the Division of Social Science and of The College of the University of Chicago helped me meet incidental costs connected with the study and made possible a year of study and reflection in England. Coming at the formative stages of the project, that year was valuable not only for the freedom from other duties which it provided but because it made possible conversations concerning obligation and related problems with, among others, Brian Barry, W. H. Greenleaf, H. L. A. Hart, and above all, J. C. Rees.

Throughout the development of the study, colleagues and students at the University of Chicago sustained what must be a uniquely supportive and stimulating intellectual environment. My work has undoubtedly benefited from that environment in many ways that I never recognized or have forgotten, but I must at least thank Leonard Binder, Gerhard

Casper, Harry Kalven, E. W. Kelley, Theodore Lowi, Nancy Hartsock, James Nyman, Frederick Siegler, Herbert Storing, and Aristide Zolberg for their interest and for the ideas and criticisms they contributed. I am particularly indebted to J. David Greenstone and Duncan MacRae, Jr., for many stimulating discussions and for their efforts to improve a long, opaque, and badly organized manuscript.

In their role as editors of the Nomos Series, John C. Chapman and J. Roland Pennock did much to improve a paper on obligations and ideals, and, along with Atherton Press, kindly granted permission to reprint it as Chapter Two of the present book. Michael Walzer read the manuscript for Atheneum Publishers and helped me to clarify my thinking concerning the relationship between consent theories of political obligation and the argument that I try to develop in the following pages. I am also grateful for the searching criticisms provided by anonymous readers of the manuscript, and to Marcella Bryant for her superb work in preparing the manuscript.

My wife Nancy provided not only helpful criticisms of the manuscript at several stages of its development but also the support and encouragement which did much to make writing it a considerable pleasure.

I have quoted short passages from a number of works, and thanks are due to the following persons and publishers for granting permission to do so: *The American Political Science Review* for permission to quote passages from Hanna Pitkin, "Obligation and Consent—II," Vol 60, pp. 39–52 (1966). Basil Blackwell for permission to quote a short passage from Elizabeth Anscombe, *Intention*. Cornell University Press for permission to quote a short passage from Kurt Baier, *The Moral Point of View*. Routledge and Kegan Paul and Humanities Press for permission to quote a short passage from Peter Winch, *The Idea of a Social Science*. Macmillan Company, London and Basingstoke, The Macmillan Company of Canada, and St. Martin's Press, Inc., for permission to quote passages from Ludwig Wittgenstein, *Philosophical Investiga-*

tions and from Friedrich Waismann, *The Principles of Linguistic Philosophy*. Methuen & Co. for permission to quote from P. F. Strawson, *Introduction to Logical Theory*. The Clarendon Press, Oxford, for permission to quote passages from H. L. A. Hart, *The Concept of Law* and a passage from R. M. Hare, *Freedom and Reason*. Oxford University Press of New York for permission to quote a passage from Joseph Tussman, *Obligation and the Body Politic* and short passages from the paperback edition of Alexander Sesonske, *Value and Obligation*. Full references to the quoted passages are provided in the appropriate footnotes.

Portland, Oregon
July 20, 1970

Contents

Introduction

U NDER WHAT CONDITIONS are obedience and disobedience required or justified? To what or to whom is obedience or disobedience owed? What are the differences between authority and power and between legitimate and illegitimate government? What is the relationship between having an obligation and having freedom to act? What are the similarities and differences among political, legal, and moral obligations?

The foregoing are among the questions that arise under the rubric of political obligation. Their importance, both from the standpoint of the practical concerns of the citizen and the theoretical concerns of the political philosopher, requires no demonstration.

These questions have been discussed by most of the great political philosophers of the western tradition. Much can be gained by examining their discussions and we will do so at various junctures in this work. But the concern of the great political philosophers with these questions, and the answers they gave to them, although no doubt heavily influenced by the discussions of thinkers who preceded them, were rooted in features of the political societies in which they lived and of which they knew. Aristotle, Hobbes, and Hegel learned much *about* authority, law, and obedience from Socrates and Plato, but neither they nor Socrates and Plato learned *of* authority, law, and obedience from political philosophers. They believed that their theories were rooted in knowledge and understanding of the institutions, arrangements, and patterns of belief and action that obtained in various forms in the political societies with which they were familiar.

If the tradition of reflection concerning political obligation is to continue, and indeed if we are to know whether earlier reflections are relevant to understanding political obligation as we confront it in our political societies, we must acquire knowledge about and understanding of the arrangements and patterns of action that constitute the phenomenon of political obligation in our societies. In this essay we hope to contribute to this end. One of our primary purposes is to identify and analyze the constellation of concepts, rules, institutions, and arrangements, and the beliefs, judgments, and conventions concerning them, in which and through which political obligations are assigned, explained, discussed, accepted or rejected, and discharged or defaulted upon. We will label this constellation "the practice of political obligation," and we will try to prepare the way to answering the questions listed above by identifying its main features and its relationships to other social and political arrangements, institutions, and practices.[1]

1. Owing primarily to the work of John Rawls, the term "practice" has great currency in contemporary philosophy. Rawls uses it as "a sort of technical term meaning any form of activity specified by a system of rules which defines offices, roles, moves, penalties, defences, and so on, and which gives the activity its structure. As examples one may think of games and rituals, trials, and parliaments" ("Two Concepts of Rules," *Philosophical Review*, Vol. 64 [1955]: 2 n.) As we are using the term, "practice of political obligation" includes these elements. Parliaments and trials are among the institutions that are part of the practice, and the practice also includes the roles of citizen, judge, and legislator. Similarly, we will try to identify the "moves" that are appropriate and inappropriate in reaching and justifying decisions about political obligations. But our use of the term "practice" is broader than Rawls's at least in that our notion of the practice of political obligation includes several practices in his

In Chapter One we will discuss the approach we have employed in exploring the practice, stating the assumptions on which it rests and examining some of the problems that arise in using it. Chapters Two to Seven explore various features and characteristics of the practice and attempt to resolve some of the theoretical problems that are posed by them. In Chapter Eight we attempt to assess the practice in more explicitly normative terms and to advance some criteria for deciding practical questions (such as whether to obey the law or not) that arise for participants in the practice. The purpose of this Introduction is to provide the reader with an overview of the essay by presenting a brief account of the main themes and arguments that are presented in the course of its development.

A central theme of the work is that the practice of political obligation operates only if men *choose* or *decide* to do or refrain from doing certain *actions* because they believe that there are *good reasons* for accepting and obeying or rejecting and disobeying *rules* that require or forbid those actions. This theme or thesis is developed in large part through analysis of the key concepts in its formulation, especially the complex notions "a rule," "following a rule," and "guiding conduct by calling attention to a rule." [2] The fundamentals of the analysis of the latter notions is presented in Chapter Three, but the topic will be under discussion throughout the work.

The significance of this thesis can be seen by putting it in

---

sense of the term. It is probably also broader in that we will be concerned with beliefs, judgments, and commitments to a degree that Rawls is not in the article cited. (But see Rawls's paper "The Sense of Justice," *Philosophical Review* 72 [1963]: 281–305.) In the latter respect our use is probably closer to such ordinary-language expressions as "the practice of medicine" or the "practice of law."

2. Throughout this work we will employ the (American English) convention of marking references to or statements about the use of concepts, as opposed to uses of those concepts (statements in the formal as opposed to the material mode), by putting concepts referred to in double quotation marks. The major exception is where reference to the use of a concept occurs within a sentence or phrase that is in double quotation marks because it is a quotation or to set it apart as a statement of a rule or proposition that is under discussion. In such cases concepts referred to rather than used are placed between single quotation marks.

a larger philosophical perspective and by noting some of the interpretations of political obligation with which it conflicts. The thesis that use of the concepts "decide," "choose," "reason," and "rule" (and we could add "belief," "intention," "purpose," "deliberation," "reflection," and "judgment") is a defining feature of the practice as it now operates indicates that in investigating political obligation we are concerned with what men *do* as opposed to what *happens to them* or what they *undergo* or *suffer*; with actions they take intentionally, to achieve a goal or purpose, for reasons, not with movements they are observed to make as a consequence of the operation of forces over which they have no control. This thesis implies that we can understand the practice only if we concern ourselves with the types of beliefs, reasons, intentions, purposes, judgments, and choices, held, given, framed, and made by men participating in the practice. Stated negatively, our attempt to understand political obligation would be doomed to failure if we dismissed these features of human affairs as epiphenomenal, fictitious, or for some other reason inappropriate objects of social-scientific or philosophic attention. The generic term now most widely used for the realm of human affairs that will concern us is "action" or "human action." There is less consensus concerning how to label that from which human action is distinguished. The generic term we will employ is "behavior," stipulated to refer, roughly, to events and movements that are explainable in terms of the operation of causally sufficient forces, explainable in ways that render irrelevant such concepts as reason, intention, purpose, deliberation, and choice. Thus the thesis that the practice of political obligation involves rules, reasons, and choices is also the thesis that political obligation is in the realm of action, not of behavior.[3]

3. For useful collections of important recent discussions of this distinction see A. R. White, ed., *The Philosophy of Action* (London: Oxford University Press, 1969); Norman S. Care and Charles Landesman, eds., *Readings in the Theory of Action* (Bloomington, Ind.: Indiana University Press, 1968); David Braybrooke, ed., *Philosophical Problems of the Social Sciences* (New York: The Macmillan Co., 1965).

Stating our first themes in terms of the action-behavior distinction points to controversies in social science that will be relevant to our concerns. It is evident that our argument is in conflict with the position that action is fictitious or epiphenomenal, that all there is in human affairs is what we have called behavior. If this position, sometimes called "molecular" behaviorism, were correct, the present essay, and any essay treating political obligation as involving reasons, choices, intentions, and purposes, would necessarily be so superficial as to lack social scientific or philosophic interest. It might even be regarded as an essay about a fiction that "exists" only in a conceptual heaven.[4]

At the most general level the issues raised by molecular behaviorism concern the relationships between language on the one hand and thought and action on the other. We will discuss some of these issues in Chapter One when we try to show that investigating the use of concepts (for example "obligation" and "rule") is a useful way to investigate the practice of political obligation. Moreover, throughout the work we will be concerned to show that leading features of the practice of political obligation, for example, rules, authority, obedience, and disobedience, must be understood in terms of concepts such as intention, reason, purpose, and decision, not in terms of responses to stimuli or drives and instincts—that is, in the concepts characteristic of human action, not of behavior. Much

4. The locus classicus of molecular or radical behaviorism in our time is perhaps the work of B. F. Skinner. See especially his *Science and Human Behavior* (New York: The Macmillan Co., 1953). For a brief but helpful account of molecular behaviorism (as distinct from the "molar" version) see Landesman and Care, op. cit., especially the Introduction and the selection from E. C. Tolman. For extended critical discussions of the many variants of broadly behaviorist positions in social science see for example: R. S. Peters, *The Concept of Motivation* (London: Routledge and Kegan Paul, 1964); Peter Winch, *The Idea of a Social Science* (London: Routledge and Kegan Paul, 1958); Norman Malcolm, *Dreaming* (London: Routledge and Kegan Paul, 1959); A. R. Louch, *Explanation and Human Action* (Oxford: Basil Blackwell, 1966); Charles Taylor, *The Explanation of Behaviour* (London: Routledge and Kegan Paul, 1964); T. R. Mischel, ed., *Human Action* (New York: Academic Press, 1969).

of this discussion will be concerned with difficult-to-classify notions such as habit, trained behavior, and acts done out of fear of punishment or other undesirable consequences.

But we have no desire to deny the existence or importance of what we called behavior. Indeed we will find that regularities in behavior which meet the requirements of rules of obligation (for example behavior that accords with the requirements of law) coexist with and contribute to some of the same objectives as does action taken out of acceptance of rules of obligation and done with the intention of discharging an obligation. Similarly, social and political institutions and arrangements which are intended to bring about such behavioral regularities (for example processes of coercion and habituation) coexist with and sometimes contribute to the same objectives as do such features of the practice of political obligation as authority, law, and arrangements intended to encourage and facilitate reasoned assessment of rules of obligation. Thus our concern will not be to deny the importance of behavior but to trace relationships among certain salient behavioral regularities and the patterns of action that make up the practice of political obligation.

Stating the matter as we have just done, however, is enough to indicate that the position we will develop conflicts with views concerning political obligation that go back to the earliest discussions of the topic and continue to have many adherents today. Many thinkers who never doubted the reality or importance of what we are calling human action have argued that *political obligation* is, or should be, in the realm that we have called behavior, not the realm of action. The basic thought behind the many variations on this theme seems to be as follows. Any observer of politics will be struck by its complexity and dynamism, and with the difficulty of predicting its course of development. If the flux and variation characteristic of day-to-day politics do not degenerate into chaos and disorder, this must be because they take place within, are undergirded by, a more uniform, stable, and predictable framework or foundation. If the flux, variation, and unpredictability of politics trace to the fact that human beings reason, frame intentions, and make choices, such stability and predictability as there is must trace to something else; it must be based upon some set of processes more likely to result in order and uniformity. If reasoning, framing intentions, and making choices are defining features of human action, and if their absence is the defining characteristic of behavior, then such stability and uniformity as there is must be the product of processes in the realm of behavior. In any stable society, the human action characteristic of day-to-day politics must be built upon and limited by behavioral regularities. If political obligation provides the framework or foundation, or part of it, within which day-to-day political interaction takes place or on which it is built, then political obligation must be in the realm of behavior.[5]

With the view that a successful politics requires a comparatively stable base we have no quarrel. Nor will we try to disprove (though we will raise some doubts about it) the contention that this base must be built in part if not entirely out of behavioral regularities, not out of the ingredients of human action. Finally, we do not wish to dispute the position that the practice of political obligation forms a part of or contributes to that comparatively settled base on which much of the rest of political interaction takes place. Our quarrel, rather, is with the inference that the practice of political obligation can perform this service only if, or to the extent that, it consists of behavior, not action; that it has in fact performed this service only where, or to the extent that, it has consisted of behavior, not action. Our quarrel is with interpretations of political obligation that place it in the realm of behavior or

5. For a succinct recent statement of this general line of thought see Sidney Verba, "Comparative Political Culture," *Political Culture and Political Development*, eds. Lucian W. Pye and Sidney Verba (Princeton, Princeton University Press, 1965), pp. 544–50 and passim. For a more developed formulation see Gabriel Almond and Sidney Verba, *The Civic Culture* (Boston: Little, Brown and Co., 1965).

argue that it would be better if it were in that realm. There is a considerable variety of such interpretations, and noting some of the more important of them at the outset will provide a contrasting background against which the view that we will develop here will stand out more clearly.

In the *Republic* Plato's search for a stable basis for politics led him to the question of how to obtain regular obedience from what he thought to be the inconstant and unreliable mass of the population. Although he held out the hope that the latter might be brought to appreciate, on something approaching reasoned grounds, the superior wisdom and hence authority of the philosopher-kings, his choice of methods fell on the formulation and inculation of a great myth (the myth of the metals). Acceptance of this myth and the authority structure said to be consonant with it would relieve the lower strata of the populace, the "brass," of the need to think about the merits and demerits of the laws and commands issued by the philosopher-kings. It would also relieve them of the need to think about whether to obey those laws and commands. Obedience would become, if not simply a matter of a uniform and entirely predictable response to a stimulus, at least habitual and unreflective. The philosopher-kings, in turn, could count on obedience and hence on internal stability; they would be relieved of the need to explain, justify, and win acceptance of their decisions and could concentrate on the task of reflecting, judging, and choosing so as to direct the republic to its proper goal. Here then is an exceptionally clear case of the argument that, at least in politics, the realm of action must be built upon a regular and dependable base supplied by behavior. If we could think of the obedience of the brass as obligatory, here would be an exceptionally clear case of an interpretation of political obligation as properly excluding reason, judgment, and choice from the activities of the bulk of the participants in the practice.[6]

6. See the *Republic*, esp. 388–92, 412–27, 474–501. For further discussion of Plato's argument in the *Republic* see Chapters Two and Five

Hobbes presents a picture that is more complicated but in the end proves to be very similar to Plato's. Men may reflect and choose whether to agree to an obligation to establish and obey a political authority (or so it is made to appear), but once having agreed, further reflection about the laws and other commands issued by the authority, or about whether to obey them, is strongly discouraged. Later writers who were influenced by Hobbes, for example the jurist John Austin, argued that this is in fact the way obligation works, that the practice of political obligation consists of two elements: 1. habitual obedience to law by most members of the society; 2. a sovereign who makes the laws and who has the authority and the power to punish those who do not obey him.[7]

A third variation on this theme is supplied by Henri Bergson. In his *Two Sources of Morality and Religion* Bergson analyzed obligation in the following terms:

> The members of a civic community hold together like the cells of an organism. Habit . . . introduces among them a discipline resembling, in the interdependence it establishes between separate individuals, the unity of an organism of anastomotic cells. . . . It is evident that each of us, thinking of himself alone, feels at liberty to follow his bent. . . . But this inclination has no sooner taken shape than it comes up against a force composed of the accumulation of all social forces; unlike individual motives, each pulling its own way, this force would result in an order not without analogy to that of natural phenomena. The component cell of an organism, on becoming momentarily conscious, would barely have outlived

---

below. The argument of the *Apology* and the *Crito* is very different and provides much of the material out of which we will form our own argument in Chapter Eight.

7. Austin's views are best consulted in John Austin, *The Province of Jurisprudence Determined, etc.* (London: Weidenfeld and Nicolson). This edition contains an excellent introduction by H. L. A. Hart.

the wish to emancipate itself when it would be recaptured by necessity. An individual forming part of a community may bend or even break a necessity of the same kind, which to some extent he has helped to create, but to which, still more, he has to yield; the sense of this necessity, together with consciousness of being able to evade it, is none the less what he calls an obligation. From this point of view, and taken in its most usual meaning, obligation is to necessity what habit is to nature.[8]

Bergson is not particularly concerned with politics and political obligation. But his major theme is exactly that the realm of obligation provides the stable base or foundation on which both society and morality are built. It is only where there is such a base that the more reflective, open-ended, ideal-oriented forms of morality and religion can develop. And this base is built out of prereflective, even preconscious materials.[9]

The views of the philosophers we have mentioned find a parallel in arguments that have had considerable currency in nonphilosophical political discourse. In the following chapters we will have numerous occasions to discuss the notion that one has an obligation to obey the law. This "general rule," as we will call it, must be distinguished from the particular laws or legal rules passed by legislatures. The latter require or forbid specified types of conduct described or identified in the law. The general rule, by contrast, requires obedience to any and all particular laws that are passed. Thus a person who has accepted the general rule might have no need to reflect about the content of any particular law or the consequences of obeying it. The fact that the rule is a law places it under the general rule and thus settles the question of whether to obey it.

Of course one could accept the general rule as a reasonable

8. Henri Bergson, *The Two Sources of Morality and Religion* (Garden City, N.Y.: Doubleday and Company), pp. 13–14. We discuss this passage again in Chapter Five.

9. The distinction between obligations and ideals is a central concern of Chapter Two.

and important guide to action without thinking of it as an absolute which settles all or even any questions of conduct that fall under it. But numerous writers have argued that it *should* be viewed as an absolute and that a stable political order is possible only if it is so viewed. One of the most forceful statements of this view is to be found in Abraham Lincoln's speech "The Perpetuation of our Political Institutions":

> Let every American, every lover of liberty, every well wisher to his posterity, swear by the blood of the Revolution, never to violate in the least particular, the laws of the country; and never to tolerate their violation by others. As the patriots of seventy-six did to the support of the Declaration of Independence, so to the support of the Constitution and Laws, let every American pledge his life, his property, and his sacred honor;—let every man remember that to violate the law, is to trample on the blood of his father, and to tear the charter of his own, and his children's liberty. Let reverence for the laws, be breathed by every American mother, to the lisping babe, that prattles on her lap—let it be taught in schools, in seminaries, and in colleges;—let it be preached from the pulpit, proclaimed in legislative halls, and enforced in courts of justice. And, in short, let it become the *political religion* of the nation; and let the old and young, the rich and poor, the grave and the gay, of all sexes and tongues, and colors and conditions, sacrifice unceasingly upon its altars.[10]

On Lincoln's view one might reason about and choose to accept the general rule—although Lincoln's choice of language

10. The speech is available, along with other materials concerning obedience and disobedience, in Robert A. Goldwin, ed., *On Civil Disobedience: Essays Old and New* (Chicago: Rand McNally, 1969). The passage is quoted from p. 5 of this collection. Lincoln does qualify his insistence that laws be obeyed with the phrase "if not too intolerable" (ibid., p. 6). To make very much of this phrase in interpreting the speech, however, would be to distort it. What would be important if one were interpreting the speech would be to emphasize Lincoln's distinction between the condition of the country at the time of the Declaration of Independence and at the time he gave the speech.

is hardly intended to encourage this procedure. But once having done so the question of obedience would be settled by a showing that a rule was a law or that a form of conduct was required or proscribed by law. Of course Lincoln differs from Plato and Hobbes in that he hopes for a vigorous political process surrounding the decision to pass a particular law. But this process must be built on top of absolute commitment to obedience. In this respect his argument aims to put the practice of political obligation in the realm of behavior, not action. As with the other writers we have mentioned, the argument puts forward an alternative understanding of the practice with which to contrast and compare the view we will develop here.

A corollary of the themes discussed thus far is an argument we will present by means of a distinction between political stasis and stability and the relationship of each to political change. We will argue that having a political obligation ordinarily presupposes the existence of a rule (whether a legal rule or some other type) which forbids or requires a specified form of conduct. We will also argue that the rules which define political obligations are typically thought to be the most basic or fundamental of the rules that have standing in the society or group. If these contentions are well supported, it might be thought that political change would indicate that the practice of which the rules are an integral part had broken down. This thought gains plausibility from the fact that one of the things that "rule" means is "regularity." If the "rules" keep changing, regularity disappears and it becomes misleading to say that conduct in the society is rule governed.

We will argue, however, that "rule" (in the relevant senses) and "rule-governed conduct" are tied to "reason" and "choice" as well as to "regularity." To say that there is a rule is not just to say that observers have detected that a certain number of people do or avoid doing X regularly or "as a rule." It is to say that at least some people have chosen to do X because they think that there are good reasons for doing so. And to say that B's conduct is governed by a rule is to say that B is one of those who has chosen to do X because he thinks there are good reasons for doing what the rule requires. Now to say that there are good reasons for doing X is to say that X can be distinguished from Y, Z, etc., (which may be merely not-doing-X), i.e., that there are alternatives to doing X over which X is preferred. It is also to say that doing Y, Z, etc., is potentially attractive to B such that there is a point to adducing reasons for doing X rather than Y or Z. In short, the existence of rules and rule-guided conduct presupposes the possibility of a tension in the thought of individuals, and hence in their society, between reasons for and reasons against accepting and choosing to conform to obligation rules. Moreover, the fact that reasoning and discussion concerning the rules takes place, and indeed the fact that A sometimes has occasion to use the concept "obligation" in guiding B's conduct, constitute indications that this possibility is realized. Since new developments may shift the balance of reasons in favor of Y instead of X, to the extent that conduct in a society is determined by obligation rules, a basis of social change is inherent in the very mechanism of conduct guidance.

Thus if political obligation is tied to rules, if rules are tied to reason and choice, and if reason and choice presuppose potentially attractive alternatives and hence a basis for change, then insofar as conduct in a political society is governed by obligation rules it will be marked by both regularity and by potential for change. We will call such a society a *stable* society and will distinguish it from *static* societies in which the potential for change distinctive of rule-governed conduct has been eliminated by basing conduct on prereflective commitments, habit, or fear. We will also argue that theorists, for example Plato and Hobbes, who attempted to eliminate the tension between reasons for and reasons against obligation rules have in fact endangered the very order and regularity they so earnestly desired; that a *static* society of the sort they envisioned is likely to alternate between periods of strict, rigidly imposed order and large-scale conflict and convulsion.

A fourth theme that should be mentioned at the outset is that there is a relationship of interdependence, both logical and practical, between the individual's actions and the practice of political obligation in which he participates. It is the individual who frames intentions, reasons, and makes choices. But it is the society that evolves and sustains the language, the arrangements, and the institutions which make it both logically and practically possible for the individual to act in a manner that can be described as discharging political obligations. If there are no individuals capable of choosing to discharge political obligations, the practice of political obligation as we will identify it here cannot exist. But it is both logically and practically impossible for an individual, taken alone, to have this capacity. To mention only the most obvious point, he cannot choose to accept or reject a rule defining an obligation if there are no rules to accept; but the notion of a rule that defines an obligation is intrinsically or necessarily a social notion. Working out this theme will prove to be important to clarifying the relationship between central, authoritative command or direction and decentralized social and political evolution, to the question whether it is self-defeating to attempt to "legislate morality," and to identifying the sorts of considerations and arguments that are relevant in reaching and justifying decisions to obey or disobey the law.

The last clause, which applies to the other general themes as well, points to the connection between our analysis of the features of the practice and answering practical questions such as "Should I obey the law?" and the other questions we mentioned at the outset of the Introduction. These questions arise within and concerning the practice, a practice that has a definite shape or character. Thus the kinds of considerations that are relevant to answering them are influenced, indeed limited, by the characteristics of the practice. Even the person who wishes to eliminate or reconstruct the practice radically must make his arguments for doing so bear upon the practice as it is. Some arguments will be irrelevant because they are based on a misunderstanding of the practice argued against.

In the last two chapters we will survey the main kinds of considerations that have been advanced as appropriate materials out of which to forge answers to practical questions (or to forge normative theories of political obligation) and to determine whether, or to what extent, they are in fact appropriate. We will try to show the limitations on some kinds of considerations prominent in the history of the theory of obligation, for example consent and receipt of benefits. And we will try to show the advantages of a broadly utilitarian approach to deciding questions which arise within the practice and to assessing the merits of the practice qua practice.

Political
Obligation

(1)

The Study of Language
and the Study of Politics

A LARGE PART of the discussion of political obligation in the following chapters is based upon an examination of the uses of concepts that figure prominently in the practice. We will analyze uses of "obligation" itself, of "rule," "authority," "reason," "freedom," "consent," and a number of other concepts. Use of this approach to understanding a political practice rests on a number of assumptions concerning language and its relationships to thought, action, society, and other "realities." The purpose of this chapter is to identify some of these assumptions as they are understood here and as they will operate in the chapters that follow. The matters we will discuss in this chapter are controversial and there is a large and sometimes technical literature concerning them.[1] The present discussion is necessarily partial and schematic. Its

1. A generous selection of the important writings concerning language and its relationships to thought, action, and other realities is available in Richard Rorty, ed., *The Linguistic Turn* (Princeton: Princeton University Press, 1967). Rorty's volume also includes a comprehensive bibliography and an introduction by the editor which attempts to identify major issues and the prominent positions concerning them. Rorty's bibliography lists several other useful anthologies on the subject.

primary purpose is to identify the bases of and the limitations upon claims advanced in later chapters. Some of this information can be gleaned from the later discussions themselves, especially by readers familiar with the controversies concerning language and its relevance to philosophy. Readers well versed in these matters, and readers not interested in them, might wish to proceed directly to Chapter Two.

I. LANGUAGE AND MEANING

WE BEGIN WITH what may be the most significant fact of all; namely, that human beings communicate with one another in language. Indeed in countless cases they do so successfully and without difficulty. Thus I write this sentence with every confidence that anyone who knows the English language will know what it means, with every confidence that it will have the same meaning for the reader that it has for me. How is this possible? How is it possible that the language A uses can so often have the same meaning for millions of people who do not know A as it has for him?

Sometimes it is made possible by A's explaining what he means by the language he uses. But even in the small number of cases in which such explanations are offered this answer raises the question of how the statements explaining the meaning of the first statement can have the same meaning for others that they have for A. And so on. The communication we ordinarily take for granted depends on there being a large number of cases in which our meaning needs no explanation. However we account for this fact, the fact itself must not be forgotten.

Very baldly, there can be such cases because the system of spoken and written symbols that we call language is governed by conventions that establish the correct uses of the concepts and other units of which the language consists. Knowing a language consists of knowing the conventions that govern it.

B can know what A means when he uses the language because A and B both know the conventions governing the language. A means what he says; he means what *is said* when the language he speaks is used in the way he is using it.

The type of conventions that will be of greatest interest here are those that govern the use of concepts. Sometimes called semantic rules, these conventions determine when we can properly use one concept rather than another—for example, "obligatory" rather than "obliged" or "X is good" rather than "I like X." To say that a concept can or cannot be used in a particular context is, among other things, to say that it can or cannot be combined with other concepts in various ways. Thus when a convention establishes that we can use, say, "obligation" in a particular set of circumstances (including linguistic circumstances), it places limits on what we can go on to say after we have used "obligation." For example, if A says "B has an obligation to do X," he ordinarily cannot, or cannot without making a special explanation, go on to say, "but he doesn't have to do X if he doesn't feel like it." Owing to the conventions governing "obligation" and "doesn't feel like it," combining the concepts in this way is misusing the language. In the absence of a special explanation for combining them in this way, A's remarks will be puzzling to other speakers of the language. Because there is a sense in which we can or cannot use concept Y having used concept X, many writers have been inclined to speak of the "logic" of language and the "logic" of particular concepts in language. Whether the use of "logic" is warranted will depend on the force of the claim advanced in using it and on the particular conceptual relationships to which it is applied. What is important at this juncture is that the conceptual relationships we are discussing when we talk about conventions are not merely regularities detected by observers. An observer may indeed detect them, but what he is detecting are conventions which users of the language follow when they speak.

Language is governed by conventions, using the language

consists of following the conventions, and making sense in the language is possible if the conventions are respected. If these propositions are true, it follows that an account of the conventions governing the language is an account of the manner in which people who know the language speak (insofar as they do so and insofar as they make sense). Insofar as the conventions are the same for all who use the language, the speech of any person who knows the language is, in principle, evidence concerning the conventions. With the implied qualifications, it is evidence that will support generalizations about the language. Thus if we investigate the speech of A, we investigate more than the speech of A. (Recall that the child usually does not have to test the knowledge of the language gained from his parents or teachers against the way others speak.)

II. USE VERSUS ANALYSIS OF LANGUAGE

ALTHOUGH WE CANNOT GO into the host of questions raised by the foregoing remarks in any detail, it is imperative that we identify (as opposed to develop) some of the main qualifications that need to be entered against them. Doing so will indicate some of the claims that we will *not* be advancing in the following chapters.

There are a number of respects in which we must qualify our suggestion that the speech of a single speaker will support generalizations about the language. Let us take as an example one of the generalizations that we will advance later, namely that "obligation" is ordinarily used where there is (a certain kind of) rule forbidding or requiring a specified form of conduct. We will argue that this is one of the conventions or semantic rules governing the use of the concept "obligation." But very little thought shows that this convention does not hold for all uses of the concept. To begin with a somewhat technical case, Professor Peter Geach has argued that rules of this type almost never hold for statements that express counterfactual conditionals. Thus if I say: "If Smith had an obligation to do X, it would be wrong for him not to do it," my use of "obligation" does not depend on there being a rule requiring Smith to do X.[2] A more familiar example would be that a speaker might use "obligation" knowing there is no rule but hoping that using the concept will hasten the development of one. Or he might use it to convey the impression that there is a rule when he knows that there isn't one.[3] Then too there are various ways in which concepts are stretched for special purposes—e.g., in writing poetry; there are the problems about "unintended" meaning emphasized by psychoanalytic theory; and there is the obvious fact that subgroups of a society put the language of the society to special uses unfamiliar to other speakers.

One of our objectives below will be to identify major exceptions and qualifications to the various semantic rules we will put forward, thus rendering more precise our statement of them and the conditions under which they hold. It is not our expectation, however, that we can come up with a scheme or set of rules that accounts for all "correct" or "appropriate" or "established" uses of the concept. We cannot prove that such a schema is never available, but our "sense" or "impression," based upon analysis of a few concepts, does not engender such an expectation. With Wittgenstein we do not see ordinary language as a "strict calculus" in which every appropriate move is determined or at least covered by a tightly drawn rule. The "sense" or "impression" of language which will underlie our discussion of political obligation is very close to the understanding stated by Peter Strawson a number of years ago. We cannot defend it in general terms here (Strawson defends it eloquently in the work from which the passage is quoted), but it will be well if the reader bears it in mind as he reads the chapters that follow:

2. See Peter Geach, "Ascriptivism," *Philosophical Review* 69 (1960). Reprinted in Rorty, op. cit., pp. 224–26.
3. See below, Chap. 5, pp. 158–59.

In discussing the logic of ordinary language I have frequently used the word 'rule'. The word is not inappropriate: for to speak of these and other 'rules' is to speak of ways in which language may be *correctly* or *incorrectly* used. But though not inappropriate, the word may be misleading. We do not judge our linguistic practice in the light of antecedently studied rules. We frame rules in the light of our study of our practice. Moreover, our practice is a very fluid affair. If we are to speak of rules at all, we ought to think of them as rules which everyone has a license to violate if he can show a point in doing so. In the effort to describe our experience we are continually putting words to new uses, connected with, but not identical with, their familiar uses; applying them to states of affairs which are both like and unlike those to which the words are most familarly applied. Hence we may give a meaning to sentences which, at first sight, seem self-contradictory. And hence, though some have incautiously spoken of the violation of type-rules as resulting in sentences which, though neither ungrammatical nor self-contradictory, are nonsense, it is in fact hard to frame a grammatical sentence to which it is impossible to imagine some sense being given; and given, not by arbitrary *fiat*, but by an intelligible, though probably figurative, extension of the familiar senses of the words and phrases concerned.[4]

It will be objected, however, that the qualifications we have admitted are much more damaging to our original position than we have allowed. We have in effect said that there will ordinarily be exceptions and qualifications to the conventions governing (and hence to generalizations concerning) the use of concepts. But to say this is to continue to claim to be in a position to know how language is used. If we were not in such

4. Peter Strawson, *Introduction to Logical Theory* (London: Methuen and Co., 1952), p. 230.

a position we could not make the generalizations and the necessary qualifications to them. In our original account we rested this claim on two premises: (1) that language is governed by conventions, and (2) that knowing the language consists of knowing the conventions that govern its use. If there is one set of conventions governing the language, and if I know the language, then I am in a position to generalize about it. (Or my speech is evidence that warrants others in generalizing about it.) But if the use of language is diverse and fluid, if it varies from speaker to speaker and context to context, this claim is weakened and perhaps undermined. If we are going to generalize about the use of language we have to get out of our armchair and investigate the diversity and complexity that is the actual use of language.[5]

The only possible general answer to this objection is that indeed one must get out of his armchair. But the reason why this is the only possible answer, and the practical implications that follow from it, vary in important respects according to the kind of question one is trying to answer by investigating language. It is pretty obvious that I cannot rely entirely on my own command of English in giving an account of many of the

5. For a version of this argument see the Introduction in J. A. Fodor and J. J. Katz, eds., *The Structure of Language* (Englewood Cliffs, N.J.: Prentice-Hall, 1964). The principal argument Fodor and Katz advance is that we cannot generalize about language until we have a theory of the structure or "compositional mechanisms" of language or of the language that the generalizations are about. Such a theory, they argue, cannot be developed solely from the armchair. We can readily grant that there are important issues that cannot be decided in the absence of such a theory. Granting as well that we have no such theory, the question is whether there are issues that *can* be decided, or on which light can be shed, by studying the use of concepts. Fodor and Katz concede that there are cases in which it is "intuitively clear" "what one would say (or not)" in a set of circumstances. Indeed they concede that "clear cases, intuitively determined, provide the empirical constraints on the construction of a linguistic theory" (p. 17). Given these concessions, the least that must be said is that it is difficult to see why they should object to attempts to identify such "clear cases" and to see whether doing so helps us to understand philosophical, political, or other sorts of questions and problems. (I leave aside the question of the adequacy of their characterizations of "ordinary-language philosophy.")

concepts used in discourse among skydiving buffs or among the members of the Black Panther party. I have to *learn* how to use many of the concepts they employ; I have to learn how they are used by skydiving buffs and Black Panthers.

But what about the skydiving buffs or the Black Panthers? Do they have to "get out of their armchairs" in order to give an account of the concepts they use as skydivers and Black Panthers? Quite clearly they rarely have to do so in order to use the concepts.[6] But using a concept and giving an account of its use are not the same. The latter requires that we examine *what* we do when we do the former; it requires us to identify, compare, and classify the circumstances, linguistic and otherwise, in which we use or would use a concept. With all save very specialized or technical concepts there are a very large number of such circumstances. Thinking of any substantial number of them, to say nothing of detecting similarities and differences relevant to the purposes of the analysis, requires industry and skills which the person who uses language but does not analyze its use has no occasion to develop or to employ. The analyst must examine a range of examples in a variety of contexts, search for objections, counterexamples, and ambiguities in the generalizations that the data suggest to him, and seek the implications of his findings for the problems that led him to make the analysis. There are no doubt numerous methods or techniques by which this can be done, and it may be that the techniques used by ordinary-language philosophers could usefully be supplemented by methods more typical of linguists or other social scientists.[7]

6. For arguments on this point see Stanley Cavell, "Must We Mean What We Say," in V. C. Chappell, ed., *Ordinary Language* (Englewood Cliffs, N.J.: Prentice-Hall, 1964).

7. The acknowledged master of the techniques of analyzing language among ordinary-language philosophers was J. L. Austin. His techniques are nowhere better displayed than in his *Sense and Sensibilia*, ed. G. J. Warnock (London: Oxford University Press, 1962). Austin talks about his methods in "A Plea for Excuses." This paper is available in Austin's *Philosophical Papers*, ed. J. O. Urmson and G. J. Warnock (London: Oxford University Press, 1961). It is reprinted in several of the an-

Contrary to numerous critics of ordinary-language philosophy, in other words, *analysis* of the use of language is not an a priori activity. The investigator can often "look into himself" to a degree inappropriate in many areas of investigation; that is he can often look to his own use of language as well as that of other speakers. But this must be done thoroughly, and it will almost always be necessary to look to the speech of others as well. In this respect analysis of the use of language is an empirical activity subject to the usual requirements of empirical investigation. The claim that a particular account or analysis of the uses of a concept is a correct analysis must be supported by evidence that the concept is in fact used in the manner claimed. And such claims are subject to qualifications and rebuttal by counterexamples and other forms of counterevidence and objection.

III. LANGUAGE AND CONVENTION

WHAT IS LEFT of our opening remarks about our ability to communicate with one another without difficulty and its explanation and significance? We can best clarify the relationships between our original assertions and the qualifications we have entered by giving greater attention to the key concept in our opening remarks, namely "convention." We said that we are able to communicate because the units of language are governed by conventions shared among the speakers of the language. It is the existence of these conventions that makes it possible to speak of what "is said" and "is meant" when A speaks, not merely what "A says" or what "A means." The conventions give language an interpersonal character such that

---

thologies listed in Rorty's Bibliography. Austin's methods are described in greater detail by J. O. Urmson in a paper entitled "J. L. Austin," which is reprinted in Rorty, op. cit., pp. 232 ff. Austin himself believed that the methods he had employed could usefully be supplemented by investigative techniques used in other disciplines.

B knows what A means when he speaks. Because language is governed by conventions, analyzing its use consists of identifying and giving an explicit and orderly account of something followed by speakers of the language, not merely detecting regularities which may or may not be known or followed by speakers. To adapt a phrase from J. A. Fodor and J. J. Katz, the conventions governing the language place empirical and theoretical constraints on accounts, explanations, and theories of language.

But a set of social conventions is not, or rather need not be, a strict, uniform, or complete calculus. An analogy may be useful at this point. When A. V. Dicey spoke of the "conventions" as opposed to the law of the English constitution he spoke of something for which there was solid evidence, of something that played an absolutely crucial role in the activities of lawyers, judges, politicians, and ordinary citizens, and hence in British government and politics. He was convinced, and few would disagree, that it would be quite impossible to understand British government and politics without attending to the conventions. With few exceptions these conventions were not codified and many of them were not even recorded. Dicey investigated them by examining the activities and practices of those involved in British politics, attending to what they said and didn't say, what they accepted as a matter of course and what they found objectionable or puzzling. In examining these sources of evidence he found much diversity of practice and belief and he found continuing change—sometimes rapid and radical change. But he also found well-established and stable *patterns* of activity and belief, patterns which allowed him to offer generalizations about what in fact was done and about what, given the conventions, it was appropriate to do. His account of the conventions was no doubt more orderly, and at least in this respect different from, the account that any participant in the practice would or even could give. Yet his account could be (and has been) checked, tested, and rebutted by participants and by other investigators.

The analogy is very close between the investigations of a Dicey (and of course many others could be mentioned as well) and the investigation of a language, especially the semantic rules of a language.[8] Without the concept of conventions governing use and practice, many of the salient features of language and of law and politics become inexplicable. Only a small number of both types of convention are codified or recorded. Even those that are recorded are subject to change, are understood and followed in different ways by different agents in different contexts and circumstances, and are perhaps more often characterized by open texture and even ambiguity than by strict or precise definition and delineation. Thus we must attend both to the conventions and the role they play and to the complexity and diversity so often characteristic of them. This is what we will try to do in the chapters that follow.

IV. LANGUAGE AND SOCIAL AND POLITICAL PRACTICE

EVEN IN THE QUALIFIED FORM in which we have advanced them, the propositions we have been considering might stimulate a certain fluttering in the heart of the empirically oriented social scientist. The properties of language that make interpersonal communication possible sometimes allow generalization from the actions of one man to the actions of large numbers of men. Moreover, for some purposes the social scientist can himself be that one man.

The flutter is apt to subside rather quickly, however, when the social scientist recollects that the generalizations in question would be about linguistic acts, would be about, in the usual pejorative expression, words or "mere words." In short,

8. In some respects the two activities are one. Although not cast in the jargon of conceptual analysis, many of Dicey's analyses consisted of an explication of the uses of key concepts in discourse about government and politics.

we have yet to provide grounds on which to entertain the expectation that we might learn something about the practice of political obligation by investigating the uses of the concept "obligation." We have yet to show that in tracing the linguistic conventions governing "obligation" we will do more than trace the contours of a conceptual heaven that has little or nothing to do with the realities of human affairs. As we noted earlier, the issues here concern the relationships between language on the one hand and thought, action, and other realities that may be more than linguistic on the other. Of course language is itself a reality—a rather salient and important one. But since the analysis of language is not an end in itself in this investigation (in the sense in which it might be for a lexicographer), we must show that investigating it will help us to achieve an understanding of political obligation.

Language is put to a wide variety of uses and the relationships between it and other things are correspondingly diverse and complex. The sentence "the cat is on the mat" puts language to a very different use from the sentence "you are hereby ordered to report to the induction center at noon on Friday." Regardless of the use to which it is put, the question of its relationship (if any) to nonlinguistic things must be answered by looking at language, not by looking at the things with which or to which it relates. Even in the comparatively simple case of concepts that refer to nonlinguistic objects or properties, for example color concepts, the link between the concept and the thing cannot be discovered by examining the thing. Hobbes made this point by recounting the following story:

> There is a story somewhere of one that pretends to have been miraculously cured of blindness, wherewith he was born, by St. Alban or other Saints, at the town of St. Albans; and that the Duke of Gloucester being there, to be satisfied of the truth of the miracle, asked the man, What color is this?, who, by answering, it was green, discovered himself, and was punished for a counterfeit: for

though by his sight newly received he might distinguish between green, and red, and all other colors, as well as any that should interrogate him, yet he could not possibly know at first sight which of them was *called* green, or red, or by any other name.[9]

Hobbes's story shows that we could not identify anything as green without the concept "green" or some cognate concept. And what counts as being green is determined by the rules governing the use of the concept, not by any set of properties that we perceive. Thus even in the case of color concepts there is much to be learned, much that can only be learned, by looking at the concepts we use.

From the time of Locke to well into the twentieth century, philosophical discussion of language was concerned largely with concepts that are used to talk about material objects and the properties of such objects. It is by no means the case, however, that all concepts are used for this purpose. Not all concepts are used to refer to or to stand for such "things." If we leave aside unicorns and centaurs, so-called logical words such as "and," "or," "all," and "none" are perhaps the most obvious case. But there are numerous others. When I say "hello" on meeting you in the street I do not refer to anything in the world; rather I *do* something in the world. (Statements about the world are supposed to be true or false. Consider whether it would be sensible to respond to my "hello" with "is that true?") In this kind of case the concept *is* the reality. (Of course it is not the only reality.) Thus an account of the practice of etiquette or polite conduct would consist in part of an account of when certain words such as "hello," "please," and "pardon me" are used. This account would be an account of a reality which consisted in large part of the use of language. It would be a true or false account depending on the facts

9. *Human Nature*, Chap. 6. In R. S. Peters, ed., *Thomas Hobbes, Body, Man and Citizen* (New York: Collier Books, 1962), p. 203. Also see Max Black, "Language and Reality," *Models and Metaphors* (Ithaca: Cornell University Press, 1962).

concerning when certain concepts are appropriately used. If the concepts ceased to be used the reality would change or disappear. There would be nothing to give an account of.

In many of its uses "obligation" is more like "hello," "please," and "pardon me" than it is like "green," "red," "cat," and "mat." (Although the latter concepts are also used for purposes other than referring to objects.) Of course the term is used in talking about a social and political practice. But it is also (if the reader will pardon an understatement) used in the practice. When A says to B: "You have an obligation to obey the law," he does something more than utter a sound or describe B's situation. A assigns obligations to B by using the concept "obligation." He could not assign (or discharge, or default upon, or release B from) obligations if the concept was not available to him or if it was inappropriate for him to use it in the circumstances. The practice of political obligation operates only where it is linguistically appropriate to use the concept.[10] The concept is not merely something external to the practice which is used to talk about the practice, it is an integral part of the practice. Concept and thing, language and "reality" are inseparable.

It follows that to investigate the conditions under which it is appropriate to use the concept is to investigate the practice. We do not investigate the concept and then try to discover the relationship between the concept and the practice. When we investigate the former we also investigate the latter. To know the conditions under which "obligation" is used is to know when the practice operates; to know when it is incorrect to use the concept is to know the limits of the practice. To find out how "obligation" is used is to acquire a part of that body of

10. It is not necessary that the word "obligation" actually be used for the practice to operate. If I say "I promise to do X," I have undertaken an obligation to do X without using the word "obligation." But if I did not understand that I had undertaken an obligation, that it would be appropriate to use "obligation" in describing what I had done, it would be doubtful that I had in fact either made a promise or undertaken an obligation.

knowledge which is shared among the members of the political society in which the practice operates and which gives the practice substance and allows the members of the society to participate in it.

V. LANGUAGE AND SOCIAL SCIENCE

THE FOREGOING CONSIDERATIONS suggest some reasons why investigating language can be a useful tool of social analysis. The many writers from Plato to the logical positivists and behavioralists who have dismissed ordinary language as of no philosophic or social-scientific interest have deprived themselves of a valuable source of information and insight about human affairs. In the case of the last-mentioned group, doing so has also contributed to the tendency to dismiss human action as epiphenomenal and to reduce human affairs to behavior. "Hello" and "political obligation" are representative of much of the realm of human action in that the concepts and the discourse that employ them are more than just a means of referring to some other reality. To insist that we haven't gotten at the reality of human affairs until we have identified objects or events other than concepts and their use is *thereby* to dismiss as epiphenomenal a good deal of what goes on in the realm of human action. Although we will not try to document it here, we suggest that this view of language and its relationship to other realities lies behind much of the reductionism that has been widespread in social science in the nineteenth and twentieth centuries.[11]

There is, however, an opposite danger that we must guard against. Even with the numerous qualifications we have en-

11. The discussion of Durkheim's *Suicide* later in this chapter is concerned with an (influential) example of social-science reductionism based in part on the view that language is epiphenomenal if not worse. For critical discussions of other social science theories with these characteristics see the works cited in the Introduction, p. xvii, note 4.

tered, the reasoning we have sketched might be taken to support the conclusion that language is the only reality and that conceptual analysis is the only possible approach to understanding society. Consider the following passage from Peter Winch's *The Idea of a Social Science,* a work that comes very close to such a view:

> Our idea of what belongs to the realm of reality is given for us in the language that we use. The concepts we have settle for us the form of the experience we have of the world. . . . [W]hen we speak of the world we are speaking of what we in fact mean by the expression "the world"; there is no way of getting outside the concepts in terms of which we think of the world. . . . The world *is* for us what is presented through those concepts.[12]

If the realm of reality is given exclusively by the language we use, it would seem to follow that the only way to investigate reality would be to investigate the language we use. It would also seem to follow that our conclusions or findings about reality can be valid or true only for reality as it is embodied in the particular language that we have investigated. If languages differ one from another, or if there are systematic differences among the parts or "strata" of a single language, it would follow that the world, in the only sense in which we can know it, differs as well.

This reasoning carries extraordinary implications for social science. As Winch explicitly argues, it prohibits a variety of analytic procedures commonplace in social science. It also suggests severe limitations on the possibility of generalizations about human affairs. These appearances may be due to the fact that we have stated the reasoning in an entirely unqualified manner. But however well or badly the above statement represents the views of other writers, it is not obvious that it involves an unwarranted extension of the reasoning we identi-

12. Winch, op. cit., p. 15.

fied earlier as grounds for using linguistic analysis in doing social science. If the latter approach is to be used in studying political obligation it is essential that we show how this can be done without accepting the further reasoning just sketched.

The argument for attention to language contends that we cannot identify and characterize particular things in the world without concepts in which to do so. In this respect the argument is correct and extremely important.[13] We do see, hear, smell, touch, and taste; and the perceptual operations or processes do not themselves depend upon language. But we cannot identify the processes as perceptions and we cannot perceive the world as this rather than that without language. We cannot, in other words, characterize or understand the world except in language.

The foregoing propositions, however, are compatible with the possibility that our language allows us to characterize and understand those things that we perceive in various ways, to dispute over what we have perceived, over how it should be characterized, and over what we should think about it. Consider the following simple example. Observing a crowd of people gathered in a public square, A sees 500 citizens engaging in an orderly and otherwise admirable discussion of questions of great public significance. B looks out over the same square at the same time and sees a mob of 5,000 anarchists giving vent to base impulses. Both A and B are able to characterize what they see, in an important sense are only able to see what they see, because they have a language. If they speak the same language they can communicate with one another about what they see. Their capacity to characterize what they see as X rather than Y and to communicate their characterizations to one another depends upon language. Moreover, whether their characterizations are accurate or justified depends in part on how the concepts "500," "5,000," "citizen," "mob," etc., are used in the language they speak. But an understanding of these

13. For an extremely cogent version of the argument see Julius Kovesi, *Moral Notions* (London: Routledge and Kegan Paul, 1967).

concepts is obviously not sufficient to determine whether they have been properly applied in the case at hand or to resolve the disagreements in interpretation and assessment between them. They may have a perfectly satisfactory understanding of the concepts they use and yet, because of misperception, bias, lack of imagination, or failure to think clearly, completely misdescribe the situation.

Let us now shift to the perspective of the social scientist. The language A and B use in commenting on the events in the square is a part of their response to those events. If the social scientist attempts to describe or analyze their responses apart from the language in which they took place, he omits a part of those responses. But any account omits some aspects of the reality of which it is an account. The relevant question is whether the omissions involved in a particular account are important or significant. Since it would be absurd to try to provide exhaustive general criteria of what is significant in social science, this question is answerable only in the context of discussions of particular social-science theories and their use in attempting to investigate and understand particular aspects of social life. For this very reason, it would also be absurd to state that nothing of significance would *ever* be lost by omitting the language in which social life takes place from accounts or analyses of it.

Granting that the language A and B use might be important, it does not follow that the social scientist must or should restrict himself to the language used by the actors whose conduct he is analyzing. Just as the language available to them allows A and B many choices as to how to characterize the events in the square, so the social scientist typically has a rich variety of choices as to how to characterize the actions of A and B. And those features of their conduct that make it meaningful to one another as actors in the situation are not necessarily the features that are important to the social scientist. The conduct of A and B becomes meaningful to the social scientist only when he can assign concepts to it; and the concepts he can correctly apply to it will be limited by the characteristics of the conduct. Which of the almost certainly large number of concepts that can be applied *should* be applied is a decision to be made in terms of the purposes that led the social scientist to study A and B, the theory or theories out of which he is working, and numerous other considerations that are not exclusively conceptual. Conceptual considerations restrict the ways in which the social scientist can combine the various statements that language allows him to make (a point to which we will return immediately below). They do not determine what is or should be significant to him.

VI. SOME LIMITATIONS ON SOCIAL SCIENCE

GRANTING THAT there is often an impressive range of choices available as to how to speak, in every case there is a positively vast body of language that we could not sensibly use (or more precisely, could not use without the sort of special explanation mentioned by Strawson in the passage we quoted on p. 8 above). Much of the time we abide by these restrictions without noticing them; we simply speak the language as we have learned it. But in special-purpose activities such as philosophy or social science we become self-conscious about how we characterize things, and we seek to improve upon ordinary language. Thus the literature of social science is full of concepts which, though the words are often familiar, are unintelligible to most speakers of the language (in the sense of English or French). The use of these concepts is governed by rules laid down by the social scientist, and nonsocial scientists have no occasion to learn them.

The many practical problems for both writer and reader that are created by this practice need not be rehearsed here. There is one type of difficulty that calls attention to features of language which are important for present purposes.

We can often characterize a single phenomenon in several

ways. But not all characterizations have the same logical status, can be substituted one for the other, or can be combined with one another in framing explanations or theories. To begin again with the simple example used above, assume that C observed the same square as A and B and determined that the pavement in the square was bearing a weight of 100,000 pounds, that the temperature was 105 degrees, and that the bodies in the square were emitting X amount of carbon dioxide per minute. C's observations might be highly relevant to matters of human decision and conduct, for example to a judgment whether the roof of the parking garage beneath the square would collapse or a decision to have first aid available for people who fainted. Nevertheless there are definite limits on the ways in which C's observations could be combined with those of A and B in reasoning about events and conditions in the square. In the absence of special explanations, to combine them in a single account would reduce that account to a mere list the items of which were related to one another by nothing more than that they all concerned a certain time and place.

The point we wish to make here goes beyond the commonplace that social science is concerned with explanations and theories, not mere collections of facts, and that it is explanations and theories that determine the relevance and significance of facts. The point is that language itself places limitations on explanation and theory construction. No attempt to explain the events in the square could disregard the fact that the interpretations A and B offer are interpretations to which such concepts as "belief," "attitude," "actions," "reasons," "intentions," and "purposes" are appropriate; nor could it disregard the fact that the latter concepts are irrelevant to the information supplied by C. Human beings do have attitudes and beliefs about facts such as C presents, and they act on such attitudes and beliefs. When this happens conceptual bridges can be built between the various types of statements. C's observations might be combined with or related to A's and B's reports in other ways as well; for example it might be pointed out that the attitudes A and B report always, never, or sometimes appear together with the conditions reported by C. But pounds of flesh and degrees of temperature do not have beliefs and attitudes. Nor does the presence of a certain number of people or a certain quantity of carbon dioxide sufficiently explain the fact that human beings *acted* in a certain way. To combine statements such as C makes with statements about human beliefs and actions without bridging the conceptual gaps between them is to speak nonsense.

We can characterize most phenomena in several ways, but there are conceptual restrictions on the ways in which we can combine and relate the several characterizations. The very fact that social science is interested in theories and explanations, in combinations of statements, subjects it to conceptual restrictions over and above those that limit the ways we can characterize events or states of affairs.

The example of the square involves relations among different ordinary-language descriptions. The example is trivial because it is unlikely that the restrictions involved would be violated. Who would impute an attitude to a pound of flesh? (It is perhaps less unlikely that it would be thought that the factors C mentions sufficiently explain human action.) But the point the example illustrates is not trivial. Serious difficulties in social science have resulted from violations of rules closely related to, if more complex than, those involved in the simple example we used.[14] The point also applies to the relationship among special-

14. See the discussion of the relations between statements explaining human action in terms of reasons and explaining human behavior in terms of causes in Winch, op. cit., esp. pp. 44, 45–51, and 80–83; and Alasdair MacIntyre, "The Idea of a Social Science," *The Aristotelian Society*, Supp. Vol. 61 (1967), esp. pp. 97–101. Winch holds that the two types of explanations are mutually exclusive and logically incompatible. He argues that the conventions governing the use of "reason" and "cause" are such that the same event can only be explained by one of the two types of statements. He also holds that human actions can only be explained in terms of reasons. MacIntyre argues that human actions can sometimes be explained, without conceptual mistake, in terms of causes, and that "the agent's possessing a reason" may be "an item of a suitable type to figure as a cause" (ibid., p. 100). He nevertheless

purpose concepts that social scientists are prone to invent and between such concepts and the ordinary-language concepts in which the bulk of their discourse continues to take place. Social scientists usually recognize that they must remain consistent with their original stipulations. They give less attention to problems involved in combining their technical concepts with other concepts. A classic and revealing example of the problems that can arise is provided by Emile Durkheim's procedure in *Suicide*.

Durkheim begins *Suicide* by remarking that "the words of ordinary language, like the concepts they express, are always susceptible of more than one meaning, and the scholar employing them in their accepted use without further definition would risk serious misunderstanding. Not only is their meaning so indefinite as to vary, from case to case, with the needs of argument, but, as the classification from which they derive is not analytic, but merely translates the confused impressions of the crowd, categories of very different sorts of facts are indistinctly combined under the same heading, or similar realities are differently named. So if we follow common use, we risk . . . misapprehending [the] nature of the things we investigate." [15] These difficulties, Durkheim argues, obtain in the case of the ordinary-language concept of suicide. There is the additional difficulty that the conventions governing "suicide" require the presence of an intention to take one's own life. As Durkheim puts it: "Intent is too intimate a thing to be more than approximately interpreted by another. It even escapes self-observation. How often we mistake the true reasons for our

agrees that "nothing could count as a reason unless it stood in an internal relationship to an action" (ibid.) and that this distinguishes "reason" from "cause." Hence he argues that reasons can figure as causes in the sense just indicated but causes cannot be reasons. Thus both writers hold that there are important conceptual restrictions on social-science explanation and theorizing and they both argue that these restrictions have been violated with unfortunate results.

15. Émile Durkheim, *Suicide* trans. John A. Spaulding and George Simpson, ed. George Simpson (Glencoe, Ill.: The Free Press, 1951), p. 41.

acts!" [16] Thus this feature of "suicide" constitutes an obstacle to scientific study of the phenomenon of suicide. To avoid the difficulty Durkheim proposes to stipulate his own use of "suicide" for the purposes of his investigation. He proposes to substitute a technical social science concept for an ordinary language concept. (He happens to use the *word* used in ordinary language, i.e., "suicide," but that is not material to the theoretical question before us.) The subject of his investigation will be suicide, when "suicide" "is applied to all cases of death resulting directly or indirectly from a positive or negative act of the victim himself, which he knows will produce this result." [17] Thus intention is rendered irrelevant and "the martyr dying for his faith, the mother sacrificing herself for her child" deserve to be called suicides as much as the "merchant who kills himself to avoid bankruptcy." [18]

Durkheim may be correct in thinking that there are similarities and differences among behaviors, conditions, and attitudes, "things" as Durkheim wants to call them, that are not marked by "suicide" as it is used in ordinary language. He may also be correct that these similarities and differences are important to social science. If so, and if they are not marked in a convenient manner by other concepts of ordinary language, there is a case for his inventing and stipulating the use of a technical term to facilitate his work as a social scientist. But there is at least one point on which it is Durkheim who is confused, not ordinary language or the people who speak ordinary language. That point is what constitutes suicide. What constitutes suicide is not given by or derivable from any arrangement of "things" in the world. It is given by the conventions governing the use of "suicide." Suicide is that to which it is proper to apply the concept of "suicide." A speaker of the language might misuse the concept by applying it in a manner not allowed by the conventions governing its use. Or he might attempt to bring about a change in ordinary use. But misuses

16. Ibid., p. 43.   17. Ibid., p. 44.   18. Ibid., p. 43.

and changes are possible solely because there are conventions that determine correct use. Concepts such as "misuse," "confusion," and "change" have application only because there are conventions governing the language. In suggesting that the crowd is confused in other senses Durkheim demonstrates his own fundamental lack of understanding of the relationship between thought and language.[19]

The fact that the crowd cannot be confused (except in the sense indicated) about suicide is the basis of the difficulties created by Durkheim's stipulated definition of suicide as "doing anything that the agent knows will bring about his own death." There are a great many actions that satisfy Durkheim's stipulation but do not count as cases of suicide in the ordinary language sense. Thus when Durkheim talks of suicide he is talking about something other than what speakers of ordinary language talk about when they use "suicide." Logically speaking, this fact need not create problems. (The practical problems are likely to be considerable.) But given the differences between the two concepts there are restrictions on the way statements using the one can be combined with statements using the other. As Durkheim recognizes, in ordinary language we cannot identify a case of suicide without evidence about intention. Moreover, the concept "intention" brings with it the concept of reasons for acting.[20] Since intention to take one's life is a defining feature of suicide we cannot explain or theorize about suicide without evidence about intention. An explanation or theory that did not use the concept "intention" would not, as such, be an explanation of suicide. Of course if we had identified a number of cases of suicide (in the ordinary-language sense) and hence had at least tacitly brought the concept "intention" into the discourse, we could search for

19. The misunderstandings involved in Durkheim's discussion of "intention" are equally serious but need not concern us at this juncture. We deal with closely related misunderstandings in discussing consent theories of political obligation in Chapter Seven below.

20. See the discussion of "intention" in Chapter Seven below.

factors that correlate with suicide. These factors would not themselves have to involve intention. If we found that there was a high correlation between cases of suicide and factors that did not involve intention (and if we were willing to use the covering law or statistical generalization model of explanation), we might say that the presence of those factors explained the occurrence of the suicides.[21] But this would be possible only because the conceptual conditions prerequisite to an explanation of suicide had in fact been satisfied. If the concepts in terms of which the data were gathered and discussed did not satisfy those conceptual conditions, those data could not—logically could not—be used to explain suicide. Statements based on those data could not be combined with statements about suicide without bridging the conceptual gap between them.

We are not suggesting that the use of technical concepts necessarily creates such difficulties. Investigators sensitive to ordinary language might construct their technical concepts so as to avoid the sorts of difficulties we have been discussing. The complexities of ordinary language make this difficult—more difficult than social scientists have recognized. The difficulties increase when dealing with actions that take place in languages of which we are not native speakers and increase yet

21. In fact this is what Durkheim did in most of his study. Cases of suicide—in the ordinary-language sense and hence involving intention—had been identified and recorded by governmental agencies. Durkheim accepted the government statistics as valid indicators of the occurrence of suicide in his sense. He then searched for correlations that would explain—in what would now be called the covering-law or statistical generalization sense—variations in the rates at which suicides had occurred. Owing to his willingness to accept those indicators most of his book is in fact about suicide in the ordinary-language sense. Strictly speaking, Durkheim should not have accepted these indicators as adequate for his purposes. While the statistical data he used do indicate the occurrence of suicides in his sense, the very cases that he wished to bring into his study by redefining the concept are systematically excluded by those data. In order to explain suicide in his sense he would have had to gather data about those cases of death that fall within the category of suicide as he defined it but are excluded by the ordinary-language concept of suicide.

further when we do not know the language at all. (This is all but certain to be the case when concepts are used universalistically.) But a difficulty is not the same thing as a logical impossibility.

VII. SOME OPPORTUNITIES FOR SOCIAL SCIENCE

THE LAST THREE SECTIONS (IV, V, and VI) parallel sections I through III, the difference between them being that I through III are concerned with language in general while IV through VI focus on questions more particularly related to social science. I and IV discuss some of the properties of language and their significance, II and V qualify the propositions advanced in I and IV, and III and VI reaffirm, with examples, the significance of the propositions of I and III as qualified in II and V. The argument of VI, however, is primarily of therapeutic or prophylactic significance. It calls attention to some types of conceptual problems that commonly arise in social science. In this respect the argument of VI is in accord with the thrust of much linguistically oriented work in Anglo-American philosophy. The later Wittgenstein and many writers influenced by him have argued that philosophical analysis of language is primarily if not exclusively of therapeutic or prophylactic value. It allows us to avoid mistakes and to dissolve pseudo-problems that result from misuse of or inattention to language. The task of building positive knowledge and understanding of human affairs and of reality more generally should be left to one or another of the branches of science.

In the chapters that follow we will criticize previous theories of political obligation, and we will try to show that some standard puzzles about political obligation, though not pseudo-problems, have been badly formulated. But we also wish to advance an account and an interpretation of the practice of political obligation. It is our objective to move beyond therapy toward a more positive theory. Conceptual analysis is one way of pursuing this objective. The propositions discussed in sections I, III, and IV of this chapter constitute the foundation on which this view rests; and the chapters that follow are an attempt to build on these foundations. It may be well, however, to provide a preliminary indication of the ways in which this will be done.

The limitations discussed in section VI are by no means the only type of restriction that language places upon us. Even when no conceptual disjunctions will result from using or combining a concept or concepts in a particular manner, it may be inappropriate or infelicitous to do so. Analyzing the conditions of felicitous and infelicitous use of concepts such as "obligation" can be illuminating concerning social and political practices and the human action that takes place within and concerning them.

Consider the following example.[22] On meeting B approaching a mail box with his completed tax return in hand, A says: "It is your obligation to submit an income tax return." We will assume that A's statement is true, that B *is* under an obligation to submit a tax return. A's statement would nevertheless be infelicitous in the circumstances described. The usual purpose of statements such as A's is to guide conduct. But it is inappropriate to attempt to guide a person's conduct when there is every reason to think that the person's conduct will be satisfactory. More schematically, the conventions governing "obligation" ordinarily allow A to use "obligation" to guide B's conduct only if B gives him reason to think he (B) is disinclined to discharge the obligation in question. Because he knows this convention, B will be puzzled by A's statement. He will be in doubt as to how to "take it" and how to respond to it. Depending on how A says it and what A says if the conversation continues, B might be insulted by it.

Knowing the English language, and hence knowing (even if

22. The example is discussed at length in Chapter Five.

he could not state the proposition systematically) that use of "obligation" to guide conduct ordinarily requires evidence of disinclination, B is apt to think that A is questioning whether B will actually mail the return, whether it is an honest return, or whether B's motives in submitting the return are the right motives. We emphasize the phrase "knowing the English language" because B's knowledge of the way "obligation" is used in that language is enough to create puzzlement and suspicion in his mind. The notion of an inappropriate or infelicitous use makes no sense without a standard that differentiates appropriate from inappropriate uses, and knowing such a standard (convention) is knowing the language. In this sense it is language that makes A's statement infelicitous; it is a linguistic convention that is violated by this kind of infelicity. Understanding the linguistic convention is what allows the observer to understand why B is puzzled.

But this is only the beginning of the theoretical significance of the convention. Knowing that A can use "obligation" only where B displays disinclination to discharge the obligation in question, and knowing that "obligation" continues to have use as a conduct-guiding concept, we know that such disinclination is an integral part of the practice of political obligation. We see that the practice does not operate in matters of conduct that are so thoroughly "matter-of-course," so completely habitual, for the members of the society that disinclination never develops. Thus we will not be tempted by accounts that treat the practice as consisting entirely of habitual behavior or seek to reduce it to such behavior. And we will be compelled to reconcile the fact that disinclination is a part of the practice with such notions as that the practice of obligation is one of the if not *the* foundation on which the rest of politics is built and that obligations are thought to be binding in a particularly stringent sense. More broadly, we will be led to examine the question of stability and change in a political society. The knowledge that use of "obligation" ordinarily implies evidence of disinclination will not itself be a sufficient basis for grappling with these questions. It will surely be highly relevant when attempting to do so.

VIII. CONCLUDING REMARKS

LANGUAGE IS NOT a strict calculus that allows us one and only one way to speak in every circumstance. It does not imprison our thought and discourse in sui generis, unalterable, or inescapable categories. But neither is it a loose, indeterminate, or undifferentiated instrument that places no restrictions whatever upon us. Durkheim is an example of a positivistically oriented philosopher and social scientist who did not pay sufficient attention to its rule-governed character. Such writers have underestimated the extent to which language has a logic that limits what we can say and which allows us to learn from it. Post-positivist thinkers such as Winch, on the other hand, have laid such emphasis on the determinate and restrictive character of ordinary language that they forbid procedures and practices that are not only familiar but very valuable.

Both of these views of language and of the relation between language, thought, and action carry unfortunate consequences for social science. Positivists thought that philosophy and social science could learn little or nothing from ordinary language. They urged philosophers and social scientists to follow (what they took to be) the example of natural science and construct new language better adapted to their special needs. The many social scientists who have been influenced by these views have been deprived of a valuable source of information and understanding concerning human conduct, and they have been rendered peculiarly liable to difficulties of the sort we discussed in the case of Durkheim. By contrast with positivist thinking, arguments such as those of Winch are a valuable corrective. But Winch would deprive the social scientist of valuable methods of investigation and analysis that his capacity to use language in fact make available to him. Social scientists need not accept either of these restrictive views. They can draw upon the evidence ordinary language supplies concerning human action and, with the exercise of due care, they can put ordinary language and specialized social-scientific language to the service of their distinctive needs and purposes. Bearing certain general considerations in mind, perhaps the best canon in these regards is supplied by Wittgenstein's trenchant aphorism: "Don't think, look."

Our discussion in this chapter is also relevant to some of the political themes we mentioned in the Introduction. Positivist philosophy of language and radically behavioral social science on the one hand and views such as those of Winch on the other carry some surprisingly similar implications concerning human action. Durkheim would eliminate intention from the notion of suicide (and presumably from notions concerning other human actions as well). Since concepts such as "deliberation," "choice," "judgment," and "purpose" pose the same problems for social science as does "intention," he presumably would want to eliminate them as well. His aim is to be able to explain the occurrence of suicide in terms of generalizations about social things. By hypothesis these generalizations would exclude reference to intention or to the other concepts just mentioned. Of course Durkheim's prescriptions concerning social science are not necessarily relevant to non-social-science thought and action. Indeed he insists that he is talking about tendencies in society and not trying to explain the actions of individuals or to alter ordinary understanding of action by individuals. But if Durkheim makes a convincing case that suicide can be more economically explained and understood if "intention" is removed, why should this gain in understanding be restricted to social scientists? Why shouldn't all of us bring our understandings of ourselves into conformity with Durkheim's findings? If correct, his account shows that nonscientific understandings of the social phenomenon of suicide are full of redundancies and unnecessary entities. More particularly, it shows that the behavior of members of a society is the result of causal forces at work in the society. I may think of what I do in terms of intention and reason, but I should recognize that the range of behavior in society, of which my behavior is part, is limited by forces identified without reference to intentions. At least to this degree Durkheim's arguments imply limitations on the significance of intention, reason, deliberation, and choice in human affairs. And of course not all later writers have shared Durkheim's reluctance to talk about individual conduct.

By contrast Winch and writers of his persuasion make a great deal of intention and reason and sternly deny that human action can be sufficiently explained by the sort of causal forces Durkheim emphasized. But they present a picture of *conceptual* restrictions so tightly drawn, so palpable, as to suggest narrow limitations on the paths which human thought and action can follow. The limits are not set by causal forces but by the "bounds of sense" laid down by the conventions governing our language. Thus, as we will see in Chapter Three and later, it has been argued that we cannot raise categorical questions such as "Why should I ever keep promises?" and "Why should I ever obey the law?" Such questions are said to be nonsensical, and raising them is said to be an indication of "philosophical disorder." If these questions cannot be raised, they cannot be answered, and the answers to them cannot be acted upon. Thus we cannot act to eliminate the practice of promising or the practice of political obligation. These practices might disappear, but we cannot act to eliminate them.

Neither of these understandings is adequate. In this chapter we have tried to suggest some of the elements of a more defensible view of language and the possibilities created by language. In the remainder of the work we will draw upon this understanding in analyzing political obligation.

(2)

Obligation and Ideals

you can only have an obligation if it is within your capacity to achieve it (handwritten note)

A PERSON CAN HAVE an obligation to do X only if it is within his capacity to do X. Accordingly, it makes sense for A to *tell* B that he has an obligation to do X only if A believes that it is within B's capacity to do X. "You (B) have an obligation to contribute $1,000 to your political party" is senseless if A knows that B has no funds to give. A's purpose (we will assume) is to guide B's conduct, but B could not possibly act upon the guidance A offers. This convention governing the use of "obligation" to guide conduct is summarized in the generalization " 'Obligation' implies ability."

" 'Obligation' implies ability" reminds us of a more widely discussed convention-cum-generalization concerning another concept often used to guide conduct, namely " 'Ought' implies can." For A to say that B ought to do X would seem to imply, very often does imply, a belief on A's part that B is able to do X. But there are well-established exceptions to " 'Ought' implies can." In particular the generalization does not hold concerning discourse about what are sometimes called moralities of ideals and aspirations, a kind or type of morality commonly defined by contrast with so-called moralities of obligation.

We will begin the task of identifying and analyzing the practice of political obligation by examining this contrast. Initially our procedure will be to look at some cases in which "ought" does not imply "can" and to make comparisons with uses of "obligation." Doing so will bring out, at a general level, some of the features of and problems that arise concerning the practice of guiding conduct by using "obligation." After attempting to delineate the use of the expression "political obligation" and identifying some of the problems that arise in connection with its use, we will examine some arguments as to how those problems should be solved. We will focus on one version of the argument that they should be solved by eliminating or discouraging individual reflection and deliberation concerning political obligations. This argument seems to be supported by the features that distinguish "ought" as it is used in discourse concerning ideals and aspirations from "obligation" as it is used in the expression "political obligation." The former leaves great scope for, indeed places great emphasis upon, individual reflection and choice in understanding and pursuing an ideal. The latter is used where there are established rules which forbid or require closely specified forms of conduct on the part of (usually) large numbers of people. Its effective use seems to presuppose commonality, stability, and even uniformity in the relationships among those who have the obligations—commonality and uniformity of a sort that individual reflection and choice has been thought to threaten. We will try to show, however, that this argument against reflection and choice concerning obligations, an argument which has the effect of putting the discharge of political obligations in the realm of behavior rather than action, misconstrues this distinction and its significance. We will also suggest that the argument threatens the very stability that those who have advanced it have wanted to maintain. In addition to introducing the topic of rules and the roles they play in the practice of political obligation, our discussion of this point will also allow us to make a start toward the broadly utilitarian argument about obedience and disobedience which it is our aim to develop.

I. OBLIGATIONS AND IDEALS

ASSUME THAT B regards the life of St. Francis as an ideal to which he should aspire. If so, he might fervently exclaim "I ought to live as he did." He might say this despite considerable experience indicating that such a life was beyond his capacities. Ideals set by the great religious teachers, and the religious teachings modeled upon them, often explicitly reject the convention that "ought" must imply "can." These ideals hold up the life and teaching of a religious leader as the life model to be imitated. But they recognize, or rather insist, that mere men are unable to do so completely. In some versions of the Christian teaching, for example, men ought to be Christlike (and they are held blameworthy, that is, sinful, when they fail) but they cannot. The force of the "ought" is indicated by the fact that inability to achieve the ideal would be damning if it were not for divine love and undeserved forgiveness. The force of the "cannot" is indicated by the fact that it would be damning to claim to have lived as Christ did. Rejection of "'Ought' implies can" is an essential part of the doctrine. (The exact interpretation placed upon this doctrine varies among the several Christian denominations. The position described here is most characteristic of Lutheranism.) It is true that men ought *to try* to be Christlike, that they have the capacity to try, and that they have the capacity to achieve limited successes. If these statements could not be made, the teaching would be unattractive if not senseless. But to try and yet fail, or to try and succeed only in part, satisfies only the "ought" that says one ought to try. If this were the only "ought" involved, failure to succeed could not be accounted sin. On the other hand, if one ought to succeed, and if "ought" did imply can, the doctrine would imply that men could achieve salvation by their own efforts.[1]

1. Nor is it the case that religious ideals are concerned only with feelings, for example love and gratitude, that are peculiarly outside of the

This exception to " 'Ought' implies can" is most clearly illustrated by but is not restricted to religious ideals. The convention does not hold in discourse about many ideals. The reasons why this is the case provide an enlightening contrast with the use of "obligation." We will mention two such reasons and then draw comparisons with "obligation." First, an ideal is something we strive toward, something that inspires us to improve our present level of performance. Once an ideal has been realized it no longer serves this purpose and a new ideal is needed. Thus ideals are either set so high as to be unattainable, as in the case of "Imitate the life of Christ," or revised upward periodically so as to stay ahead of actual achievement. Second, ideals typically have a loosely specified and open-ended character. Consider "Imitate the life of Christ," and the ancient Greek "Realize the highest human potential." Each directs attention to a life model that has many facets, that can be approached by many courses of action, and that develops and enlarges for the individual as he pursues and reflects upon it. The individual is to contemplate the model, seek to become imbued with its spirit, and make choices that seem likely to bring him more closely in accord with it. The choices will be affected both by the circumstances in which they are made and by the facet of the ideal grasped by the actor in question.[2]

---

control of the individual who experiences them. The Christian ought to act as Christ acted (or would act), not just have the feelings that Christ had (or would have).

Of course a man who thinks that "Ought *must* imply" can" might argue that these uses are somehow improper. Although he does not enter into the general questions raised by this view, William Frankena has disposed of it to our satisfaction: "For we can seriously defend [uses of "ought" that don't imply "can"] just as we can seriously defend the use of "dear" in "She is very dear to his heart," if we do not *assume* that "dear" always implies "expensive." William Frankena, "Obligation and Ability," *Philosophical Analysis*, ed. Max Black (Englewood Cliffs, N.J.: Prentice-Hall, 1963), p. 151.

2. In the second respect, though not in the first, ideals differ from goals. The goal of a fund-raising drive is usually set higher than the amount raised in previous drives in the hope of spurring the fund-raisers and the contributors to greater efforts. But the goal will be specified quite

"Obligation" is the most stringent of our conduct-guiding concepts. To say that A has an obligation to do X is to say that it "must be performed," that A is "bound" to do X (*Oxford English Dictionary*). As several commentators have noted, etymologically the concept traces to "ligare" which means "to bind," perhaps physically. The suggestion of physical constraint is analogical, but it brings out the strong connotations the concept carries.[3] To say that B has an obligation to achieve an ideal would be to suggest that B must, or is bound, to achieve it. It is analytic to say that it would be good or commendable or meritorious for B to achieve an ideal (though not to claim to have achieved it). It would be inappropriate to say that he had an obligation to achieve it. Short of a special explanation (or indications that A was not choosing his words with minimum care), B would be puzzled by such a remark.

The same conclusion is suggested by the loosely specified, open-ended character of ideals. There is no single formula or set of rules that will tell a man how to pursue the Christian ideal or how to fulfill his highest potential as a human being. Since some actions promise more in this respect than others, there are good and even best actions in a set of circumstances. But when we say that an action is obligatory we are saying that it is the one action that the man must do to fulfill his obligation. Notice that we often use the verb "discharge" with "obligation." To be able to say that a man has or has not discharged an obligation requires a closely specified understanding of what it is that is obligatory, an understanding that allows us to distinguish performance of the obligation from other actions

---

exactly so that everyone will know when the drive has been successful. An *ideal* fund-raising drive, on the other hand, would probably exceed its goal—by an amount not specified in advance—and would have other virtues as well, perhaps harmonious relationships among the fund-raisers and between the latter and the larger community.

3. Cf. David Gauthier, *Practical Reasoning* (London: Oxford University Press, 1963) Ch. 12. This feature of "obligation" is discussed at length in Chapter Six below.

and that allows us to identify a terminal point at which the obligation has been discharged. Thus "The Christian is obligated to imitate the life of Christ," is odd because it is too indefinite and open-ended for "obligation." By contrast, "It is your obligation to register with the Selective Service System," and "Having promised to meet X at 5:00 p.m. you are under an obligation to do so," are appropriate. We know what must be done and we know when the obligation has been discharged (or not).[4]

These differences between "obligation" and the use of "ought" in discourse about ideals embody a number of the differences between two segments of morality, segments that some moral philosophers have regarded as so different as to constitute distinct types of morality. The exception to " 'Ought' implies can" that we have been discussing is common in what have been called "moralities of aspiration." If effective, such moralities elevate human beings and societies above their present level and spur them on to achievements over and above what they think they can achieve and over and above mere survival or even mere satisfaction of their needs and desires as presently conceived. They are moralities that urge men to press beyond a satisfactory life to a life of excellence, to aspire to the achievements of saints and heroes.

Accounts of the lives of saints suggest that there have been men for whom a morality of aspiration constituted a sufficient guide to conduct. They genuinely sought to make their every action accord with or bring them closer to a very high ideal, and they were prepared to sacrifice all lesser satisfactions to the ideal. There may even have been societies and groups of men

4. Another feature of the use of "obligation" that we will discuss in Chapter Five is relevant here. Use of "obligatory" ordinarily implies that failure to do the action will be blamed and perhaps punished, but performance of the act will not be praised. To assign blame, and especially to punish, requires clear specification, usually specification in advance, of what constitutes acceptable and unacceptable conduct. Once again this is a condition not usually satisfied by ideals or discourse concerning ideals. But it is almost always appropriate to praise people for acting in a manner that brings them closer to an ideal.

within societies (for example utopian communities) that sought to base all relations on a morality of aspiration. Such men or such a society would have no occasion to employ the concept of obligation as it is now used in English. (Or rather they would have no occasion to use it to guide conduct in their own society. They might use it for descriptive or analytic purposes or to guide the conduct of others.)

For most men and most societies, however, the morality of aspiration is built upon a morality which, if effective, contributes to making human life tolerable, to making it possible for men to live together in reasonable peace and order and to satisfy the material needs and desires common among them. The requirements of this second kind or aspect of morality are often embodied in rules and laws that apply to all or most of the members of the society. These rules and laws bind the members to specified types of conduct. Failure to conform to the rules usually meets with some form of sanctions.[5]

---

5. Thus this second kind of morality has often been labeled "law-" or "rule-governed" morality. On the distinction between the two kinds of morality see for example: H. L. A. Hart, *The Concept of Law* (London: Oxford University Press, 1961); Lon Fuller, *The Morality of Law* (New Haven: Yale University Press, 1964); Henri Bergson, op. cit.; Lord Lindsay, *The Two Moralities* (London: Eyre and Spottiswoode, 1948); J. O. Urmson, "Saints and Heroes" in A. I. Melden, ed., *Essays in Moral Philosophy* (Seattle: University of Washington Press, 1958). The distinction between the two moralities, and between obligation and ideals, was beautifully employed by Carlo Weber in a discussion of birth control. Weber wrote:

I readily subscribe to the ideal that the natural processes ought not to be impeded or thwarted or frustrated, in any quarter, not in conception, nor in childbirth, nor in the growth of the child, nor in the movements of nature. Nature is to be prized, cradled, loved, not blocked. I believe, therefore, that it would be wrong to obstruct the natural process of conception when there is not actual conflict with a higher goal. But to legislate that ideal is to condemn those who cannot honestly attain it, and incidentally to rob them of the right to pursue the goal as well as they can, simply and precisely because it is seen as good, and not because it is an obligation. The danger in making laws of ideals is that one then begins to think in legal categories, a problem that has beset Catholic moral theology for centuries. It is the responsibility of the Church to state the ideal as clearly and beautifully as possible, to inspire people to pursue it,

This second kind or segment of morality is the usual home of the concept "obligation." The requisites of such a morality are among the requisites of the use of the concept to guide conduct. One of these would seem to be the existence and identification of a degree of commonality or some common denominators among all or most of the members of the society. Some sense of commonality of interest and/or need would seem to be necessary if a judgment that a type of conduct should be required of all members is to be widely accepted. Moreover, for a type of conduct to be obligatory for all the members of a society they must share the capacities necessary to discharge the obligation.[6] Thus by contrast with a morality of ideals or aspirations, a morality of obligation must be built upon and must emphasize characteristics common to groups of men, must minimize individual differences.

As we noted in the Introduction, a number of philosophers and statesmen from Plato to Bergson have argued that the points emerging from the foregoing comparison carry definite implications concerning obedience. They have urged that, at least as regards political obligations, the commonality, indeed uniformity, necessary to a morality of obligation can be achieved and sustained only if or to the extent that the rules

---

to provide them every means, by grace, education, and social reform to do so. It does no good, however, to make criminals and sinners of those who cannot, for social or personal reasons, achieve the ideal no matter how honestly they seek it. I do not have in mind those who piteously clamor that they cannot attain the ideal, when in fact they are rationalizing their own narcissism. But I do believe that people should be motivated to discover for themselves how close they can approach the ideal, and not how legitimately or illegitimately they may deviate from it. Carlo Weber, "The Birth Control Controversy," *The New Republic,* 23 November 1968.

6. Assigning obligations has of course been regarded as a way to *create* a common denominator among the members of a society, as a way to weld a diversity of men into a unity sufficient to make political life possible. At the very least, however, this practice presupposes commonality of latent or potential capacity sufficient to make it possible for men to accept and discharge the assigned obligations. In this respect at least the practice of assigning and discharging obligations is grounded in and limited by what is common to the members of a society qua members of the society.

defining obligations are treated as absolutes which are to be obeyed under virtually all circumstances. They have also argued that such obedience, and hence the requisite uniformity, are best achieved when the members of the society eschew critical reflection and choice concerning the content of the rules which define obligations—when they commit themselves to, or are in some way brought to conform with the obligation rules simply because they are rules or on even less reflective grounds. Reflection concerning the rules and the exercise of choice as to whether to obey them, the argument runs, serves to enlarge or emphasize individual differences and to threaten both commonality and uniformity.

Granting that obligation rules form a comparatively settled part of a stable political order, and granting that it is desirable that they should do so, we will argue that unreflective conformity with them may in fact threaten stability. We will suggest that critical reflection and decision contributes to stability. Or rather we will try to show that some commonly used arguments against this position are not cogent and we will begin the task of developing a counterargument.

II. POLITICAL AND OTHER OBLIGATIONS

WE MAY BEGIN by recalling that not all obligations are common to all members of a society. Among the important sources of obligations are practices such as promising and contracting. As Hume and others have argued, the obligation to keep promises depends upon wide acceptance of a rule to the effect that to make a promise or a contract is to undertake an obligation.[7] The existence and effectiveness of such a rule presupposes that the members of the society are able to understand and act according to the rules and procedures that constitute promising and contracting, including the rule that one ought not to make

7. See David Hume, *Treatise of Human Nature*, Book III, Part II, Section V. See also Hart, op. cit., pp. 42–43; John Searle, "How to Derive 'Ought' from 'Is,'" *Philosophical Review* 73, pp. 43 ff.

promises and contracts that are beyond his capacity to keep. To this degree such practices presuppose commonality among those who participate in them. (Those who are assumed not to have the requisite capacities, for example young children, are excluded from the practice.) But the procedures constituting the practice place only very general limits on what, substantively speaking, one can promise or contract to do. Moreover there are few if any actions that members must promise or contract to do. In these respects the capacity required is as diverse as the substance of the promises and contracts actually made. It would be bizarre to suggest that maintaining stability or commonality requires that the individual not reflect about which promises or contracts he should make.

Some commentators have treated promising as paradigmatic of all obligation-generating practices. They have argued that we use "obligation" only in situations that are like promising contexts in at least two respects: (1) the obliger [8] must undertake the obligation, and (2) the content or substance of the obligation will be determined by and hence will vary with the content of the agreement, promise, or undertaking.[9] It seems undeniable, however, that "obligation" is also used in situations that not only lack these features but in fact involve assigning substantively identical obligations to a very great many people who have never agreed to or undertaken them. There is nothing odd about the statement "Christians may . . . choose to serve the cause of racial justice by disobeying a law that clearly violates their obligations as Christians," [10] nor, to take a more immediately relevant case, the statement "Citizens of the

8. We will use "obliger" to refer to one who has an obligation. Compare "debtor," one who has a debt, and "contractor," one who has made a contract.

9. See for example Gauthier, op. cit., Ch. 12, and Alexander Sesonske, *Value and Obligation* (New York: Oxford University Press, 1964). But see also Richard Brandt, "The Concepts of Obligation and Duty," *Mind* 73 (1964). For an extended discussion of the views of Gauthier and Sesonske see Chapter Seven below.

10. "Race Relations," Statement adopted by the Biennial Convention of the Lutheran Church in America, 1964. Published as an occasional pamphlet by the American Lutheran Church. No date or place of publication indicated.

United States have an obligation to submit an income tax return each year." Indeed it has been widely thought that the modern nation-state is distinguished from its feudal predecessors by the fact that it assigns a substantial number of obligations to all of its citizens, obligations that many of the citizens would not undertake if left to their own devices. In feudal societies such political obligations as there were had been defined through personal relationships of a contractual or quasi-contractual type and were adapted to local and individual conditions. In the post-feudal state there are obligations that are common to all members. This feature of the nation-state has been thought to be one of the main sources of its strength. Common obligations bind all of the members of society together in a unity that feudal societies were unable to achieve. Thus they contribute to making the massed power of the members of the society available for collective action.[11]

It is precisely these characteristics of the nation-state, however, that have prompted some writers to argue that the notion of obligation should not be used concerning the requirements which such states make of their citizens or subjects. These features may be a source of strength, but they also render the notion of political and legal obligations "inapposite." [12] Of course the very act of criticizing the notion of "political obli-

11. Note that this generalization assumes that there are concepts (concepts, not words) in French, German, Dutch, etc., that are comparable in the relevant respects to the English "obligation." This has to be the case if we are to say that the practice of ascribing identical obligations to all members is a feature of the nation-state. To the extent that it is the case we are justified in generalizing from our findings concerning "obligation" and obligation in English and English-speaking societies to other political societies. We are of course equally justified in generalizing to any other society that has a concept relevantly similar to the English "obligation." We have not made the investigations of French, German, etc., to say nothing of non-Western languages, that would be required to verify the generalizations (nor have we seen the results of such investigations by others), and hence strictly speaking we must regard the generalization as an assumption.

12. See esp. John Ladd, "Legal and Moral Obligation," in J. R. Pennock, ed., *Political Obligation* (New York: Atherton Press, 1970), Nomos 12.

gation" concedes that it has had use in the language that the writers in question have been able to understand. But they argue that the notion distorts the logic of what John Ladd calls the "paradigm" or "strict" uses of the concept and hence produces muddles. Among other things, they assert that it renders one of the conditions necessary to the use of "obligation," namely individual choice, irrelevant or inappropriate.[13]

We do not wish to deny that political and legal obligations are more general and require more commonality than obligations undertaken by promising. It is worth noting, however, that such obligations are rarely entirely general. Through the familiar device of legislative classification differing obligations are assigned to people with differing capacities. Thus "common denominator" and "uniform" often means common or uniform among a class of the population, not the entire population. For example most of the provisions of the Selective Service Act in the United States apply to males between eighteen and thirty-five years of age.[14] This procedure expands the versatility of the device of assigning obligations as a means of social control and direction. Since legislators cannot know the capacities of all of the members of their society in the way a man making a promise can know his, the very fact that "obligation" implies ability makes it clear that it is valuable for the citizen

13. We should note that this argument seems to presume that there is (and must be?) one and only one set of conventions governing all uses of "obligation." It is true that there must be a set of conventions governing the use of a concept. It is also true that if there are differing conventions governing different uses, e.g., as regards promising and as regards obeying the law, the *concept* differs from use to use. But it would hardly follow from these facts alone that one of the uses is appropriate and the others are not. Also, the argument that "political obligation" is both inapposite *and* morally objectionable is somewhat hard to follow. If the use is inapposite it can have *no* implications, morally objectionable or otherwise.

14. All laws apply to all residents in the society in at least the following respects: they are promulgated by an authority common to all; no one is legally permitted to interfere with their operation; and all residents can be required to support them by paying taxes and in other ways that are adapted to the varying capacities of those from whom support is demanded.

to reflect about and discuss critically the classifications employed in passing laws that generate obligations.[15]

The suggestion that political and legal obligation are inapposite notions, however, raises a question which cannot be dealt with by making further comparisons between political obligations and ideals or political obligations and obligations undertaken by promising. The objection raises the question of what exactly we mean by the expression *"political* obligation." How does the use of this expression differ from the use of "obligation" in connection with promising or when qualified by "religious" or "familial"? Answering this question will involve a slight detour, but the detour will lead us to an important form of the argument that reflection and choice about political obligations is undesirable.

Since the answer to the question will turn in part on interpreting the qualifier "political," we should concede that any answer will involve an element of stipulation. "Politics" and "political" are not among the more precisely delineated concepts in our language. Argument concerning their proper use constitutes a veritable subfield of political philosophy and political science. But these concepts cannot be used in any manner whatever; there are some uses which no one would question and some which no one would allow.

From the *Antigone* and the *Crito* forward the obligation most commonly described as political has been the obligation to obey the law and other authoritative commands emanating from the state. Similarly, the question most commonly discussed under the rubric "political obligation" is "Should I obey the law?" Quite clearly, legally defined obligations constitute the bulk of what has been thought to be political obligation.

These facts might suggest that political obligation and legal obligation are coextensive phenomena; perhaps even that "po-

---

15. It is of course by no means the case that all laws either require or prohibit behavior. Thus it is not the case that all laws assign obligations. On this point see H. L. A. Hart, op. cit., Chaps. 3 and 5, and passim.

litical obligation" and "legal obligation" are synonymous terms. We can, however, speak of obligations to political parties or interest groups as political, and it is widely thought that there are obligations arising out of citizenship which are not defined by law but which would be called political. It is certainly common, for example, to hear it said that the citizen has a political obligation to vote, to keep himself informed about public affairs, to support and defend the constitution.

For present purposes, however, the more important point is that the notion of legal obligation can never stand alone. Of course it has often been argued that the notion of legal obligation is incomplete or even vacuous without the notion of moral obligation. But the point relevant here is broader than the argument that political obligations must be supported by or even equivalent to moral obligations.

Let us recur to a feature of promising mentioned above. If B says "I promise to do X" he undertakes an obligation to do X. He does not have to *say*, very rarely does *say*, that he undertakes an obligation. Yet B and everyone who knows the language knows that to say "I promise" is ordinarily to undertake an obligation. ("Ordinarily" covers a multitude of exceptions which we will not go into here. One example: A [a prosecuting attorney]: "What exactly did C say to D as they left the restaurant?" B [a witness]: "He said 'I promise to . . .'.") If B does not know that this is the case he does not know the use of "I promise" in the language. We noted that Hume had accounted for this feature of "I promise" by saying that there is a rule or convention established in B's society to the effect that to promise is to undertake an obligation. The status and the logical characteristics of rules such as this one will concern us in the following chapter. Here it is enough to say that in the absence of something like what Hume called a rule, B's obligation to do what he promised to do would be inexplicable. B's obligation does not arise magically from his making a certain sound or set of marks on paper. We might say that the notion of a promising obligation does not stand alone. It presupposes a socially established rule or arrangement according to which to promise *is* to undertake an obligation.

Legal obligations pose a closely analogous problem. Such obligations are established when (though not only when) a legislature or other authoritative agency of the state passes or issues a law or other authoritative command which forbids or requires a class of individuals to do a certain action. But just as B rarely uses the concept "obligation" in promising, so legislatures, executive officers, and judges rarely if ever use it in framing laws and orders. Nor do legislatures enact laws stating that citizens or subjects have an obligation to obey laws. Whence, then, the idea that there is an *obligation* to obey the law?

The answer to this question is much more complicated than the answer to the analogous question about promises. From a conceptual standpoint it involves the relationships among the concepts "law," "authority," "obligation," and perhaps others. The complexities will concern us in the following chapter. At this juncture we will rest with the same answer we gave concerning promising, namely that there can be legal *obligations* where there is an established rule to the effect that there is an obligation to obey the laws and other authoritative commands of the state. We will call this "rule" the *general* rule to distinguish it from the *particular* rules or laws passed or promulgated by legislatures, courts, etc. Behind statements such as (1) "Citizens of the United States have a legal obligation to submit an income tax return" there lies not only (2) a law requiring them to submit such a return, but also (3) the general rule "Citizens of the United States have an obligation to obey the authoritative commands, of which laws are one species, of their government." [16] When we state the first two we imply the third. The first two can be said only because the

16. On the relation between "obligation" and "authority," see esp. Hanna Pitkin, "Obligation and Consent—II," *American Political Science Review* 50:1 (March 1966). For further discussion of the relationship, and of Pitkin's arguments concerning it, see Chapters Three and Seven below.

rule stated by the third is established in the society. (For brevity we will hereafter formulate the general rule as "Obey the law.")

The one point that is clear about this "general rule" is that it is not a legal rule. To repeat, legislatures do not pass laws which make it obligatory to obey the law. As Hobbes saw, passing such a law would only raise the question why there is an obligation to "obey" the law creating an obligation to obey other laws. It is in this sense that we are arguing that legal obligation does not stand by itself.

How then should we characterize the general rule? The answer to this question will depend in part on our purpose in characterizing it. If we wish to present an accurate description of the way the rule works in a given political order we will want to know how the members of that political order regard it or act in relation to it. The best evidence on this question will be what they say about why they obey and/or disobey the law. If they say that there is a moral obligation to obey the law, or if they describe obedience to law in terms that satisfy the criteria of the use of "moral" (as opposed to nonmoral) among them, then we can say that the rule is a moral rule for them. If their talk about or action vis-à-vis law shows that they think of it as something that "you better obey or else" then we can say that it is a prudential or expediential rule. There are other possibilities as well. There is no reason to think that only one of them will be realized in any society.

We might also wish to assess or evaluate the rule in various ways, for example decide whether it is effective or whether we as analysts think it is a moral rule in the sense of a rule that is morally good or right to obey. In these cases the testimony given by the members of the society will be relevant but not conclusive.

A third possibility is that we might want to analyze the rule in the sense of locating it among the various types of rules, arrangements, and practices at work in the society. It is in connection with this third objective that it would be most natural to call the rule a political rule and the obligation a political obligation. To characterize them as political would be to say that the rule and the obligation are a part, presumably an important part, of the political (as opposed to the economic, religious, familial, etc.) aspects of the society. Whatever else we might want to include in the category of political arrangements, few of us would quarrel with the suggestion that government, law, and the requirement that government and law be obeyed are an important part of them. Thus however else we might characterize the general rule, we can certainly characterize it as a political rule. If we are right that the notion that there is an obligation to obey the law lies behind all particular legal obligations, it follows that all legal obligations, regardless of the content of the particular law in question in this case or that, are political obligations. To say this is not the same as to say that it is a legal obligation although it is of course entirely consistent with saying that it is a legal obligation. It is also consistent with saying that it is a moral obligation, and even a religious or familial obligation. (Thus in a theocracy many obligations would at once be political, legal, religious, and moral.) It is also consistent with the obligation having been undertaken by promise or consent, inherited, assigned, accepted, or otherwise acquired or justified. The obligation is political because it is an integral part of the political arrangements and practices of the society. Such other obligations as there may be, which are not defined by law—for example to support a political party or to take an active interest in public affairs—may be called political for the same kind of reason. They too may vary widely in content, in manner of development, definition, and acquisition, and in justification.

III. POLITICAL OBLIGATION AND THE CONTAGIOUS EFFECTS OF DISOBEDIENCE

WE NOW RETURN to the question whether individual reflection and choice is undesirable or inappropriate as regards political obligations. We will concentrate on the case of political obligations that are also legal obligations. In the present chapter the focus of our examination of this many-faceted question will be some of the ways in which the general rule has been used in framing arguments about obedience and disobedience to law.

It is impossible to obey or disobey a particular legal rule—e.g., "Stop at red lights," "Do not transport women in interstate commerce for immoral purposes,"—without violating the general rule as well (and the converse). But the standing of and justification for the general rule is very different from the standing of and justification for any particular rule. It is not uncommon to act in the manner required by both while accepting the justification for only one. An anarchist might refrain from carrying concealed weapons because he believes it a good rule of conduct and despite being unconvinced by the argument for the general rule. As the argument quoted in the Introduction indicates, Abraham Lincoln might have been entirely unconvinced by the arguments for, say, not carrying concealed weapons and yet have obeyed the law forbidding it because it was a legal rule which he could not disobey without disobeying the general rule.

Even Lincoln's sweeping argument concerning the importance of the general rule leaves open the question of whether there should be a legal rule on this point or that and whether it should be this rule or that. One cannot infer from the argument for the general rule the importance of any particular rule as such. It is more plausible to infer from the argument for the importance of the general rule the importance of *obeying* particular rules. This is the use to which the argument for the general rule is most often put. The man who objects to a particular rule and is inclined to disobey it is told that he must not do so. Even if his objections to the particular rule are sound, to disobey it is necessarily to disobey the general rule. If disobedience to the latter threatens the system of legal rules and everything that depends upon them, it is wrong to disobey it. In large, diverse political societies that promulgate many laws, some of which inevitably affect some members adversely, the argument continues, the general rule is of great importance. If the case for obedience rested entirely on the argument for each particular rule there would be a higher incidence of disobedience.

In this manner arguments for the general rule become a vehicle for arguing that reflection and choice concerning obedience to political obligation rules must be severely limited. Once a legal rule has been passed it falls under the general rule. Thus questioning of it, to say nothing of actually disobeying it, acquires a significance far greater than the subject or content of the particular rule itself might suggest. (Note the parallel with deontological arguments about keeping promises. Keeping this or that promise may not, in itself, be of great importance. But the rule "Promises should be kept" is of great importance. Since breaking any particular promise violates "Promises should be kept," keeping each and every promise acquires great significance.) Acceptance of and strict conformity to the general rule becomes the way in which the society achieves and maintains the commonality and uniformity required by a morality or practice of obligation.

Reliance upon the argument for the general rule has disadvantages that have not been given sufficient attention. The most obvious of these obtain in unstable regimes, regimes that have not won the loyalty or firm support of their members. Emphasizing the general rule has the effect of making the question of obeying any and every particular rule a question of supporting or undermining the political order itself. If a group of men objected to a particular rule, and if they had no great respect for or attachment to the regime, emphasizing the general rule might raise the question most dangerous for the regime. In such a regime, the stronger the objection to the particular rule, the greater the danger of relying upon the argument for the general rule to win obedience to the particular rule.

In a well-established, stable political order enjoying strong support from its members, reliance upon the general rule is not likely to create the problem just mentioned. Appeals for obedience based on the general rule can be supported by reference to the benefits and advantages generated by the political order. If it is true that the political order is threatened by disobedience to the general rule as it applies to particular legal rules, then the argument against doing so is both cogent and likely to be persuasive.

But is it true? Does the argument provide a cogent case for obedience to particular legal rules? Granting that I cannot disobey a particular rule X without disobeying the general rule as it applies to X (which is the indisputable logical point at the core of the argument), why should I expect that my disobeying X will influence others to do so or influence myself or others to lose respect for the general rule? The argument that I should not disobey X because doing so will lead to disobedience to X' obviously involves an extension of the logical point just mentioned. Most of the attempts to defend this extension have made use of some version of the assertion that disobedience is contagious. A priori one would expect that some kinds of disobedience are contagious and some not, and that those that are so are contagious under some circumstances and not under others. Points that we have already discussed, especially the point that "obligation" is used of matters thought to be of fundamental importance to the society, suggest some distinctions among types of cases in which men may be inclined to disobey particular legal rules. These distinctions may shed some light on the question of when and why disobedience is likely to be contagious in stable regimes and hence likely to undermine the commonality and uniformity characteristic of the realm of obligation.

Insofar as particular legal rules are widely agreed to be good rules and addressed to matters thought to be of importance to society, the relationship between particular rules and the general rule is not a source of difficulty. The law against homicide, for example, serves one of the most fundamental objectives of virtually all societies. When the law is broken society has, to that degree, failed to achieve one of its basic objectives. We don't condemn homicide by showing that one homicide will lead to another or that breaking the law against homicide will lead to violations of other laws. Legal rules that are approved and widely thought to be important can be defended, and disobedience condemned, without relying upon the case for the general rule *in isolation from* the case for the particular rule in question. The general rule remains essential because it provides the basis for saying that there is an obligation to obey the particular rule. But there may be little need to appeal to the general rule in order to persuade men to obey the particular rule or to justify compelling obedience or punishing disobedience on the part of the occasional disobedient. If the case for the general rule is used for the latter purposes, it can be argued that it (the rule) should be respected because it provides ancillary support for particular rules extremely important to society.

In a stable regime these points hold even for laws addressed to what are agreed to be important matters but to which some members have strong objections. If the matter is both important and controversial, a case can be made that it is essential that there be a law, even an unsatisfactory law, regularizing conduct concerning it. If there was no law, or if the law was widely disobeyed, the members of society might act at cross purposes and conflicts and inequities might result. Thus once again the argument for obeying the particular rule need not depend on showing that disobeying it will influence men to disobey other laws as well. Disobedience to this law is directly productive of undesirable consequences.

The second type of case involves the use of law to require or prohibit types of conduct not thought to be of great import or thought to be important only by small segments of the populace. As the function of the state has enlarged, the statute books have been swollen by measures that may be well drafted and useful but that could hardly be said to be essential to the basic objectives of society. Moreover, much of this legislation is directed to problems special to limited segments of society. The segments of the populace directly affected by it may think it important, but large parts of the population may not even be aware of it.

Noticing these facts, H. L. A. Hart has argued that one of the differences between moral and legal obligations is that rules defining moral obligations "are regarded as . . . of great importance to maintain," while "importance is not essential to the status of all legal rules." [17] But if a law is not important to maintain, why should I obey it? And why should others who observe my disobedience disapprove of it? More urgently perhaps, if a law is unimportant what is the justification for punishing my failure to obey it? [18] Perhaps even comparatively unimportant laws should be obeyed because it is important to

17. Hart, op. cit., pp. 170, 171. Hart recognizes that many legal rules are thought extremely important to maintain. In addition, however, we should note certain complexities and qualifications that Hart does not discuss. Hart's argument applies most clearly to the case of "laws" that have fallen into desuetude, laws that remain on the statute books only because an occasion to repeal them has never occurred. Such "laws" are certainly not thought to be important. Other laws, for example parking regulations, are as a general matter not thought very important—as indicated by the fact that violations are penalized but do not prompt other forms of disapproval. But in some circumstances, for example where there is very heavy use of available parking space, the rules are taken seriously and violations are strongly disapproved. Again, the man who persistently violates parking regulations, who incurs many many parking tickets each year, might meet with expressions of disapproval that would be unusual and even thought inappropriate in the case of the person who receives an occasional ticket. In the first case Hart is right but his argument is uninteresting. In the second it is certainly true that parking regulations are thought less important than, say, laws against homicide, but there is nevertheless a social purpose that is served by them and in some circumstances they take on considerable importance. Presumably this would be true of almost any law that had not fallen into desuetude. Thus the sort of justification that would be appropriate for violating even the less important legal rules would vary according to the circumstances in which the violation was committed, as would the sort of disapproval appropriate to violations. The third case illustrates the connection between particular rules and the general rule that we discuss immediately below. Persistent and willful violation of even an unimportant law is thought to flout and show lack of respect for law in general.

18. In the case of laws that have fallen into desuetude, of course, the answer given by all but the most insistent legal absolutists is that I need not obey and that disapproval and punishment are neither required nor appropriate.

obey the law. The apparently *paradoxical* character of this reply vanishes when we draw the distinction between the general and the particular rule. The latter may be unimportant, but the former is of great importance. And the latter cannot be disobeyed without disobeying the former and perhaps without influencing others to disobey the former as well. But if there is no paradox in the relationship between the general rule and particular rules, the peculiarities of that relationship might mean that reliance on the argument for the general rule will actually contribute to the likelihood of contagious disobedience.

Whatever the abstract arguments for accepting the general rule, if the specific result of doing so is that men are regularly required to act in ways they think it unimportant to act, commitment to the general rule might be expected to weaken. Reliance upon the general rule to support the demand for obedience to particular rules not thought important might weaken the sense of the importance of the general rule itself. B perceives that the general rule requires him to do X, X', X", all of which he considers trivial. He generalizes from these cases and draws the conclusion that the general rule is unimportant. He then brings this conclusion to his deliberations concerning all cases that fall under the general rule.

We can give this speculation somewhat greater cogency by stating it in terms of points discussed earlier. We say there is an obligation to obey the law, an obligation to conform to the general rule. "Obligation" and "obligatory" are typically used of types of actions thought to be of great importance to the society or social group, and they are especially forceful conduct-guiding concepts because they are used in connection with types of actions thought to be of great importance. A sense of the importance of the allegedly obligatory action is one of the conditions which makes it appropriate to use "obligatory" and "obligation" with their implication that the actions "must be performed." Occasional use of the concepts in the absence of those conditions, as when "obligation" is made to do for the whole range of action-guiding concepts, is not likely to alter the conventions governing or the implications of "obligation." In the case of trivial legal rules, however, the relationship between the general rule and particular rules creates a pervasive tension among the conventions governing the use of "obligation." The availability of "authoritative" and "law" to characterize the particular rules make it appropriate to use "obligation" in conduct-guiding discourse about them. But the sense of the unimportance of the conduct required by the particular rules deprives "obligation" of sources of support that make it cogent and forceful. Use of the concept under these conditions violates or at least strains the logic of the concept. It might weaken its conduct-guiding force as compared with its use under conditions that accord more completely with its usual logic. Continued violation of the logic of a concept is likely to change its logic, at least for the class of uses in question. In this case the change is almost certain to be in the direction of reducing if not eliminating the implication that obligatory actions are actions that "must be performed." The *word* will remain the same but the *concept* will have undergone a change. Thus members of the society may continue to use "obligation" in connection with legal rules but the inference that those rules must therefore be obeyed would no longer follow from use of the concept.

There is indirect evidence that such a development has in fact occurred in the case of legal rules such as parking and traffic regulations, antilitter ordinances, and regulations of a more specialized kind, for example those governing profit reporting by corporations, antitrust legislation, regulations concerning contracts with the government, and many others. These laws are often violated and disapproval of violations is less than uniform or insistent; one should pay the penalty if caught, but to disobey without being caught is sometimes thought a kind of achievement or success. Strictly speaking the disobedience is criminal but the disobedients are not thought of as criminals. Yet the belief that one should pay the penalty tacitly concedes that these regulations are authoritative and hence that it is linguistically appropriate to say there is an obligation to obey them. Thus it would seem that the logic of "obligation" in these contexts is not always thought to include "must be performed." In its application to such rules the general rule can be said to generate an obligation, but the concept does not have the same conduct-guiding force it has in other contexts.

Linguistic developments of the sort we have been discussing are more symptomatic of changes in attitudes than causes of the latter. Despite what we said above, it is not likely that the tension between the general rule and particular rules would itself constitute a sufficient explanation for a significant number of acts of disobedience. At best the explanation could account for the comparatively uninteresting case of disobedience to laws not thought to be important in society. It would be implausible to argue that the sense of the unimportance of the general rule as it applied to unimportant particular rules would carry over to its applications to laws agreed to be important.

IV. THE CONTAGIOUS EFFECTS OF
DISOBEDIENCE AND REFLECTION AND CHOICE

ASIDE FROM CLARIFYING the relationship between the general rule and particular legal rules (and perhaps casting some light in a small corner of the practice of political obligation), our discussion of "important" and "unimportant" legal rules directs attention to a related but different class of cases, those in which men obey particular rules out of habit or in some other unreflective or uncritical manner, that is in just the manner that the distinction between ideals and obligation has been thought to suggest they should and do. Here the particular rule might in fact be important, but it is not *thought* to be important; it is not thought to be important because it is simply not thought about. Men obey it, or rather the behavior of men conforms with it, but they do so unreflectively or uncritically.[19] Because

19. On the differences between following a rule and acting habitually see among many recent discussions: Peter Winch, op. cit. (London:

men do conform to the rule (and hence to the general rule as it applies to the particular rule in question) it would seem that the question of explaining their disobedience simply would not arise in a practical way (a situation that many would think difficult to improve upon).

Despite its apparent virtues, habitual, unreflective conformity with particular rules on the part of any very sizable segment of a populace can be a source of difficulties. Law is an instrument that human beings use to serve their purposes, to assist them in achieving their objectives. Particular legal rules are ordinarily passed to solve some problem or meet some need. The fact that they do so is what justifies the belief that they are important and should be obeyed. But when men conform to them in an unthinking manner the basis of this belief is lost. One result of such a development is that the importance of laws is not conveyed to new generations. Since the latter may find the habits of their elders unattractive, and since the elders have lost the capacity to defend their own behavior, conflict may develop between generations. Similarly, technological and other types of change may take place that render the laws inappropriate. Since conformity to the laws has become unthinking, these changes and/or their implications for the laws may go unnoticed and neither the laws nor the behavior patterns associated with them will be changed to adapt to them.

The most general and most dangerous outcome of such a situation is the accumulation of social problems until a crisis is reached. The crisis may be sufficient to jar people out of their habitual modes of behavior but it is apt to do so in a costly and unpleasant manner. Such a situation could strain the relationship between the general and the particular rule in a manner not unlike (but much more significant than) the strain created by parking regulations and antilitter ordinances. Those

Routledge and Kegan Paul, 1958), esp. pp. 57–65; Hart, op. cit., esp. pp. 54–59; and Max Black, "Rules and Routines," in R. S. Peters, ed., *The Concept of Education* (London: Routledge and Kegan Paul, 1967), esp. pp. 97–98. These distinctions and their significance are discussed at greater length below. See esp. Chapters Three, Four, and Six.

who are skeptical of the established modes of behavior and the particular rules that correspond with them, whether members of a younger generation or others, will find a defense of those rules hard to come by and will find it difficult to initiate discussion concerning them. Habits are not defended. So long as modes of behavior remain habitual for a group of men they will be puzzled if not irritated by requests that they defend them and they will be unable to respond to such requests. (If they are in fact forced to defend them the habits will thereby have ceased, at least for the time being, to be habits.)

Unfortunately the unavailability of a defense of the particular rules will not alter the fact that they remain legal rules which there is an obligation to obey. Indeed if the modes of behavior in question are habitual for a large segment of the populace, the fact that no defense is forthcoming and no discussion is possible will increase the likelihood that the rules will remain legal rules. Unless those skeptical of the rules satisfy *themselves* concerning their value and importance they will be thrown back on the case for the general rule as a ground for obeying them. (We deliberately pass over the possibility that they will decide to obey the particular rule simply to avoid inconvenience or punishment.) The case for the general rule will not be supported by the case for the particular rules to which it applies. Unlike the case of parking regulations, however, in this situation the skeptic is not likely to dismiss the matter as insignificant; "obligation" will be attenuated in its application to important cases.

Once again there is evidence that such a process has been at work in this and other countries in recent years. Consider the case of laws on such subjects as relationships between races, the use of drugs, abortion, and sexual behavior. Many people accepted these laws under conditions that no longer prevail and they continue to conform to them (and the nonlegal norms and rules concerning the same subjects) in what, judging from their response to critics, is often an habitual manner. As a consequence it is difficult for critics of those laws to initiate discussion concerning them, and criticisms of the laws (to say nothing of tendencies to depart from the modes of conduct prescribed by the laws and the related social norms) meet with hostile and sometimes repressive responses. Of course large numbers of people have continued to obey these laws despite skepticism concerning their value. This fact may be testimony that the general rule can be effective even when it receives little or no support from arguments for the particular rules to which it applies. But disobedience has been widespread and approval of disobedience (or at least refusal to express disapproval) even more so. Moreover, such disobedience has often been accompanied by expressions of generalized doubt concerning the importance of obeying the law (concerning the general rule).

Whether or to what extent any of the cases of disobedience alluded to can be explained in the terms of the present discussion is a question that could not be decided without making an investigation of the intentions, purposes, and reasons of those who have disobeyed and supported disobedience. Our purpose in mentioning them has been less to comment on some fairly obvious social phenomenon than to bring out some of the features and implications of arguments for obedience based on the general rule. Stated in the most general terms, the point suggested by the foregoing discussion is that the views of the citizenry concerning particular legal rules should and do influence their assessment of the general rule. This is hardly surprising and is worth emphasizing largely because it has been denied or, where its existence has been recognized, condemned as unfortunate by influential theorists of political obligation. As noted, Plato, Hobbes, Bergson, and Lincoln have argued that political obligations are in fact or should be discharged without reflection about or even concern with the content of the obligation, perhaps habitually or even "somnambulistically" (Bergson). Our discussion of habitual obedience and its relation to the general rule is intended to suggest that, so far from being appropriate to "obligation," such obedience is systematically at odds with the logic of that concept. So far from contributing to the order and stability craved by the theorists just mentioned such behavior might contribute to an increase in disobedience.

From a more explicitly evaluative perspective, the foregoing considerations suggest that those who obey laws habitually or mechanically share the responsibility for any contagious effects of disobedience by those who question or disobey the laws because they disapprove of them. They also suggest that the argument that one should not disobey particular rule X because doing so will undermine the general rule and regime—that this argument is least cogent where the law is regarded as important and where criticism and disobedience of it prompts vigorous discussion and controversy.

Contrary to what seemed at first sight to be the implication of the distinction between ideals and obligations, it now appears that critical awareness, reflection, and discussion concerning the rules that define the bulk of our political obligations are no less important in the practice of political obligation in a stable society than in any other aspect of politics in such a society. In the absence of such reflection, acting out of a sense of obligation may degenerate into acting habitually, out of fear, or in some other mechanical manner. A political society nourished by reflection and discussion concerning its obligation rules is not likely to be brought down by epidemics of disobedience. In such a society a measure of disobedience might even contribute to the capacity of the body politic to remain aware of what it is doing and to solve the problems that arise for it. By the same token, reliance upon arguments for obedience that are grounded in the importance of the general rule may be symptomatic of a stagnant or stagnating political process and political society, a society in which the practice of political obligation is degenerating into something else.

V. CONCLUDING REMARKS

OUR INITIAL CONTRAST between obligations and ideals served to emphasize that "obligation" is used of forms of conduct which are rule-governed, which "must be performed," that are believed to be fundamental to the society or social group, and that are general in application. It also called attention to the fact that effective use of "obligation" to guide conduct presupposes a considerable degree of commonality in the society or social group and contributes to stable patterns of conduct. "*Political* obligation" is best used of forms of conduct that are required by rules which are thought to be of fundamental importance to the political arrangements of society. If the political arrangements are thought to be basic or essential to society, then political obligations will be regarded as the most fundamental obligations (as for example in the thinking of Hobbes).

Most political obligations are defined by rules that have standing in law. But law is dependent upon a variety of conventions, arrangements, and understandings that do not themselves have legal status. In this chapter we discussed one of these, which we called the general rule. We examined arguments that make explicit or implicit appeal to this rule in urging strict obedience to law. We implicitly conceded the importance of a stable pattern of obedience to law (we will argue for this view in the final chapter) but we argued that such a pattern can best be achieved and maintained if the rules that define political obligations are subjects of critical reflection and discussion. Commonality and stability, we suggested, are threatened by unreflective conformity to particular legal rules and the general rule. They are best maintained when the conviction of the value of these rules is continuously renewed through critical examination of their content and the consequences of accepting and obeying them.

In the next chapters we will develop this argument by examining more closely various kinds of rules, the roles they play in political obligation and related practices, and the relationships between them and such concepts as obligation, authority, law, and community. One of our objectives in doing so will be to show that the argument for critical reflection and choice is not merely a recommendation but an analysis of the way the concept "obligation" is used and the way the practice of political obligation operates. We will try to show that concepts such as reason and choice are conceptually linked to "obligation" and "authority." Despite our suggestions and speculations in this chapter, there might be political uniformity and order with little reflection and choice on the part of the members of society in question. But in such a society uniformity and order would not be achieved through the practice of political obligation.

The last point brings us back to the distinction with which we began, namely between ideals and obligations. The argument of the present chapter might be viewed as setting forth an ideal practice of political obligation, one in which reflection and choice play a substantial role. The thrust of such an interpretation would be that reflection and choice do not play a significant role in the practice as we know it. Even this interpretation concedes a minimal version of one of the basic points we have been arguing, namely that a morality or practice of obligation does not logically or in any other necessary manner exclude reason and choice. If it did so, a practice such as we have argued for could not be a practice of political obligation—ideal or otherwise. Reason and choice may in fact be more prominent in moralities of ideals and aspirations than in moralities and practices of obligation. But if this is a fact, it is a contingent fact, not a necessary characteristic of moralities or practices of obligation.

As indicated, however, we do not accept the view that the present chapter argues for an ideal practice of political obligation. We wish to show that in point of fact reason and choice are an integral part of the practice of political obligation. Rather than say that the concept of obligation does not necessarily exclude reason and choice, we want to argue that it necessarily includes them. Of course the practice of political obligation is not a necessary part of a political order. Political societies sometimes achieve a degree of order and uniformity of behavior by force, deception, and manipulation; other political orders are marked by a degree of order and uniform behavior owing to the habitual, unthinking conformity of their subjects. Thus if we are making a recommendation it is a recommendation for a political order in which the practice of political obligation plays a prominent part in achieving stability and commonality; it is a recommendation against those practices and procedures which various writers have confused with political obligation and which will, at best, produce order and uniformity.

(3)

Obligation and Rules

OUR DISTINCTION between obligations and ideals was drawn in part in terms of the fact that rules of conduct figure prominently in the former but do not figure prominently or at all in the latter. We argued that reason and choice are part of the practice of political obligation, but we did not take up a major objection to that argument, namely that they are excluded, or that their significance is narrowly limited, by the very fact that rules are prominent in the practice. The main task of the present chapter is to analyze the concepts "rule," "rule-governed conduct," and "guiding conduct by calling attention to a rule." We will try to show that so far from excluding reason and choice from the practice of political obligation, the fact that these concepts figure in the practice renders reason and choice not only a desirable but a necessary part of it. The most difficult part of this task will be to analyze further what we called the general rule ("Obey the law") and to show in what respects it is possible to give reasons for accepting or rejecting it.[1]

1. Throughout this chapter and in the remainder of this work we will be assuming that Hart is correct in his thesis that in most of its conduct-guiding uses "obligation" is a rule-dependent concept; that we ordinarily use "obligation" (as distinct from "ought," "right," "good," etc.) where

Since our discussion of these questions is lengthy, it will be well to indicate in advance the route we will follow and the major theses we will advance. We will begin by attempting (in section I) to identify some of the characteristic features of the generic phenomenon of conduct-guiding rules and to distinguish such rules and conduct guided by them from various related phenomena with which they have been confused. One purpose of this discussion is to show that rules are a feature of human action not of behavior. Rules of conduct ordinarily indicate the presence of a regularity or pattern in the activities of those to whom they apply. But they also presuppose that the activity to which they apply will be susceptible of guidance in the sense that the individuals to whom they apply must be able to choose or decide whether to accept them and conform to them. Similarly, rules set a standard or criterion of proper action. Hence they presuppose that the conduct in question is thought to matter sufficiently to warrant distinguishing proper from improper conduct and holding people to the former. Most important, we will argue that we can speak of rules only if those who are guided by alleged rules, or who use alleged rules in guiding the conduct of others, think that there are good reasons for accepting them and conforming to them. Developing these points will involve distinguishing rules and rule guided conduct from the use of force, threats of force and behavior out of fear of force, from trained behavior and from habitual behavior.

---

there is an established rule requiring or forbidding a type of conduct. (See H. L. A. Hart, op. cit., esp. pp. 79–88.) This thesis is obviously correct in the central class of cases before us, namely obligations defined by law. We have also suggested respects in which it is true of obligations undertaken by promising and contracting; there are rules requiring us to keep promises and fulfill contracts. In all of these cases the problem is not to decide whether there is a rule but to identify the kind or type of rule there is, to determine how the type of rule in question compares with other types, to assess the logical and practical implications and consequences of the fact that there is a rule of a certain kind. If we sort out the kinds of rules and their implications in the cases in which we would readily agree that there is a rule, we will be in a much better position to decide whether there are established uses of "obligation" which do not presuppose the presence of a rule.

Section II develops distinctions among six types of rules. The distinctions are taken with modifications from work of Max Black. They are central not only to this chapter but to the argument of several later chapters as well. Section III is the heart of the chapter. The question at issue there is why the presence of a rule provides a ground, warrant, or justification for doing what the rule advises, directs, or requires. More particularly, why does the presence of particular legal rules and the general rule provide a ground for acting in the manner required by these rules? Does the fact that a statement that X should be done has achieved the standing of a rule add to the case for doing X? Does this fact limit the kinds of considerations that are relevant to deciding whether to do X? If it is true that political obligations are defined by rules, these questions are ways of asking whether, and if so why, political obligations should be discharged. If the latter question is to be discussed in general terms (and one of the issues before us in this section and later is whether it is profitable to discuss it in general terms), we suggest that the above questions about rules are the best way of asking it. They are the best way of asking the question about political obligations because they direct our attention to the kinds or classes of considerations relevant to answering it.

From the standpoint of a theory of political obligation the crux of the matter is whether reasons can be given for accepting and rejecting the general rule. There is often great controversy over the merits of particular legal rules but there is little or no controversy as to whether reasons can be given for and against them. It is less obvious that the notion of giving reasons for accepting or rejecting the general rule is a cogent notion. We will grant that doing so is quite a different sort of activity from reasoning about particular legal rules. This is because of (1) the extremely abstract character of the rule and (2) the relationship between it and the semantic rules governing the concepts that figure in its formulation. The first requires that reasons for or against the rule be cast in extremely general terms, terms that can easily be so vague as to justify nothing or so inclusive as to justify too much. Owing to the relationship between the rule and semantic rules, questioning the general rule involves questioning semantic rules as well. Thus there is a sense in which merely stating the general rule, even for the purpose of questioning it, seems to reinforce and even endorse it. It is difficult, or it appears to be difficult, to find linguistic ground, as it were, on which to stand in questioning the general rule. In this chapter our attention will focus on the second of these difficulties. We will try to show that much of the difficulty can be resolved if we make the distinction just mentioned, namely between the semantic rules governing the concepts that figure in the formulation of the rule and the (conduct-guiding) general rule itself. We will also suggest that the first difficulty can be and has been overcome. The burden of our argument on this point, however, is carried by the discussion in Chapter Eight where we will try to *give* reasons for the general rule.

I. CHARACTERISTICS OF RULES

WE WILL NOT GET FAR in understanding conduct-guiding rules and rule-guided conduct without distinguishing among the major senses in which "rule" is used. But there are some characteristics common to most of the senses of "rule," and identifying them now will provide perspective on the ground that we will explore in greater detail below.

First, talk of a rule in the sense of a rule of conduct usually indicates the presence of observable regularity in the conduct to which the rule applies. This point has been a source of confusion because "regularity" is one of the things that "rule" *means* (in one of its uses). For example we say: "As a rule B does X on Saturday morning," meaning that anyone who observes B on Saturday mornings will notice that he usually does X. Of course the fact that as a rule B does X on Saturday morning is not enough to show that there is a conduct-guiding rule that B knows about and that requires or forbids that he should (must) (ought to) do X on Saturday morning. B's regularly doing X is not even a necessary condition of there being a conduct-guiding rule that he do so. But if no one to whom the conduct-guiding rule applies in fact does X on Saturday mornings, doubt will be cast on the proposition that there is a rule requiring that X be done. We usually say there is a rule (noun) requiring X only if there is evidence that the alleged rule in fact *rules* (verb) the conduct of at least some of the persons to whom it applies most of the time. At a minimum, evidence that the alleged rule does not rule the conduct of those to whom it applies will lead us to *qualify* the statement that there is a rule. We might say that there is a rule requiring X but that it has fallen into desuetude, or that a rule requiring X has been proposed but has not become effective.[2]

Second, there can be conduct-guiding rules, and talk of conduct-guiding rules, only where the conduct to which the rules apply is susceptible to guidance by second parties. This requirement means that it must be possible for the agent to whom the rules apply to choose to do what the rules require in the circumstance(s) in which the rules require it. Thus there is no sense to a rule (except in the sense of a regularity) requiring or forbidding patellar reactions or other involuntary movements and impulses.

Third, the concept "rule" involves the notion of a standard or criterion which discriminates between right and wrong, correct and incorrect, proper and improper, wise and unwise. (Which of these adjectives apply depends on the type of rule at issue. We will discuss the question further as we examine different types of rule.) The development and application of such a standard presupposes that the type of conduct in question is thought to be important enough to the society or group for there to be some point in having and enforcing the standard. The notion of right or wrong conduct has no application to conduct that everyone agrees is trivial. Thus we do not have

2. On this point cf. Hart, op. cit., esp. pp. 23–24, 140–41.

rules governing many matters of personal taste and avocation. Of course we do have rules concerning some matters of personal taste, and other societies have rules concerning matters that we think too trivial to warrant regulation by a rule. The thesis that it must be thought to matter how people act for there to be a rule does not involve any specification of what is or could be thought to matter. It is not uncommon for it to be thought to matter that people do X *because* there is a rule requiring it. This is sometimes the case when a rule first develops because it is thought to matter that people do X for one reason, that reason loses its cogency, but the rule has come to be an accepted part of social arrangement. As objectionable as these views and arrangements often are, they do not upset the thesis that there are rules only where it is thought to matter how members of the society or group conduct themselves in a particular respect.

The conditions we have discussed thus far are not sufficient to distinguish making and calling attention to rules from a variety of other methods of influencing conduct, even including physical compulsion such as pulling a man from X to Y by a rope and threats of unauthorized use of force. Threatening a man with harm and deliberately pulling him by a rope presuppose a belief that it is possible to influence his behavior by doing so. They also presuppose a belief that it matters that the person act or behave in the required manner. To distinguish all ways of guiding conduct that do not involve rules would take us well beyond our present concerns. But there is one further characteristic of rules that is of the utmost importance in the present context. A can properly be said to have guided B's conduct by calling attention to a rule only if he thinks that there are good reasons for accepting the rule as a basis of conduct. B can claim to have been guided by the rule that A cited only if he (B) thinks there are good reasons for accepting the rule as a basis of conduct.

We are not suggesting that the agent's belief in the availability of good reasons for giving, accepting, and acting upon guidance is exclusive to rules. An agent may think that there are, and there may be, good reasons for making and complying with a threat. Likewise there may be good reasons for submitting to training, hypnosis, and even compulsion (though there are problems with the last) and there certainly can be good reasons for training, hypnotizing, and compelling others to do X. What we want to suggest is that absence of a belief that there are good reasons does not render talk of compulsion, threats, and trained behavior inappropriate. By contrast, belief in the availability of good reasons for an alleged rule is a necessary condition of the proper use of "rule" and "rule-guided conduct."

Clarifying and defending this thesis is the main task of the present chapter. We can make a beginning by considering some descriptions of actions of A and B which clearly do not require that A or B think they have good reasons for doing what they are doing. The clearest case is describing A as having compelled B to do X by using physical force against or upon him. A may have reasons for compelling B to do X and, logically, B can inquire into them and accept or reject them. His acceptance of them will, as a practical matter, facilitate A's task. But it is not necessary for A to have a reason (much less a good reason) for doing so in order for it to be said that he compelled B to do X. Nor is it necessary that B know and accept A's reason (assuming that he has one) for it to be appropriate to say that B's behavior was influenced or even determined by A's use of force. Presumably there is some explanation, perhaps in terms of motive or impulse, for A's compelling B to do X, and B will not understand *why* A compelled B unless he knows what the motive or impulse was. But not knowing *why* A compelled B to do X is no obstacle to knowing *that* he compelled B. We do not expect the bully or ruffian to have, much less to give, reasons for pushing other people around. Nor do we expect people pushed around by bullies and ruffians to know, much less to accept, the reasons why they are pushed around.

The same analysis applies in all but one respect to the case of influencing conduct by making unauthorized threats. B is threatened with certain consequences if he does not do X, but he is not actually compelled to do X. Therefore he must decide whether to do X. Knowing why A wants B to do X and why A is using threats may help B decide whether A will actually make good on the threats. Thus such knowledge may help him to decide whether to do X. If B has good reason to believe that A will not carry through on his threat doubt would be cast on the propriety of explaining B's action as a response to A's threat.[3]

A third and more interesting class of cases is when A trains B to do X. Assume that A trains B to do X whenever Y, such that the appearance of Y becomes a sufficient condition of B's doing X. If so, saying that A's causing Y influenced B to do X or that B did X because of the influence of A does not require evidence that A or B had good reasons. We would probably not say that A had trained B (assuming B is an adult) to do X when Y unless A gave and B accepted reasons for doing so during the training process. If A gives no reasons during the training process it would be more appropriate to say that A conditioned B to do X. (This is one of the differences between the use of training in connection with human beings and its use in connection with animals, and perhaps between training adults and training young children. It is also another area in which we need a good deal of information in order to know whether to use action concepts or behavior concepts.) But once the training had been completed having and giving reasons would become unnecessary.

3. Using the concept "decide" in describing B's response to A's threat slurs over a problem in the distinction between action and behavior. So long as A does not literally force B to do X there is ground for saying that B decided to do X and hence that X was an action of his. A major implication of using this description is that B can be held responsible for doing X. But if A threatens B with extremely grave consequences we sometimes say that B "had no choice" but to do X. If we say this we put X in the category of behavior rather than action. In this kind of case to say that B "had no choice" is usually to say that the choices (other than doing X) are so unpleasant or hard to accept that we could not expect B to choose them. Thus in order to make the action-behavior distinction we must know a good deal about the alternatives to doing X, the consequences of choosing them, and the circumstances in which the choice must be made.

An example may clarify the point here. A veteran shortstop, A, trains a rookie second baseman, B, always to angle behind him (A) when they are both pursuing a ground ball hit over second base. At the outset A explains that: (1) they must always do it the same way so as to avoid collisions; and (2) the rule he suggests is best because (i) the second baseman is necessarily moving away from the base to which he must throw the ball (first base) while the shortstop is moving more or less toward it; and (ii) the degree to which the shortstop is moving toward first base will be maximized if he cuts in front of the second baseman. The rookie then practices adjusting his angle of pursuit to that of the shortstop until he has learned to estimate the latter very quickly and to set his own course accordingly. Thus by setting his own path of pursuit A also determines B's path of pursuit (X).

Of course a conduct-guiding rule continues to be available to A and B and they might mention the rule and the reasons for it in explaining their practice to others. But we could say that A influenced B and that B's behavior was trained, even if, after several seasons, B had entirely forgotten the reasons for the arrangement. But if B had forgotten the reasons we could not say that he was following a rule when he did X. An observer could discover a rule in the sense of a regularity in B's behavior, and he might discover a rule in additional senses if he investigated the history of B's behavior. He would not now find the characteristics of conduct guided by a rule.

Our reasons for this contention can be brought out more clearly if we consider the closely related case of habitual behavior. A period of training is one possible origin of a habit. When this is the case—as in the baseball example above—there is little to distinguish habitual from trained behavior. But a mode of behavior can become habitual in other ways as well, for example simply by unguided repetition of a behavior over a period of time. Most of us are not trained to smoke tobacco or drink alcoholic beverages but these are among the most commonly mentioned examples of habits. What is characteristic of habitual behavior is that the person who does X habitually has ceased to think about doing X; he has ceased to be aware of alternatives to X and to choose to do X after considering alternatives. It is not that there are no alternatives available. The availability of alternatives that *could be* chosen, objectively speaking, distinguishes habitual behavior from behavior that is compelled or determined. Nor is it that the person could not choose to do other than X in the sense in which we say that an addict could not, unaided, choose to cease using heroin or an alcoholic could not choose to give up alcoholic beverages. It is physically possible for B not to do X. But he does not consider whether to do X or not, he simply does it. Alternatives are available but he does not consider them.[4]

We have already noted that a part of the notion of a rule (save in the sense of a regularity) is the notion of a standard or criterion which distinguishes right from wrong, correct from incorrect. Stated in the most general terms, the notion of a rule involves choosing among alternatives. Thus the person who is unaware of alternatives to what he is doing cannot be following a rule. The man who unthinkingly lights up a cigarette every time he gets in the car or sits down to coffee is not following a rule. His behavior is habitual.

Following a rule, then, involves an awareness of alternatives and a choice between or among them. Combined with the point that the conduct must be thought to matter, we get the conclusion that the existence of rules that *rule* conduct pre-

4. It is true that we use the noun "habit" in cases where a person does consider alternatives but nevertheless does X. Since we have learned of its ill effects on health, smoking tobacco has become a leading example. If we say that a person has the habit of smoking we are usually saying (a) that the person thinks that smoking is undesirable and (b) that, though not addicted, he is weak-willed. Statement (a) is not a general feature of the use of "habit." There is nothing odd about the notion of good habits. Statement (b) brings out the distinctiveness of this use of the noun. It would be odd to say that a person who "had the habit" of smoking smoked "habitually." His smoking is a matter of distress to him, he worries about it, tries to avoid it or at least alleges that he is trying to avoid it, but continues to do it. A man behaving habitually does not engage in such self-examination.

supposes a degree of reflection on the part of some substantial number of those to whom the rules apply.[5]

If the foregoing analyses of "rule" and of compulsion, threats, trained behavior, and habitual behavior are valid, and if it is true that "obligation" is rule-dependent, it follows that compulsions, threats, trained behavior, and habitual behavior cannot be among the necessary or defining features of the practice of political obligation. They may or may not be associated with the practice in various circumstances, but their presence does not establish that the practice is operating and their absence does not establish that it is not operating. Thus we have made progress in delimiting the area in which the practice of

5. Later we will elaborate upon the kinds of reflection appropriate to different types of rules. But we should stress immediately that there are degrees of awareness and reflection, and that there are important distinctions to be drawn, in terms of degrees of awareness and reflection, within the category of rule-following conduct. There are many things that we do routinely, as a matter of course. Routine, matter-of-course actions are distinguished from actions we take deliberately, with close attention to each step in the process. With the most obvious marks of reflection and deliberation missing, it is sometimes difficult to distinguish such actions from habitual behavior. Contrary to Winch, to whom I am indebted in the previous paragraphs, it is not enough that "it makes sense to distinguish between a right and wrong way of doing things in connection with what [the agent] . . . does." (Winch, op. cit., p. 58). The fact that an observer can make such a distinction does not establish that the actor is aware of the distinction or is acting upon it. The actor must give us evidence that *he* is aware of the distinction. There are a *great many* ways in which he might do this. He might recognize a mistake—whether his own or that of someone else. He might teach the activity to others. He might make adjustments in his conduct in response to changed circumstances. He might, perhaps with assistance through questioning, state the rule. And there are numerous things which he would not do which a man behaving habitually might do, for example continue with a form of behavior in inappropriate circumstances, find requests for explanations or justification puzzling or upsetting. Tests such as these often allow us to make judgments, but they do not state the defining criteria of rule-following conduct and they are often difficult to apply in actual cases. Here again we must recognize that we are working with distinctions which cannot be sharply drawn and which can often be applied only with a good deal of information about the particulars of the case to which we are applying them. On these points see L. Wittgenstein, *Philosophical Investigations*, E. Anscombe trans. (London: The Macmillan Company, 1958), esp. I, 82–83 (pp. 39–40). See also Max Black, "Rules and Routines," op. cit.

political obligation operates and in identifying its characteristics. Since prominent theories of political obligation have analyzed the practice in terms of compulsion, threats, and trained and habitual behavior (we are thinking primarily of Plato, Austin, and Bergson) we have also made progress in disposing of influential misunderstandings of the practice. The next task is to analyze more closely the relationship between rules and rule-guided conduct on the one hand and reasons and reasoning on the other. Granting that rule-guided conduct is reflective conduct, we must try to determine what kinds of reasoning are appropriate in connection with the rules that generate and define political obligations.

II. TYPES OF RULES

MAX BLACK has distinguished four main senses in which "rule" is used and hence four main types of rules: (1) regularity, (2) instructions, (3) regulations, (4) precepts.[6] In addition there has been a good deal of discussion in recent years of a fifth type of rule for which there is no convenient term in ordinary language but which has been called "practice-type" (Rawls), "constitutive" (Searle) and "regulative" (Black).[7] Finally, there is a sixth type of rule which cuts across the first five categories, namely the semantic rules or conventions that we discussed in Chapter One.

For reasons already indicated, regularities are not conduct-guiding rules and will be of interest only as they figure in the formation and justification of rules of types 2–6. Instructions guide conduct but they do not generate obligations. We will be concerned with them only because it is enlightening to compare them with rules that do generate obligations. Regulations,

---

6. Max Black, *Models and Metaphors* (Ithaca: Cornell University Press, 1962), pp. 109–15.

7. See Rawls, "Two Concepts of Rules," op. cit., pp. 3 ff; John Searle, loc. cit.; Max Black, "Rules and Routines," op. cit.

of which laws, judicial decrees, and executive orders are leading examples, are of obvious importance in the present context. The question of the *kinds* of reasoning appropriate in connection with them, however, is quite straightforward and they will not occupy us for long in this chapter. The most difficult questions arise concerning precepts and their relationships to constitutive-type rules and semantic rules. We will argue that what we called the general rule is best thought of as a precept. But it takes some of its force—and acquires much of its complexity—from the semantic rules that govern the uses of the concepts that figure in its formulation. This and other precepts have some of the characteristics of constitutive rules, but we will argue that it is misleading to place them in that category. Some regulations can be thought of as constitutive rules, but they do not define obligations.

The major question before us in discussing these types of rules will be the following: in what respects, and why, does the fact that there is a rule that X be done provide a reason for deciding to do X? Does the fact that there is a rule add to the case for doing X? Does it limit the kinds of considerations that are relevant to deciding whether to do X?

We will begin by putting enough flesh on the bones of the above categories to make them useful for our purposes.

As Black has defined the term, instruction-type rules differ from regulations (as do precepts) in that they are not passed or promulgated by an authority. Rather than being "laid down" at a determinate moment of time by an authority they evolve or develop in the course of experience. It is usually impossible to say when they were formulated and when they took effect. They can and do undergo change and can and do cease to be rules, but we do not speak of their being altered or rescinded. Refusing to follow them can have adverse consequences, but it does not lead to the imposition of penalties or punishments except in a metaphorical sense. By contrast with constitutive rules, however, they do not constitute or define activities or practices and following them or not does not affect the logical status of the action. Examples of instructions are: "Do not use a screwdriver to do the work of a chisel," "In five-card stud bet heavily after the second card if you have the only ace or king showing," "Do not plant tomatoes until after the last frost."

Examples of regulations would be laws passed by a legislature and some of the rules of games that are governed by an authoritative body. About rules of this type we can usually ask such questions as: "Who *made* the rule and by what *authority?*" "How *long* has the rule been *in effect?*" "What would be required to *rescind* or *alter* the rule?" [8] We can also speak of such rules as having been enforced, obeyed, and violated, and the idea of a penalty or sanction is most at home in the case of rules of this type.

Some typical precepts are: "Do not lie," "Do not cheat," "Put charity ahead of justice," "Honor your father and mother." As with instructions, precepts are not promulgated and are not subject to alteration or rescindment. Nor do notions such as enforcement, penalties, and punishments apply to them. It is appropriate, however, for A to hold B to conformity with precepts in ways he cannot do with instructions. Blame, censure, and other nonlegal sanctions can sometimes be applied if B does not conform to them. It has been argued that precepts define or constitute practices and arrangements so that failure to conform with them, or at least to give weight to them in de-

---

8. There are borderline cases in which it is difficult to answer the questions just mentioned and in which doubts arise as to whether the questions have point. Are these *historical* questions appropriate in the case of rules of common law that are alleged to have existed since "time out of mind"? The point of saying that they have existed since time out of mind is at once that questions of authorship cannot be answered, *and* that the rules have a lengthy history at least a part of which can be recounted. A similar difficulty arises in the case of games, for example poker, the playing of which is governed by rules but for which there is to my knowledge no recognized governing body that promulgates the rules. Shall we classify rules of common law and rules of poker as regulation-type rules? The answer is that it matters very little how we classify them so long as we are aware of their features and their significance. A system of classification should help us to identify standard cases and to manipulate them efficiently. But such a system should also increase our sensitivity to differences and special cases.

ciding how to act, affects the logical status of the action. Thus "Do not lie" might be thought of as a constituent part of the institution or practice of morality. To refuse to give weight to the rule *is* to show a lack of understanding of the institution and to act amorally. Again, "Obey the law" might be thought a constitutive of the practice of political obligation. If so, a person who didn't give weight to the rule in relevant circumstances would show a lack of understanding of the practice and would not be participating in it when he acted. The importance of these interpretations for present purposes is that, if valid, they limit the kinds of considerations relevant to deciding whether to tell a lie or obey a law.

Clear examples of constitutive rules would be laws that establish the procedure that must be followed in order to take a certain legal action. Thus the law of wills and testaments determines what must be done to make a will. The person who does not follow the rules simply does not make a will. The law which indicates what must be done to make a will does not create obligations to make wills. The man who fails to follow the rules laid down by the law may suffer adverse consequences but he has not failed to discharge a legal obligation and he is not subject to punishment.[9] Some rules of games also provide relatively clear cases of constitutive rules. If a man has two pairs in a poker game and his opponent has three of a kind, the man loses the hand. If he claims to have won the hand he shows that he does not know the rules of poker. The rules concerning the rank order of hands are one of the constitutive parts of the game of poker.

In this case, however, the distinction is less clear-cut, and it has less significance than in the legal example. The law of wills and testaments can be changed only if established procedures are followed by agents with proper authority. Thus what counts as a will and as making a will is quite clear-cut. But the rules of

9. For an excellent discussion of legal examples of constitutive rules, see Hart, op. cit., esp. pp. 26–48, 78–79, 238–40. Hart calls them secondary rules.

games can be changed, at least for the purpose of playing the game here and now, by those who happen to be playing it here and now. If the seven of us decide that two pairs will beat three of a kind in this evening's game, then two pairs *will* beat three of a kind. It might be argued, of course, that owing to this change in the rules the evening's game is not a game of poker. Unless this argument is just a somewhat indirect way of objecting to the change, to make it would be to claim that there exist a set of necessary conditions, perhaps necessary and sufficient conditions, of a game being called a game of poker. Hart has argued persuasively that such conditions cannot be identified for such tightly defined concepts as "valid will" and "valid contract." [10] It would clearly be much more difficult to identify them for "poker." Not anything will count as a game of poker, but which or how many of the usual rules can be changed or disregarded before the game ceases to be poker cannot be settled abstractly. It cannot be settled because there is no established criterion by which to settle it. Thus the logical tie between the rules of poker and "poker" is not as tightly drawn as in the case of legal rules about wills. This point, which holds for many alleged examples of constitutive rules, will be important when we discuss the kinds of reasoning that are appropriate in connection with such rules.

Since we discussed some of the general characteristics of semantic conventions in Chapter One, we will take them up here only as they are important in connection with the other types of rules.

III. RULES AND REASONS

APART FROM the case of regularities, one of the *meanings* of the noun "rule" is "guide to conduct." Can we say more than

10. See H. L. A. Hart, "The Ascription of Responsibility and Rights," *Logic and Language*, First Series, ed. A. G. N. Flew (Oxford: Basil Blackwell, 1963), esp. pp. 146–56.

this as to why the existence of a rule provides a ground or warrant for acting in the manner directed or required by the rule?

At one level of discussion this question is most easily answered in the case of constitutive rules. Such rules provide a reason for acting because it is only by acting in the manner specified by the rules that one can engage in the practices or play the games that are constituted by the rules. If B (a batter in a baseball game) asks A (the umpire) why he should retire from the batter's box after the third strike has been called, A's proper reply is simply: "Because the rules (of baseball) require that you do so." Of course A's reply counts as a reason for B to retire only if it is indeed a game of baseball that is in progress and only if B and the other players wish to continue to play that particular game. If these conditions are satisfied, for B to question whether the rules give him a reason to retire from the batter's box would be to demonstrate a lack of understanding of baseball (or of the notions of a rule and a reason as they are used in the type of case at hand).

Put another way, in the case of constitutive rules the rule itself constitutes a reason for acting in the manner specified by the rule. It might also seem that there is no room for a distinction between a statement of the rule qua rule and reasons for the rule or for acting in conformity with it. The notion of a reason for the rule or for accepting the rule involves a misunderstanding.

We mention this argument about constitutive rules at the outset because it provides a kind of limiting case as to why the presence of a rule provides a warrant for acting in a certain manner. It is a limiting case in the sense that it says that this type of rule provides a warrant for acting because it is a rule of this type. Put another way, it is a limiting case in that it suggests that any and all considerations other than that it is a rule of this type are irrelevant and perhaps otiose. We will be in a better position to assess this argument later, but having it in mind will facilitate the discussion of instructions, regulations, and precepts.

A. *Instructions and Reasons*

If B does not bet heavily after the second card when he has the only ace showing, A may rightly infer that B is not playing poker well; he is not justified in inferring that B is not playing poker. The rule does not itself constitute a reason for following the rule in the way constitutive rules have been said to do. But instructions do advise us as to how to conduct ourselves; they advise us how to maximize the likelihood of achieving our ends or purposes. Failure or refusal to conform to such rules, though it does not render our conduct irrelevant to any practice or activity, might make it self-defeating. Assume that my purpose in playing poker is to win money and my purpose in carpentry is to make useful and attractive articles out of wood. If following the rules mentioned above contributes to those ends, and if failure to conform to them causes me to lose money or to produce useless and ugly articles, I have reason to conform to the rules.

The rules themselves, however, provide a reason only in what we will call a derivative sense. "Don't use a screwdriver to do the work of a chisel" provides the carpenter with a reason for fetching the chisel from the garage only if doing so will enable him to do a job he couldn't do to his satisfaction with a screwdriver. "Bet heavily after the second card . . ." provides the poker-player with a reason to risk a large sum only if doing so maximizes his chances of coming out of the game a winner. By contrast with the relationship between "The batter shall retire from the batter's box after the third strike" and playing baseball, there is no logical relationship between the rules in question and the ends in view. The standing of the rules depends not on logic or facts about concepts but on experience in carpentry and poker playing. I accept these rules not because of any feature internal to their formulation but because experience with working with wood has shown that using a tool with the characteristics of a chisel has regularly allowed me (or others) to do certain jobs better than using a tool with the characteristics of a screwdriver. If I want to persuade another person to accept these rules, I recite the relevant experience.[11] Thus in the case of instructions the notion of giving reasons— in this respect evidence—to support the rule is not only cogent but essential to the idea of accepting and acting upon the rule. If B asks A why he should bet heavily after the second card and A replies: "Because there is a rule that says you should do so," B will do well to look for a new instructor in the fine art of poker playing.

Evidence that acting according to the rule will bring about the predicted and desired result is only a necessary, not a sufficient condition of there being good reasons for accepting and conforming to an instruction-type rule. When this condition is satisfied (and when the end-in-view is accepted) an agent has *a* reason for accepting and conforming to the rule. But for him to have good reasons for accepting it and acting upon it he must believe that there is no better way to achieve the end in view. Perhaps following rule X makes it possible to achieve Y but excludes achievement of Z, following rule X', or following no rule at all, makes it possible to achieve both Y and Z. If so, there is a reason for following X, but not a good reason. Of course if A is not aware of X' he will have a good reason for following X. Note that this distinction between a reason and a good reason has no application to constitutive rules. If I am going to play baseball, the existence of a rule that the batter must retire after the third strike is at once a reason and a good reason for retiring. But given the availability

11. By "reciting the experience," of course, we do not mean that it is necessary to recount each instance on which a carpenter messed up a job by using the wrong tool. Over time the results of experience become embodied in what we might call "abbreviations," of which instructions (and instruction books) are themselves examples but which also include the design of tools such as chisels and screwdrivers. A man learning carpentry today can be persuaded that he should use a chisel for this job and a screwdriver for that by being *shown* the differences in the design of the two tools. But he can "see" that he should use the chisel for this, the screwdriver for that only because of his experience with sharp and blunt tools; and there is something for him to "see" only because of the experience that lies behind the development and differentiation of the tools.

of (well-supported) X', for a poker-player to conform to X because it is a rule would be absurd. We would suspect that following X had become habitual for him or that he was following X because A ordered him to do so, out of fear of disapproval or out of some other motive that was related to "rule" only in the sense of regularity-type rules.

Rules in the sense of instructions, in short, presuppose evidence for a rule in the sense of a regularity; a regularity which supports a prediction that following the instruction will be the most efficient means to a certain end. But reasons in the sense of this kind of evidence are not a sufficient basis for accepting an instruction (and hence not sufficient for understanding the concept "rule-governed conduct" as it is used in connection with instructions). Instructions are guides to conduct, not merely stated regularities. Accepting them involves more than accepting certain empirical generalizations as true. One cannot accept an instruction as a guide to conduct if he does not accept the end or purpose to which it directs conduct. Empirical generalizations on the one hand and ends and purposes on the other are of course distinct entities. But instructions bind the two together into a logical whole that one cannot accept without accepting both the generalization and the end or purpose. Thus in order to complete our account of instructions we must examine the notion of accepting an end or purpose.

We will do well to begin by recalling Kant's distinction between hypothetical and categorical imperatives, with instructions corresponding to the former (and, as we will see later, precepts to the latter). Both hypotheticals and categoricals advise agents how to achieve some end or goal, the difference between them, as Black puts it, is that an agent can exempt himself from a hypothetical (instruction) "by disclaiming interest in the relevant purpose." [12] Perhaps a better way to make the point is that the decision whether to accept or reject the end or purpose is not, in the pure case, subject to challenge by

12. Max Black, *Models and Metaphors*, op. cit., p. 112.

second parties. If I play poker simply to have an occasion to drink beer with my cronies I can rightly dismiss the rule: "Bet heavily after second card if . . ." as irrelevant. Moreover, I will be justified in regarding criticism of my decision as an unwarranted interference in my affairs.[13]

Defining "instruction" in this way has two implications. The first is that a person can accept the end served by an instruction because he deems it to be in his interest to do so, because he has an impulse to do so, because it would benefit others to do so, or for any one of a large number of reasons. In the case of instructions, proper use of the concept "rule-guided conduct" requires the availability of good reasons for accepting the rule only as regards evidence that conforming to the rule will serve an end or purpose that the agent accepts. B may have reasons for accepting the end but he need not have them and he need not give them if he has them.

The second implication of the definition is that instructions are not obligation-generating rules. Of course B might be *obliged* to act upon instruction X. Since it is inappropriate for others to question his decision not to do so, B cannot be said to have an obligation to act upon X. (I am assuming that the notion of an obligation to oneself is not a cogent notion. For discussion of this point see Chapter Six.) For this reason instructions are of interest here mainly because examining them helps us to understand types of rules that do generate obligations.[14]

13. There are few "pure" cases. My wife might object that while it is all very well that I risk family funds by playing poker, I might at least make some attempt to reduce the risk. Or another player might object that my attitude toward the (instruction-type) rules of play make the game less interesting for the other players. Insofar as my dismissal of the rule has significant consequences for others they can rightfully question it. Since there are few types of action that could never have significant consequences for others (or at least few such actions about which rules have developed) the distinction between instructions and precepts is not sharp. It is based on the fact that there are many situations in which the consequences for others of my rejecting an instruction are so insignificant —at least by comparison with their consequences for me—that challenges to my decisions or actions would be thought unwarranted.

14. Note the relationships between the foregoing discussion of instructions and the case of constitutive rules such as the legal rules as to how

B. Regulations and Reasons

We turn now to the type of rule that defines most political obligations, namely regulations. In discussing regulations in this section, and precepts in the next, we will be returning to issues concerning obedience to law which we first took up in Chapter Two. There we discussed some aspects of the relationship between legal regulations and the general rule "Obey the law." We entered some objections to uses to which that relationship had been put in arguments about obedience. One of our purposes in the next two sections will be to carry ahead the arguments of Chapter Two by showing how and why reasoned argument concerning obedience to particular legal rules and the general rule is both possible and appropriate.

We noted in Chapter Two that legal rules can be said to define *obligations* because there is a general rule according to which there is an obligation to obey the law. If there was no such rule legislatures would have to pass a law that created an obligation to obey the other laws they passed; and doing so would only raise the question of why there was an obligation to obey the law creating an obligation to obey the other laws. But the fact that particular rules are supported by the general rule hardly excludes the possibility of supporting particular rules in other ways as well. Laws are passed by individuals or groups of individuals at a specific moment in time. Hence it is

---

to make a will and rules of baseball such as retiring after the third strike. In the latter two cases we said that one must follow the rules only if one wanted to make a will or play baseball. Just as the instruction "Don't use a screwdriver to do the work of a chisel" applies only to the person who wants to achieve certain objectives in working with wood, so the law of wills and testaments and the rule of baseball apply only to the person who wants to make a will or to play baseball. The cases differ, of course, in that in the one the relationship between following the rule and achieving the objective is empirical, in the other it is logical. But in neither case does the rule itself provide a sufficient reason for following the rule or for thinking there is an obligation to follow the rule. Thus if, say, "There is an obligation to keep promises" or "There is an obligation to obey the law" are practice-type rules, something more than the characteristics which make them rules of this type must be brought forward if it is to be said that there is an obligation to follow them.

clearer than in the case of instructions and precepts that men decide to pass them. Which in turn makes it obvious that we can ask for a justification as to why they were passed. Many of the institutions and procedures characteristic of our political and governmental arrangements are designed to facilitate asking such questions, to facilitate an exchange of reasons for and against existing or prospective laws. Consider how we would respond to a legislator who thought he could give a sufficient justification for his support of bill X by pointing to the fact that after passage it would fall under the general rule. Presenting such a "justification" would constitute a conclusive demonstration that he did not understand the representative institutions under which he held his office.

Thus it is clear that reasons can be given and that we expect them to be given for or against particular legal rules. Much of the discussion of law that takes place in politics involves the exchange of such reasons. By contrast, much of the discussion of law and obedience that takes place in treatises on political obligation concerns the argument that the absence of good reasons for a particular law is not enough to show that that law should not be obeyed. Once passed the law falls under what we are calling the general rule. This rule creates an obligation to obey the particular law even if there are no good reasons for, or if there are good reasons against, the particular rule as such. Thus the question arises whether it is possible to give reasons for accepting and obeying the general rule and how such reasons relate to reasons for doing the action which the particular rule in question requires us to take.

C. Precepts and Reasons: The Case of "Obey the Law"

The general rule is not made or passed by an authority and it would make no sense to say that it had been rescinded or even amended. For these reasons it should not be classified as a regulation-type rule as we are using that category. In this respect it is similar to "Promises should be kept" and to rules of games which are not governed by an authoritative ruling body. Yet, with the qualifications noted above, a man who does not understand and accept the rule "Promises should be kept" cannot participate in the practice or activity of promising and a man who does not understand and accept the rules establishing the rank order of poker hands cannot play poker. The institution or practice of ruling conduct by law, and of having one's own conduct governed or ruled by law, is more complex than promising or than the most complicated of games. Accordingly, the relationship of the rule "Obey the law" to law is more complex than the relationship of "Promises should be kept" to promising. As with promising and playing games, however, one does not understand the practice of governing conduct by law unless he understands that to say of a rule that it is a law is to say of it that there is an obligation to obey it. To say of a rule that it is a law is to say that it has been promulgated by an authoritative agent or agency who or which has the authority to promulgate the particular rule in question. And to say that a rule has been promulgated by an agent or agency with the authority to pass the rule is to say that there is ordinarily an obligation to obey the rule. As Pitkin, to whom I am indebted on these points, puts it: "It is part of the concept, the meaning of 'authority' that those subject to it are required to obey, that it has a right to command. It is part of the concept, the meaning of 'law,' that those to whom it is applicable are obligated to obey it" [15] The best way to see this is to notice that denying it would create the difficulty noted above, namely that legislatures would not only have to pass laws, they would have to pass laws that required obedience to the laws that they had passed. Thus although the general rule "Obey the law" or "There is an obligation to obey the law" is not itself a law or any other species of authoritative command, use of the concept "law" (and hence implicitly the concept "authority") in the rule make it impossible to reject the rule without challenging the rules governing the (relevant) use of "law" and "authority." "There is ordinarily an obligation to obey the law" is an explication of one feature of "law" and "authority." A person who doesn't

15. Hanna Pitkin, loc. cit., p. 48.

understand this doesn't understand the semantic rules governing the concepts in question.

Given these features of "law" and "authority" it might seem to follow that we are faced with a case in which there is and can be no logical distance between the rule and the reason for accepting the rule. The formulation of the rule (or any formulation of equivalent meaning) itself seems to constitute the reason for accepting the rule.

1. APPLYING THE RULE

Pitkin, Searle, Rawls, and the other writers who, to my knowledge, have discussed these matters, do not conclude that these characteristics of "Obey the law" and "Keep promises" justify the conclusion that conduct governed by them is or even could be entirely mechanical. Difficult questions arise in applying the rule to particular cases. These writers insist, however, that such difficulties are properly resolved by examination of the rule itself, not by appeal to considerations external to the rules. There are occasions on which promises need not or even should not be kept and laws not obeyed. But whether a law is to be obeyed is a question to be decided by looking to see what exceptions or excusing conditions are allowed by or established as part of the rules, not by looking to considerations external to the rules. If this argument is correct it shows that there is at least one important sense in which the rule and the reason for accepting the rule are one and the same.

This position assumes rather more clarity concerning the boundaries of the practice constituted by the rules than is often justified. Any rule-constituted activity is itself a part of and is meaningful only because it is a part of a larger context of human practices, arrangements, institutions, and relationships. Baseball, chess, and poker, for example, are distinct activities constituted by rules unique to each of the games in question. But none of these games could be understood by a person with no grasp of the general concept of a game that is at once cooperative and competitive.[16]

16. Cf. Wittgenstein, op. cit., I, 29–33 (pp. 14–16).

In the case of political obligation these problems have most often been brought to our attention in connection with the work of courts in interpreting and applying constitutional provisions and statutes. A man would be a poor judge indeed if he did not understand that the fact that the provision before him was a constitutional or statutory provision constituted a reason for accepting and conforming to it. But a judge who knew nothing but the letter of the constitution or the statute books, who refused to consider anything "external" to those sources in interpreting and applying the latter, would be little better. (Again, if we take the first clause literally, he would be no better at all since in both cases the judge would be unable to do the work of a judge.) It is worth mentioning that the problems of the judge typically reach him only after they have first been faced by the legislator, the citizen, and the policeman. In law we have an authoritative agent to whom we look to "decide" issues in the interpretation of rules. But this does not free the citizen of the need to make judgments on the same issues, judgments that he makes in a more final way in the case of promising and other moral and social practices that have not been made a part of a system of law. Thus the citizen who accepts and attempts to conform to "Obey the law" must also understand and take account of features of the larger setting in which that rule exists, that is of considerations that are, in various degrees, external to that rule. His reasoning concerning his political obligations, like the judge's reasoning, must include consideration of matters external to the rules that define them. To argue that it is inappropriate, logically or otherwise, for him to consider such matters is to reduce conduct guided by the general rule and the particular rules that fall under it to a logical impossibility or to an absurdity. The conceptual connections between "authority," "law," and "obligation" do not support the inference that decisions to accept and act upon the general rule in this case or that must or even can be based exclusively upon features or characteristics internal to the rule.

2. ACCEPTING THE RULE

The foregoing discussion deals with problems of applying

rules to particular cases. Since the question of applying a rule does not arise in a practical way unless the rule has been accepted, the discussion tacitly assumed that the rule had been accepted. We now come to the question whether sense can be made of the notion of giving reasons for or against accepting the general rule categorically. Pitkin and others have argued that this notion is based on confusions, is evidence of "philosophical disorder." If this is true, the fact that the general rule is an integral part of the practice of political obligation means that there are definite limits on the use of reason in making judgments about one's political obligations. As we noted at the end of Chapter One, this argument is also an instance of a thesis about ways in which language sets limits to thought and action.

a. "Obey the law" as a semantic rule Pitkin begins her argument by distinguishing the two questions just identified; "Why should I obey this law in these circumstances?" and "Why should I ever obey laws?" She accepts the view that the first question will be familiar to any person with a modicum of awareness of his role as a moral and political agent. Although there are hard cases in which there is dispute about the answer, we know how to go about finding an answer and we reach agreement in a large number of cases. The second question, on the other hand, has been raised mainly in philosophical works and there is great disagreement among those who have tried to answer it. She then suggests that "if none of the theories of political obligation is able to deal adequately with that question, it must be quite peculiar, not nearly as straightforward as it looks. Perhaps it is a question that cannot be fully answered in the ordinary way. But what sort of question is that; . . . I would suggest . . . that it is a symptom of philosophical disorder, the product of a philosophical paradox." [17] If this

17. Pitkin, loc. cit., p. 46. For a very similar argument see Margaret Macdonald, "The Language of Political Theory," in *Logic and Language*, First Series. We might note in passing that most of the philosophers who have put forward answers to this question give every indication of being

is the case the most immediate task is not to resolve the problem or answer the question, but to dissolve the paradox.[18] This can be done by placing the appropriate emphasis upon facts that those caught up in the paradox are fully familiar with, indeed which are available to them from their knowledge of the very concepts in which they state the question, but which they haven't brought to bear on the question that is bothering them. The "answer" to the question "Why am I (ever) obligated to . . . obey laws?" is "that this is what 'legitimate government,' 'genuine authority' *mean*. It is part of the concept, the meaning of 'authority' that those subject to it are required to obey, that it has a right to command. It is part of the concept, the meaning of 'law,' that those to whom it is applicable are obligated to obey it. As with promises, so with authority, government and law: there is a prima facie obligation involved in each, and normally you must perform it." [19] The theorist who is not satisfied with this answer, who quests "for some 'higher,' absolute, deductive, justification is misguided. Insofar, then, as the grammatical point does not seem to still the question, does not get at what someone philosophically puzzled wants to ask, what is needed is not a better justification, but an account of why the philosopher is driven to ask the question in the first place." [20]

---

quite satisfied with their answers to it. They typically criticize previous answers (thereby indicating that they thought previous theories meaningful but mistaken) and give what they take to be cogent reasons for accepting their own answer. Moreover they seem to think it of considerable practical importance that other men accept their answer. It is perhaps also worthwhile to remind ourselves of what we all know, namely that the failure of all previous attempts to answer a question does not itself entail the conclusion that the question is meaningless and for that or some other reason unanswerable.

18. In Pitkin's words, the task is to "show how and why it [the paradox] arises, why anyone should so much as suppose that political obligation in general needs (or can have) a general justification." This would "require a discussion of the nature of philosophical puzzlement" (Pitkin, loc. cit.).

19. Ibid., p. 48.

20. Ibid., p. 49. Cf. Wittgenstein's remarks that when we have stated and taken to heart the meaning of the concepts involved we have iden-

We have no quarrel with Pitkin's account of "authority," "law," and "obligation." The correctness of that account explains why legislatures do not have to state that there is an obligation to obey their laws. It bears repeating that we cannot come to grips with the practice of political obligation if we do not understand "law," "authority," and "obligation" as they are used in the ordinary language(s) in which that practice is conducted. Any attempt to discuss the question "Why am I obligated to obey the law?"—whether in this case or ever—that is not grounded in an understanding of the uses of these concepts will not be discussion of that practice. Insofar as it is intended to be discussion of that practice it will be meaningless. As H. A. Prichard put it, to ask why I have an obligation is to assume that there is some sense in which I have one, which is possible only if I understand the concept "obligation." [21] Thus far Pitkin's argument is correct and important.

It is a long and unwarranted step from these premises to the radical conclusion that any and all attempts to answer or even to discuss seriously the question "Why do I (ever) have an obligation to obey the law?," no matter how firmly grounded in understanding of the linguistic facts to which Pitkin points, must be misguided and must be meaningless except as a symptom of philosophical disorder. The first problem in assessing the argument is to determine just how to interpret the crucial but ambiguous notion "philosophical disorder." What precisely is the nature of the disorder involved in categorical questioning of the obligation to obey the law? The strongest interpretation, which is suggested by the fact that the conclusion is built upon an analysis of concepts, would be that it is impossible to raise this question without systematically misusing concepts so as

tified a "form of life." And forms of life are "What has to be accepted, the given. . . ." Wittgenstein, op. cit., II, xi (p. 226). Again, "If I have exhausted the justifications I have reached bedrock, and my spade is turned. Then I am inclined to say: 'This is simply what I do.'" Ibid., I, 217 (p. 85).

21. See H. A. Prichard, *Moral Obligation* (London: Oxford University Press, 1949), esp. essays 4 and 5.

to render the discussion literally without meaning or sense. Interpreted in this way, Pitkin's argument constitutes no less than a delineation of the "bounds of sense" in one (not so little) corner of human activity; an attempt to identify, as Plato would have put it, the limits of intelligibility.

This strong interpretation is not the only one that finds a warrant in Professor Pitkin's text. Siding with Cavell against Rawls's view that there could be intelligible discourse about the utility of the practice of promising qua social practice, she says that Rawls's view "implies a degree of freedom of choice on our parts which we do not in fact have. To evaluate the practice of promising pro and con, we would have to envision alternatives. And how shall we envision a society which knows no obligation to keep one's word? . . . We seem to have no choice about the pros and cons of such an institution. It is not socially useful; it is indispensable to the very concept of society and human life." [22]

Now this passage is itself ambiguous and could be used to support the first interpretation we suggested. To say that the institution is indispensable to the *concept* of society might be construed as a remark not about human needs or the way men interact in a society but about the conventions governing the use of "society"; a remark in the formal mode to the effect that "society" is misused if it is applied to arrangements or relationships that do not include the practice of ascribing and assuming obligations and holding people to their word. The point at issue would not be whether men have lived or could live together without this institution, but whether it would be proper to describe such an arrangement as a society. And that issue would be settled by looking not at how men live together but how the concept "society" is used.

The passage could also be interpreted to be about some kind of contingent, perhaps physical necessity; to be an assertion that it would be impossible for men to live together without

22. Pitkin, loc. cit., p. 48.

the institutions in question, or perhaps impossible to attain the benefits that result from life in a society with those institutions. This interpretation is most clearly suggested by Pitkin's extension of her remarks about the necessity of the institution of keeping one's word to the case of law, government, and authority. She concedes that "here, I suppose, there may be somewhat more room for discussion [of the merits of these institutions qua institutions] than with promises. For it is not at all obvious that government and law are indispensable to human social life." [23] The passage continues in a manner that could be taken to withdraw the concession as regards authority. But the important point is that the phrase "*concept* of society and human life" has been dropped in favor of "human social life." This phrase creates problems of its own, but there is nothing in Pitkin's use of it that tempts us to interpret her remarks as an abbreviated analysis of the use of "society" (as remarks in the formal mode). Thus any necessities or impossibilities that are discovered will have to be the consequence of facts about man or society and thus contingent not necessary. The "philosophical disorder" involved in categorical questioning of the obligation to obey authoritative commands will be a result of mistakes concerning facts about human beings and societies, not mistakes in the use of language.

The third and weakest interpretation of "philosophical disorder" is bound up with Pitkin's discussion of the quest for and impossibility of an "absolute, deductive justification" of such institutions as promising, law, government, and authority and hence of the obligations generated by those institutions and practices. Having noted that "classical consent theories" did attempt to provide a utilitarian justification for authority and obligation by first describing a society which lacked them, Pitkin passes directly to the assertion that "even a recognition of the necessity or utilitarian advantages of such things as authority, law, and government is no absolute answer to the

23. Ibid., p. 48.

man who is questioning his particular obligation to obey. . . . There is no such absolute answer, and can be none. Nothing we say is absolutely beyond question." [24] Here Pitkin does not deny the possibility of meaningful categorical questioning of authority and obligation. Her criticisms are directed against a particular type of categorical questioning and more especially to a particular type of attempt to reply to such questioning. A man who was dissatisfied with Pitkin's grammatical answer to the question "Why should I (ever) obey the law?" but who was not in quest of an "absolute, deductive answer," could attempt to assess the institution of law, authority, and obligation without evidencing the philosophical disorder that Pitkin has in mind. If it could be shown that Plato, Hobbes, Locke, Green, etc., did not hope to provide an "absolute, deductive" answer to the questions they raised about obligation, their philosophizing could be, so far as Pitkin's criteria go, meaningful and free of "disorder." On this interpretation Pitkin's argument, at least insofar as it is concerned with categorical questioning of obligations, is primarily directed not to obligation but to a particular sort of perplexity or puzzlement, the kind that persists in the face of every sort of answer or response save the one that logically is unavailable.[25] As she says—and we agree with her although it would require an immense digression even to begin to state clearly and defend our position— "nothing we say is absolutely beyond question." (But then we must ask whether this ringing declaration applies to Pitkin's own assertions concerning the impossibility of meaningful categorical questioning of political obligations. Unfortunately we must also ask whether it applies to the ringing declaration "Nothing we say is absolutely beyond question.") If this is the case, the sort of perplexity with which she is concerned is not unique to obligation or to normative matters. The same

24. Ibid., p. 49.
25. She is interested, in other words, in the sort of puzzlement that was of great concern to Wittgenstein and which has been discussed so brilliantly by John Wisdom.

sort of perplexity and questioning could arise concerning "2 + 2 = 4" or "The atomic weight of lead is X." Thus the arguments about impossibility should be understood as indicating what it is, in the case of obligation, that this particular form of perplexity and questioning overlooks or fails to take to heart, not as establishing a bar to any and all categorical questioning of obligation. This is a "weak" version or interpretation of the argument in that it does not establish a bar to all categorical questioning of the institutions in question and in that it does not distinguish the problem of justifying these institutions from the problem of justifying or supporting any other practice, rule, proposition, or conclusion. Interpreted in this way the argument is of no interest here and we will say no more about it.

Let us now examine the merits of the argument interpreted in the first and strongest sense we identified, namely as asserting that all attempts to question categorically the obligation to obey the law involve conceptual errors that render the discussion meaningless.[26] Insofar as this argument depends on the assertion that it is logically or conceptually impossible to conceptualize an alternative to the present arrangement, the argument has no serious claim to our allegiance. We are talking about the concepts "authority," "obligation," "law," and "society." For there to be concepts that we can use there must be rules or conventions establishing the proper use or uses of those concepts. As we argued above, the notion of a rule of conduct presupposes an alternative to the required conduct; the notion of following a rule presupposes awareness of an alternative. Rules establishing the proper use of a concept necessarily exclude some uses as improper. Thus to know how to use "authority" is, among other things, to know how not to

26. Pitkin never asserts this of attempts to question the obligation to obey the law and our judgment is that it is not her intention to assert it concerning the obligation to keep promises. The challenge thrown up by her discussion suggests the question—which is of obvious importance —and provides a convenient opportunity to examine it.

use it, to know how to distinguish the use of authority from the use of other concepts. Which is to be able to conceive of alternatives to arrangements involving authority at least in the sense of being able, so far as logic is concerned, to conceive of arrangements that do not involve authority, including entire societies in which no authority is to be found. More pointedly, people who know the English language are not tempted to apply "authority" to anything and everything to which it does not apply. They are tempted to apply it to phenomena that bear certain similarities to authority, for example power or influence or prestige. In learning how to use it we learn how to distinguish its use from the use of related concepts. A man who lives in a society in which there is both authority and power and who knows how to use both "authority" and "power" is in an excellent position to conceive of a society in which there would not only be no application for "authority" but in which he would properly use "power" in all the situations that resemble those in which, in his society, he properly uses "authority."

Assuming, then, that it is possible to conceptualize an alternative to the arrangement that involves the relationships between "authority," "law," and "obligation" as we now use them, let us inquire whether there is any other sense in which categorical questioning of that arrangement necessarily leads us into "philosophical disorder." Interpreted in the "strong" sense, the argument before us is an example of a type of argument that has been called—not altogether out of a benevolent attitude toward it—"descriptivism." [27] It involves the contention that it is possible to derive a normative conclusion (T), that B has a prima facie obligation to do X (obey a law), from two factual premises, namely: (1) There is a law that is authoritative for A that requires X; and (2) The statement (which is a statement of the semantic rules governing the concepts in question) "R is an authoritative law" entails the statement "All

27. See R. M. Hare, "Descriptivism," *Proceedings of the British Academy* XLIX (1963).

those for whom the law is authoritative have a prima facie obligation to obey the law." Indeed the argument implies that in such cases premises other than 1 and 2 are irrelevant to supporting T and otiose in any argument intended to support T. Once again this is an impeccable account of the inferences allowed by the concepts as they are now used. Moreover, these inferences must be understood in order to participate in the practice in question. A man who did not understand that these are valid inferences could not fully understand the actions, verbal and otherwise, of participants in the practice; a man who simply chose to ignore the inferences would not be understood by other participants.

But a man need not simply ignore the inferences. He might deny that he (ever) should have had or should ever have an obligation to obey the law, explain that he issues his denial in full knowledge that it flies in the face of established conventions, and try to *justify* his denial by presenting arguments intended to show that the conventions that allow the inference T, including the linguistic conventions, are unfortunate or pernicious and should be altered or repudiated. If he simply said, flat out, so to speak, that he had no obligation, other members of the society might find it difficult to understand him.[28] If he explained what he meant and tried to justify his position we might find his views unpersuasive, wrongheaded, or even shocking and pernicious. Is there any ground whatever for thinking that we would find them unintelligible? We would, rather, realize that the man was engaged in the radical enterprise of questioning and trying to alter some of the most fundamental conventions—both linguistic and otherwise—in our society. It is a logical point that we cannot question and/or try to change all of the conventions, linguistic or otherwise, of

28. But of course if this happened, and if the conversation were a serious one, couldn't they, and wouldn't they be likely to, ask him what he meant? When a man says something that we find puzzling don't we ordinarily assume that he is trying to say something meaningful—if not necessarily something sensible—and try to discover what it is? And aren't we usually successful?

our society at one time. If we tried to do so we would have no usable concepts in which to form our questions. But holding most of the concepts constant, that is using them in the conventional manner to think about the uses of selected concepts, we can question and try to change the use of any given concept.[29] Given the elaborate web of conceptual relationships that extend out from a concept such as "authority" this is a sensitive task.[30] But there is no reason to think it a logically impossible undertaking. Wherein lies the logical or conceptual error in the following statement: "The more I reflect about political authority and the obligations generated by its exercise the more convinced I become that society as a whole would do better to imitate the example of my poker club and do without it. According men a claim to obedience independent of the reasons they can give for the particular rules they suggest hampers and erodes the process of discussion and diminishes our humanity. Leadership, influence, even power, these we need. But there is nothing I would like better than a society in which the concept of authority as we now know it would have no application." [31]

We will conclude the discussion of the first and strongest interpretation of Pitkin's thesis by quoting again a passage that supplies a general perspective from which to view the thesis and the points we have tried to make against it.

In discussing the logic of ordinary language I have frequently used the word 'rule.' . . . The word is not in-

29. Recall the more general discussion of this question in Chapter One. And see John Searle, loc. cit., p. 57, n. 8.

30. Recall Wittgenstein, op. cit., I, 106 (p. 46). "We feel as if we had to repair a torn spider's web with our fingers."

31. Even Hare, to whom I am indebted here, gives too little weight to the possibility of questioning and trying to change the uses of concepts which in present use represent cases of a logical tie between what he calls the descriptive and commendatory meaning. That I cannot (now) describe a rule as an authoritative law without implying that there is an obligation to obey it does not prevent me from questioning and trying to change the conventions that constitute the basis of that tie. Cf. R. M. Hare, loc. cit., esp. p. 127.

appropriate: for to speak of . . . 'rules' is to speak of ways in which language may be *correctly* or *incorrectly* used. But though not inappropriate the word may be misleading. We do not judge our linguistic practice in the light of antecedently studied rules. We frame rules in the light of our study of our practice. Moreover, our practice is a very fluid affair. If we are to speak of rules at all, we ought to think of them as rules which everyone has a license to violate if he can show a point in doing so. In the effort to describe our experience we are continually putting words to new uses, connected with, but not identical with, their familiar uses; applying them to states of affairs which are both like and unlike those to which the words are most familiarly applied. Hence we may give a meaning to sentences which, at first sight, seem self-contradictory. And hence . . . it is in fact hard to frame a grammatical sentence to which it is impossible to imagine some sense being given; and given, not by arbitrary *fiat*, but by an intelligible, though probably figurative, extension of the familiar senses of the words and phrases concerned.[32]

Strawson's point is that the rules governing ordinary language do not constitute a rigid or strict calculus such as is constituted by the rules of a system of formal logic. We must be able to account not only for the stability and continuity of ordinary language, for the respects in which its development to the present influences the ways in which we talk, but also for its fluidity and the possibilities of variation and change that are contained in it.[33]

We turn now to the argument that categorical questioning of the obligation to obey the law is impossible because, for some reason other than logical impossibility, we are unable to "conceive of alternatives" to the existing practice, unable to

32. Peter Strawson, op. cit., p. 230.
33. Cf. Wittgenstein, *The Blue and Brown Books*, pp. 24–25, 82; *Philosophical Investigations*, I, 64–75 (pp. 31–35), and esp. I, 107–9 (pp. 46–47).

conceive of men living together without law or authority and an obligation to obey them. This argument looks suspiciously like the argument of the naturalist who watched the bumblebee fly away and said: "It's impossible." For what else is the state of nature described by Glaucon, Hobbes, Locke, and Hume but such a conception? And what else have anarchists been putting forward as an ideal? These thinkers have not only conceived of an alternative, they have worked an alternative out in considerable detail and have *put it to use* in thinking about society and politics. Indeed they have used it for the very purpose that the argument we are considering dismisses as a symptom of philosophical disorder, namely as a means of evaluating, in general or categorically, the practice involving authority, law, and obligation. Given the fact that to all appearances men *have* conceived of an alternative, and given the absence of logical or conceptual barriers to doing so, the least we are entitled to say is that the person who argues that it is impossible to do so takes on the burden of showing in detail what is wrong in each of the numerous cases that seem to refute his position.

But this is not all we are entitled to say. We are also entitled to inquire into the status of the proposition "It is (nonlogically) impossible for men to conceive of men living together without authority, law, and obligation." The most obvious point here is that since the impossibility we are now considering is contingent, not logical, it is contingent upon something or some set of things that might change. Thus the proposition can only be a (somewhat hyperbolic) way of saying "It is impossible for men *as they are* living in the world *as it is* to conceive of an alternative." But further, what does it mean to say that it is (nonlogically) impossible for men to *conceive* of something? Grammatically the statement looks like "It is impossible for men as they are (and the gravitational forces being what they are) to jump twenty-five feet straight up." As is often the case, however, grammatical similarity is not a good guide to logical similarity. In the case of jumping twenty-five feet straight up we know what would count as evidence that the act in question is or is not impossible. Is the same true in the case of the contention that it is impossible to conceive of an alternative to the practice we are discussing? Can we measure and determine the present limits of our "powers of imagination" in the way that we can measure and determine the present limits of the strength of our muscles? If we cannot do so, what sense (other than that no one has yet done so—if contrary to fact that was the case) are we to give to the idea that it is impossible for men as they are to conceive or to imagine something. The conditions necessary to the use of "impossible" and "cannot" are not satisfied in this case.

At the very best, then, the assertion that it is (nonlogically) impossible to conceive of men living together without authority, law, and obligation (to conceive of an alternative to present arrangements) is an assertion about the past that cannot bind the future. At worst the assertion depends on a misuse of "cannot" and "impossible." Thus the arguments we have been considering do not show that we cannot conceive of alternatives to present arrangements. If the capacity to question those arrangements categorically carries with it the possibility of distinguishing between the rules that constitute those arrangements and reasons for or against accepting those rules, these arguments do not show that there is no logical room for such a distinction.[34]

This conclusion is of great importance. It means that there are alternatives to simply thinking and doing what the semantic rules governing our language, even very fundamental features of our language, influence us to think and do. It means that

34. The matter is nicely disposed of by Jane Austen in a speech she gives to the very conventional Mrs. Bennet: "My dear Jane, Mr. Collins is a conceited, pompous, narrowminded, silly man; you know he is, as well as I do; and you must feel, as well as I do, that the woman who marries him cannot have a proper way of thinking. You shall not, for the sake of one individual, change the meaning of principle and integrity, nor endeavor to persuade yourself or me, that selfishness is prudence, and insensibility of danger security for happiness." Jane Austen, *Pride and Prejudice* (New York: The Pocket Library, 1940), p. 149.

our thought and action in the area of law and authority are not bounded by impassable conceptual or logical restraints. In order to know *what* we are faced with when faced with a law and *what* we are doing when we obey it or disobey it we must understand the concepts involved. But to understand them is to understand the possibilities open to us concerning them.

b. "Obey the law" as a precept The general rule is potentially of great significance in our lives. There are a very large number of laws requiring and forbidding a very large number of actions. If the general rule gave us good reasons for obeying all laws it would be the basis of a substantial part of our conduct. If it is logically and conceptually possible to ask for reasons for accepting the general rule we certainly have good reason to do so.

The first question that arises is whether those features of the rule that Pitkin has rightly emphasized provide good reasons, or reasons at all, for obeying the law. If we treat these linguistic facts as materials for answering the question rather than stilling it, should they have weight with us? Does the existence of these linguistic rules add anything to the case for obeying the law?

The answer is pretty obviously "No." Pitkin reminds us of what the words "law" and "authority" mean. But the fact that words have a certain established use is in itself hardly a reason for acting in a manner that affects other people. If instead of saying "That was what I was ordered to do" Eichmann had said "That is what the words 'authoritative command' mean" he would hardly have added to the strength of his case. "That is what the words mean; therefore that is what I have an obligation to do" is so abject a form of conformism as to be altogether outside of the realm of moral reasoning. Of course Eichmann could not reason about whether he had an obligation to obey if he did not know what the words meant. He could not do so because he could not know *what* he was reasoning about. But to know what one is reasoning about is a precondition of reasoning about it; it is not the same thing as reasoning about it. (This is not to deny that in fact we are often *influenced* by the semantic rules governing the concepts that we use in reasoning.)

If the fact that "This is a law" means "There is an obligation to obey it" is to count as a reason for obeying the law it must be shown that it is desirable that the words be used in this way. Or better, it must be shown that it is desirable that society have arrangements that include laws and the rule that people have an obligation to obey them. In terms of the breakdown of types of rules that we are using, the semantic rule must coincide with a precept-type rule for which there are good reasons.[35]

Putting the matter this way helps us to see that the question "Why should I ever obey the law?" is indeed a very special kind of question. As Pitkin says, we are familiar with it primarily from the work of political philosophers who have been concerned to understand and evaluate political practices seen in a very general perspective. The infrequency with which the question is asked is perhaps now explained in part by the con-

35. This would also be true of constitutive rules (if they are a distinct category). It should be clear from the discussion in the text that we regard "There is an obligation to obey the law" as a semantic rule which coincides with a precept. To digress briefly concerning the general question of constitutive rules, we suggest that a number of the examples that have been put forward as instances of such rules are better thought of as semantic rules. "There is an obligation to keep promises" is a case in point. It is not clear how this rule is distinguished from "Do not lie," "Do not cheat," "Do not act in a rude manner," and many other rules which can be viewed as explications of the concepts of which their formulation consists. The person who does not know that lying and cheating are things that one should not do does not know how to use the concepts "lie" and "cheat." We could not engage in the practice of lying or cheating, or criticize it, if we did not have the concepts. (Cf. Philippa Foot, "Moral Arguments," *Mind* [1958], pp. 502–13, and "Moral Beliefs." *Proceedings of the Aristotelian Society* 59 [1958–59], pp. 83–104.) We would reserve the category "constitutive rules" for rules which not only identify what must be done to engage in a certain activity but which can be laid down, and changed, only by an authoritative procedure. Compare in this respect John Rawls's remark that "the practice conception [of rules] is more relevant to understanding legal and legal-like arguments than it is to the more complex moral arguments" (John Rawls, loc. cit., final footnote).

ceptual facts we have been discussing. Language is often misused in ordinary speech (that is this or that part of language is misused) but few men step outside of and self-consciously assess (part of) language in the manner now involved in categorical questioning of the obligation to obey the law. But it may also be that a very large number of people would agree with the view that authority, law, and obligation are "indispensable" to social life. Since they would have in effect answered the question we are considering, they would have no reason to discuss it explicitly.

A more important sense in which the question is special can be seen by recurring to the distinction between the general rule and particular legal rules. The very grammar of the general rule conveys the impression that there is some one thing, law, that people are to obey, and hence that there is some one reason for obeying it or not. This is profoundly misleading. There is one concept that has numerous applications, all of which may share certain features (for example, having authoritative standing), but which may differ from one another in important respects. We have already noted the distinction between laws that require or forbid and laws that enable or empower. The corollary of this distinction is that the notions of obedience and obligation have no application to laws of the latter type. In addition, some obligation-generating laws are vastly more important than others. It is not only implausible but pernicious to think that the reasons for obeying laws against homicide are in all respects the same as the reasons for obeying parking ordinances; that the reasons for obeying the laws of contract are in all respects the same as those for obeying the laws forbidding mistreatment of children. We have to ascend to an extremely high and general level, to a level to which our ordinary experience with law rarely takes us, to find a single purpose or set of purposes common to all laws or a single set of reasons for obeying all laws. Categorical questioning of the obligation to obey the law draws us away from the considerations involved in day-to-day thinking about law.

Insofar as such questioning obscures the differences among laws, it is not impossible or meaningless, it is dangerous.

It does not follow that we should dismiss such questioning. To dismiss it would be to exclude an important part of the practice of political obligation from our consideration. If we rarely encounter men *asking* the question "Why should I ever obey the law?," and if we rarely find men actually rejecting the obligation to obey the law categorically (as opposed to reflecting, say in writing political philosophy, about whether there are good reasons for rejecting it), it is not at all uncommon for men to *answer* the question affirmatively. This is in fact what is happening when acceptance of the general rule "Obey the law" is inculcated in the young, extolled in discussions of the achievements of a society, or offered as a reason for obeying laws that are thought to be objectionable. Offering this kind of advice presupposes not reasons for thinking that a particular law is a good or defensible law, but reasons for thinking that the practice which includes authority, law, and obligation is a good practice. There is no reason to think that the very large number of people who hold this view and give such advice can only be or in fact are merely explaining the meaning of the concepts they use in giving the advice.[36] Such people might accept the view that authority and law are indispensable to society, but this could just as well mean (as Pitkin recognizes) that there are a great many reasons that support it, not that it cannot be supported (except by giving facts about language). These reasons do not add up to an absolute, deductive justification; but they might provide a cogent argument for accepting the rule, an argument that would have to be met by anyone who claimed that he was

36. Pitkin's view in this regard is very much like the position of David Hume. Hume said that moral guidance is often no more than reports about the meaning of words. "The merit of delivering true general precepts in ethics is very small. Whoever recommends any moral virtues really does no more than is implied in the terms themselves." David Hume, "Of the Standard of Taste," *Essays: Moral, Political, and Literary* (London: Oxford University Press, 1963), pp. 233–34.

justified in rejecting the rule. Political philosophers have tried very hard to state such reasons. That we find some of these reasons unpersuasive does not show that they are not reasons or that the exercise of working them out is futile or misguided. Reasons of the sort philosophers have presented have persuaded a great many men that authority and law qua authority and law are valuable and should be maintained even at the cost of considerable sacrifice of other values in particular cases. Competing reasons have persuaded a much smaller number of men that authority and law are of little value and that nothing should be sacrificed to maintain them (this seems to be Thoreau's view) or even that they are of no value or are a positive evil that should be done away with (this seems to be Bakunin's view). Thus categorical questions and answers about authority and law taken alone, that is independent of their relation to the more particular questions that arise in connection with authority and law, not only have meaning and sense but have practical application and significance.

It is not the case, however, that reasoning about law and authority qua law and authority is only possible about or relevant to categorical acceptance or rejection of them. The categorical question "Why should I ever obey the law?" does not have to be answered with reasons why I should *always* obey the law or why I should *never* obey the law. Reflection about the categorical question can lead to the conclusion, did lead Socrates to the conclusion, that there are important benefits and advantages to be derived from the practice and that it is worth maintaining. As the case of Socrates also shows, it can equally lead to the conclusion that there are difficulties and dangers that arise in connection with the practice, difficulties that sometimes justify disobedience.[37] If the fact that a rule is a law is relevant to deciding whether to obey it, it is difficult to see why the reasons that make law important, and hence contribute to making the fact that the rule is a law a relevant

37. Socrates' views are discussed at length in Chapter Eight below.

fact, would be irrelevant. For most of us most of the time the value of categorical questioning is not that it will help us to decide whether to become anarchists, but that it gives us general considerations to bring to the less than categorical choices and judgments which we all must make throughout our lives.

3. SUMMARY CONCERNING THE PRECEPT "OBEY THE LAW"

From one perspective "Obey the law" is a semantic rule. Stating it serves to explicate one feature of the use of the concepts "authority," "law," and "obligation." A person who does not understand the rule does not understand the relevant uses of these concepts or the social and political practices of which they are an integral part. It is impossible to understand the concepts that are used to formulate the rule, the rule itself, or the practice constituted by the concepts and the rule without also understanding a larger network of concepts, rules, and social and political practices of which the practice involving political authority, law, and political obligations are but one. Applying the rule to particular cases often requires explicit attention to that larger network as well as to the characteristics of the situation at hand.

Owing to the uses of the concepts "law," "authority," and "obligation," merely to apply those concepts to a particular rule without questioning their ordinary use is to imply that there is an obligation to obey them. The precept-type rule that coexists with the semantic rules is also well established in numerous societies and disputes about obedience often center on the case for the regulation-type rule in question not the semantic- or the precept-type rule. For these reasons the normative implications of the use of the concepts is often not explicitly defended. Because the regulation-type rules to which the general rule applies are diverse in content and purpose, it is difficult to identify a single reason or set of reasons for accepting the general rule. Indeed there is a danger of oversimplification in reasoning about the general rule and much to be said for a political process which emphasizes reasoning about the particular regulation-type rules. But it is neither impossible nor meaningless to defend or question the general rule; it is defended or questioned whenever it is recommended or attacked independently of its application to a particular legal rule, and it has been defended and attacked in a systematic manner by a number of political philosophers.

IV. CONCLUDING REMARKS

WE CAN NOW DRAW conclusions concerning the questions with which we began the chapter, namely what the existence of rules of various types adds to the case for doing an action that falls under them, and what sorts of reasoning are appropriate to supporting acceptance of and conformity with the various types we have examined.

1. An instruction-type rule supports B's acting in a manner that accords with the rule if B wants to achieve the goal or objective which is served by following the rule. Whether B will try to achieve that objective is up to him. Such rules are appropriately supported by giving evidence (from experience) that following the rule is the most efficient way to achieve the objective or objectives that B has. However B may in fact act, if he does not believe that there is such evidence it is inappropriate to say that he is following the rule.

2. Constitutive rules support B's acting in a manner that accords with the rule in that they establish what must, logically speaking, be done in order to achieve an objective or engage in an activity. The only sense in which they can be supported in a particular case is by showing that they have been correctly identified and applied. Reasons could be given for or against changing the rules and hence the practice they constitute but until such changes have been ratified by established procedures it will remain the case that B can engage in the activity only by following the rule as it is. In their character as constitutive rules such rules support B's following the rule only if B wants to achieve the objective or engage in the activity constituted by

the rules. Some of the rules that have been characterized as constitutive rules have social standing such that it is thought that individuals have an obligation to follow the rules if they have once entered into the activity. Thus if I have made a promise or contract I have an obligation to keep it or perform it. But this feature is not a general characteristic of rules with the logical properties that distinguish the category. Having entered a game of baseball does not put me under an obligation to keep on playing. Or rather, if I do have such an obligation it is generated by rules other than the rules of baseball. Hence where the feature is present it is best to say that one and the same formulation states both a constitutive rule and a rule of some other kind—for example a precept or regulation. Thus if promising is treated as a practice constituted by constitutive rules, "There is an obligation to keep promises" is *both* a constitutive rule which constitutes a part of the practice *and* a precept. Using the first to guide conduct is "supported" by showing that the rule is in fact established and has been correctly cited; use of the second is supported by showing that it is good or desirable that there is a practice of promising which includes the constitutive-type rule. B might want to engage in the practice despite the fact that he disapproved of it or disapproved of that characteristic of it which is given by the existence of the precept-type rule. If so he could be guided by the constitutive rule but not by the precept. In such a case his conduct would be reasoned in the sense that he chose to follow the rule as against alternative actions and believed that following the rule was the most efficient means to his objective. If he did not have reasons for following the rule in this sense he could not be said to have followed it.

3. The semantic rules we have examined in this chapter have a number of the features of constitutive rules. We must understand such rules if we are to know *what* we are doing in taking a particular action. Use of them in guiding speech is "supported" by evidence that they have been correctly identified. Since to speak is sometimes to act in ways over and above

speaking, semantic rules sometime guide conduct in the sense of indicating what we must do if we are to act in a manner consistent with the implications of the ways we have previously spoken. Or more precisely, they indicate what we must do if, when our actions have been properly characterized, those characterizations are to be consistent with the ways we originally spoke. Thus if B says that X is an authoritative law that applies to him, he must also say that he has an obligation to obey that law. And if he says he has an obligation to obey that law he must discharge that obligation unless he can show that the obligation is defeated or that he is excused from it in the circumstances. The force of the "must" in the three previous sentences, however, is "must do it if he is to speak and otherwise act in a manner consistent with the established semantic rules." And to show that an action is consistent with semantic rules is not to show that the action is justified.

In the cases we have considered it is useful to think of the semantic rule as coinciding with regulations or precepts. To show that the *action* of obeying the law is justified one must show that the regulations and/or the precept that coincides with the semantic rule are justified. It is logically possible to conform to the semantic rule despite rejecting the precept or regulation; someone might do so simply to facilitate communication. This fact is sufficient to show that following the one is logically independent of following the other. B can be said to be following the semantic rule if he shows that he knows the rule and shows that he knows that following it is the most efficient means to his end of facilitating communication.

In fact, of course, following the one ordinarily coincides with following the other. Moreover, semantic rules can be changed without recourse to established, authoritative, procedures. Hence the person who dislikes a precept that coincides with a semantic rule begins the process of challenging and changing the latter at the same time that he challenges the precept. (The case of regulations is more like the case of constitutive rules in this respect.) By the same token the person who follows the precept, that is shows that he acts in accord with it because he thinks there are good reasons for doing so, also follows the semantic rule. The fact that the semantic rule is so intimately related to the precept makes it appear that the semantic rule is itself a reason for accepting and following the precept. Indeed it makes it appear that there is no room for a distinction between a semantic rule and a precept and hence that the only general reason for obeying the law is "that is what the words mean." A main purpose of our argument has been to show that this is nothing more than appearance.

A rule is a regulation in the sense in which we are using the term only if it is authoritative in the sense of "promulgated by an agent or agency with the authority to do so." The question whether a particular rule is authoritative will often be decided by looking to some higher rule such as a charter or constitution. But the fact that a rule is authoritative affects its significance for conduct only because there is a precept-type rule according to which there is an obligation to obey authoritative rules. Regulations presuppose such a precept in the sense that if there were no such precept the implications of saying that regulations are authoritative would be different than they now are. Thus part of the conduct-guiding force of regulations stems from the fact that the precept "Obey the law" lies behind them. In this respect the advice that B should obey a particular law is supported by giving reasons for accepting the precept. B can be said to be guided by the rule only if he thinks there are good reasons for the precept.

But there is no such thing as obeying the law in the abstract. Any action properly described as obeying the law will also be describable as some other action as well—for example submitting an income tax return or attaching a pollution control device to one's automobile. The concept "law" and the rule "Obey the law" identify and govern only one feature of the particular legal rule and actions taken under it; they identify and govern the action under only one of the characterizations appropriate to it. Hence there is a possibility of reasoning about the rule and the conduct taken under characterizations other than "law" and "Obey the law." Putting a pollution control device on one's car can be defended or attacked independent of the fact that there is a law requiring it. Moreover, since any form of conduct that we can describe could be required or prohibited by law, the reasoning that supported or attacked "Obey the law" could be known a priori to be conclusive as to whether to obey any particular law only if it could be established that obeying the law, as such, is the greatest possible good (or evil) in all circumstances. It is something of an understatement to say that this is implausible. Thus if B is to defend what he is doing in obeying or disobeying a law he must be able to defend what he is doing under characterizations other than "obeying (disobeying) a law." Since he is obeying a rule (in addition to the rule "Obey the law") he must be able to defend that rule. Since he *is* obeying or disobeying the rule "Obey the law," being able to defend doing so gives him reasons for doing what he is doing and allows him to claim that his conduct is guided by a rule. But being able to defend "Obey the law" is not a sufficient condition of being able to defend his conduct and it is not sufficient to show that his conduct is guided by any rule other than "Obey the law."

Precepts such as "Keep your promises" and "Do not lie" are widely accepted in numerous societies and are thought to be extremely important. Indeed they are so widely accepted that to describe an action as lying, or as breaking a promise, is in itself to condemn that action. It is perfectly appropriate to regard "Do not lie" and "Do not break promises" as semantic rules governing some of the uses of "lie" and "promise." A person who does not understand these rules does not understand the use of "lie" and "promise" in the language. "Obey the law" is more controversial than "Do not lie" and "Do not break promises" but to so characterize the action is also to assess it normatively; but here too to call a rule a law which applies to B is to say that B has an obligation to obey it. The person who does not understand this fact does not understand the present use of "law" in the language.

But the case against lying, breaking promises, and obeying

the law does not consist of these linguistic facts. The person who does not know these facts cannot make a case for or against these rules or for or against acting in accord with them. This is because he does not know *what* he is making a case for or against. Moreover, making a case for or against them can be viewed as, among other things, making a case for continuing to use the concepts as they are now used. But to describe the arguments of Socrates, Plato, Hobbes, Thoreau, etc., in this way would be to trivialize them. These thinkers recognized that the rules in question concerned forms of conduct that have substantial consequences in human affairs. They were strongly for or against the rules because they thought the consequences were very good or very bad. They accepted or rejected, obeyed or disobeyed the rules because they thought that there are good reasons for doing so; because they thought that obeying and disobeying them are effective ways to achieve certain ends and because they thought that there are good reasons for valuing and trying to achieve those ends. Once we have examined the relationship between these precepts and other types of rules it is clear that they understood the matter correctly. The existence of a precept-type rule adds to the case for acting in accord with the rule to the degree that there are good reasons for thinking that doing so is an effective way to achieve certain ends and that the ends are desirable. It can be said that a person's conduct has been guided by such rules to the extent that there is evidence that the person knows what conforming to the rule consists of and thinks that there are good reasons for doing so.

(4)

The Social Bases of
Obligation Rules

I̳N CHAPTERS Two and Three we tried to show respects in
which rules and rule-guided conduct are tied to good
reasons. Since political obligations are rule-dependent the relationship between rules and good reasons creates a conceptual
tie between "good reasons" and "obligation" and thus between
good reasons and the practice of political obligation. Now the
activity of reasoning is an activity of individuals. It may be
done in cooperation with other men, but it is done by individuals. Thus if we are right that reasoning plays a role in
accepting and rejecting obligation rules, in guiding and being
guided by such rules, these activities (and the practices of
which they are part) are activities of individuals.

In arguing for the connection between rules and obligations
on the one hand and good reasons on the other we are arguing
against the view that rule-governed conduct is unreflective. We
are also arguing against the view that rules and rule-governed
conduct are social phenomena in the sense of something that

takes place apart from, can be explained or understood without reference to, reflection and deliberation by individuals. It is difficult to make this argument without implying that individual reflection takes place apart from, can be understood without reference to, arrangements and institutions that are social in the sense of being shared among individuals. We have attempted to guard against this error in various ways—for example by calling political obligation a practice, by insisting that conduct-guiding rules depend upon experience that is shared among men, and by recognizing various respects in which rules that are more than linguistic in character require the intrinsically social phenomenon of language. There is, however, much more to be said concerning the social character of rules and rule-governed conduct. To mention but one point at the outset, there is the fact that rules can apply to an individual, and can be used as a basis for criticizing and even punishing him, despite the fact that he does not accept or even know about them. We must now broaden our account by giving more explicit attention to the social dimensions and bases of rules and rule-governed conduct.

In doing so we will be concerned with controversies in moral and political philosophy that are both longstanding and very much alive today. Moral philosophers such as Kant and R. M. Hare who have emphasized the necessity of individual freedom to a genuinely moral decision, and who have wanted to put morality on a rational basis, have minimized the social character of moral conduct, especially the respects in which its social character influences and limits decisions of individual agents. By contrast, Aristotle, Hegel, Durkheim, Bradley, and a whole school of contemporary philosophers led by Philippa Foot have stressed the social dimensions of moral judgments and the limitations placed by those social dimensions on individual choice.

This debate in moral philosophy has counterparts in political philosophy proper. One of these is the controversy concerning the salience and the advantages of centralization or decentralization of political authority and decision-making. Centralists have been impressed by the prominence of centralized authority in the political societies we have known and by the advantages of decision-making by a comparatively few individuals with authority to act largely or mainly on their own judgment. Pitted against the centralists, of which Plato and Hobbes are good representatives as regards the evaluative question, are theorists who have argued that in fact the activities of political leaders are always significantly limited by the social and political conditions under which they act and by the need to win acceptance of their authority and their decisions. These theorists have also argued that it would be disastrous if political leaders were not limited in these ways. Here we can probably list Aristotle (although the great strength of his thinking is indicated by the difficulty we have in classifying him in terms of these dichotomies), Hume and Burke, Montesquieu and Durkheim, and such contemporary writers as Lindblom, Tullock, and Buchanan.

The similarities between this controversy in political theory and the issues in moral philosophy mentioned above have emerged with particular clarity in recent years owing to the emphasis upon rules in moral philosophy generally and to the understanding of the development and standing of moral rules presented by philosophers such as Hare. Thus there is reason to expect that our analysis of rules will shed some light on both controversies. As noted, regulation-type rules are promulgated or laid down at a determinate moment in time by an authoritative agency or agent. The significance of this kind of rule and this process of rule-making in politics can hardly be denied. But precepts and instructions, rules that develop and achieve standing in a very different manner, are no less important. Indeed they are an essential part of regulations. We suggest that much of the controversy between centralists and decentralists can be viewed as turning on the distinctions among different types of rules and the ways in which they achieve standing in a society. Hare's moral philosophy is especially instructive in this respect because it represents an attempt to treat rules that most of us would think of as precepts in terms more appropriate to regulations. If successful this attempt might resolve, or perhaps dissolve, some of the issues between centralists and decentralists in political philosophy. It might show that the processes characteristic of the development of regulations, processes in which decisions by individuals or small numbers of individuals are very prominent, are in fact characteristic of precepts as well and hence predominant in politics and political obligation. We will argue that Hare's attempt to establish this position is not successful. But its failures are instructive failures that will help us to understand the sorts of rules involved in the practice of political obligation and hence some of the complex and subtle ways in which individual and society depend upon one another.

Another controversy relevant here is the continuing debate concerning the role of consent in political obligation. Our emphasis on reasoned acceptance of obligation rules by the individuals to whom they apply is reminiscent of the tendency of consent theorists to stress individual choice and to relegate the social and historical circumstances in which choices are made to a subordinate if not insignificant position. A main purpose of the present chapter is to show that this is not our intention. We will try to show respects in which there is a relationship of interdependence between individual reasoning about and acceptance or rejection of obligation rules on the one hand and conditions and arrangements that are intrinsically social on the other; respects in which the notion of individual reasoning and choice presuppose certain social conditions and arrangements. In this respect our discussion in this chapter will prepare the way for the more detailed examination of consent theories that we will present in Chapter Seven.[1]

1. From a historical perspective the discussion in the present chapter could be viewed as an elaboration of the sort of points that Hume made against consent theories. See especially his "Of the Original Contract," *Essays: Moral, Political, and Literary,* loc. cit.

I. LANGUAGE AND INDIVIDUAL ACTION

WE WILL BEGIN by reminding ourselves of some respects in which garden-variety human activities, whether in the moral, political, or some other realm, presuppose a social context and are significantly influenced by social conditions and relationships.

The first points we will note hold for all activities that involve the use of language. We have discussed the fact that the concepts we use in interpersonal communication can have meaning because their use is governed by conventions that differentiate between correct and incorrect use. The notion of a convention or rule to which we can appeal to explain or validate a particular use of language presupposes a social context, a context in which there are other human beings who also know the convention and who can test any use of the language by it. To think that it is, in general, sufficient for one to develop a rule and apply it to his own use of language is, in Wittgenstein's figure, like someone buying several copies of the morning newspaper to assure himself that what he read in the first copy he bought was true.[2]

The fact that language presupposes conventions having social standing also places limitations—social limitations—on what we can treat as or include in a particular form of activity. We cannot engage in or talk about the practice of political obligation without using such concepts as "obligation," "rule," "authority," "promise," and "law." The use of these concepts is governed by conventions and to use the concepts *is* to conform with the conventions. For these reasons in most cases it is misleading to say that I choose to conform with the linguistic rules. I choose to speak or not, and I choose which part of the language I am going to use. Choosing to use a particular part of the language is to put myself under the rules governing that

2. *Philosophical Investigations*, I, 265, pp. 93–94.

part of the language. Moreover, putting myself under those rules limits what I can say later. Saying "I promise to take you to the airport at 12:00," puts me under the convention according to which to say "I promise to do X" is to undertake an obligation to do X. Similarly, if I choose to say "I gave my wallet to X simply because he threatened to shoot me if I didn't," I do not then have to choose to say that I did not have an obligation to give my wallet to X. In explaining my behavior I thereby put myself under the rule that lays down that one does not have obligations in such circumstances. Thus whether or not I have an obligation to do X in circumstances Y is not entirely a matter of choice. I have an obligation to keep my promise because the rules I have placed myself under create one, and I do not have an obligation to hand over my wallet because there are rules in terms of which I cannot have one. These conventions have a social standing and in this sense the limitations and constraints of which we have been speaking are social in character. There are as many such limitations as there are conventions of our language—an indeterminate but very high number.[3]

II. SOCIAL RULES AND INDIVIDUAL ACTION

LATER we will explore further the limitations imposed by semantic and other linguistic rules governing the concepts that are prominent in discourse about obligations. Before doing so we should note a few of the many additional respects, going

3. We do not intend to suggest that speakers of a language often feel narrowly hemmed in by linguistic rules. As we stressed throughout the last chapter, few linguistic rules are strictly or tightly defined. Applying them often requires the exercise of judgment by the individual speaker. (And where it does not we simply speak the language as we have learned it.) But as Wittgenstein said, "If language is to be a means of communication there must be agreement not only in definitions but also (queer as this may sound) in judgments" *Philosophical Investigations*, I, 241, (p. 88). Thus the open texture common to many linguistic conventions does not alter the fact that they have social standing.

beyond though not independent of language, in which human actions presuppose a broader context of social conditions and relationships. Consider the act of going to the store to buy a loaf of bread, an act that we typically (and rightly) explain in terms of the individual's desire for the loaf of bread. In describing your act as going to the store to buy bread I make implicit reference to such established social conditions as a system of economic relations and practices, a set of beliefs and preferences concerning diet such that bread is readily available in the society, a pattern of work and leisure such that the store at which you buy the bread is open for business at the time you are free to go and buy the bread, and many others.

Lest it be thought that these points hold only for acts that have substantial social consequences, consider the act of going for a walk. Going for a walk must be distinguished from walking to work, going out to feed the ducks, or checking on the condition of the bird bath at the back of the yard. Making these distinctions involves the use of the social instrument known as language. Knowing how to use the relevant aspects of the language is inseparable from understanding the social patterns to which they apply. The idea of "going for a walk" would be unintelligible in a society in which there was no leisure time, no notion of recreation, and perhaps in a society that lacked the notion that the development and differentiation of individual tastes and preferences was a good or at least an acceptable thing. (Or more strictly, it would be unintelligible in a society that lacked these items *and* had no information concerning societies that did possess them.) There would be no cases of going for walks for us to understand if no one ever decided to go for a walk; but if someone went for a walk in a society without leisure time or the notion of recreation (say a foreigner visiting the society) the members of that society would not understand what that person was doing. For the same reasons a member of the society—one with no experience of societies in which people do go for walks—could not decide to go for a walk.

Secondly, our understanding of some conduct is logically dependent on an understanding of social relationships in the stronger sense (stronger than the one just discussed) that we identify and understand the conduct *in terms of* the social relationships that it involves. So-called role-activities are the clearest case in point. In identifying, understanding and evaluating these actions we use concepts, for example "father," "judge," "policeman," "boss," "president," that refer not to individual persons and their characteristics but to established expectations concerning relationships among persons. There is much in the conduct of Judge Smith, and in the responses of others to his conduct, that we cannot understand or assess if we do not know what it is to be a judge, what it is that a judge is expected to do. The concept "judge" and the activities of judges are intrinsically social.

In general, insofar as an individual's conduct is influenced or governed by rules that have social standing (whether rules governing a social role or some other type of conduct), it cannot be understood apart from those rules. To begin with, a man who knowingly does what a rule requires (or knowingly refuses to do it) *thereby* obeys (disobeys) the rule. As Black says, there is ordinarily no "distinctive act of 'obedience' intervening between understanding [the rule] and acting."[4] This isn't to say that the existence of the rule and the individual's awareness of it are the necessary and sufficient conditions of his obeying the rule. It is possible for him to disobey it despite recognizing that it is a rule he concedes he should obey. He might also choose to act on some other rule or principle that also applies to the situation. Knowing that there is a law against resisting arrest, persons engaged in civil disobedience often choose to go peacefully to jail. They may do so not out of an intention to obey the legal rule against resisting arrest but in order to protest more effectively some other legal rule or some other policy. Just as the rules of our language allow us to de-

4. Max Black, "Rules and Routines," loc. cit., p. 94.

scribe most situations and actions in a number of ways, so our set of rules of conduct often require us to choose between two or more rules. Finally, an individual who recognized that a certain rule had authoritative standing in his society might nevertheless conclude that the rule should not have such standing, reject it categorically, and refuse to conform to it. In all of these cases, however, the individual's decision as to how to act is a decision not to act on the rule. Thus even in such cases, and the more obviously so when the individual obeys the rule, we would not understand his conduct if we did not take into account the presence of the rule and the agent's assessment of it. Thus insofar as we are dealing with rules that have social standing the choices individuals make could not be made if no rules existed and cannot be understood without reference to the rules.

We should also recall our earlier arguments that some types of conduct-guiding rules, including regulations, presuppose a regularity-type rule which supports predictions concerning the consequences of acting on the regulation. Since laws are addressed to classes of people not to individuals, the evidence must support such a belief on the part of (usually) large numbers of people acting in a diversity of contexts and situations. This evidence can only be based on experience with the type of conduct required by the rule. The judgment that a number of actions are all examples of the same type of conduct, and hence that their consequences are relevant to predicting the consequences of acting on the prospective rule, presupposes linguistic rules governing the use of "same" and of the concepts in terms of which we identify the particular types of conduct. Thus the points we have already made about the social character of language apply again at this juncture. But having the concepts is not sufficient: there must also be enough instances of the type of conduct to give us confidence in our predictions concerning its consequences. If the rule is intended to apply to a number of people in differing situations, the evidence supporting it is not likely to be convincing to those expected to obey and to support the rule unless they are able to see the relationship between it and *their* experience. If rules are to be obeyed and supported it is important that the type or class of action required by them be inclusive enough to figure in the experience of a substantial segment of the people for whom they are to be rules. Put another way, rules should concern types of conduct that are part of the *shared* experience of the members of the society or social group to whom they apply. Where they do not do so the case for accepting and obeying them is not likely to be persuasive to those to whom they are addressed.

It might seem that this argument would have little or no practical application as advice to prospective rule makers. We would expect that a rule would develop out of the experience of the group of men to whom it applies—that conduct-guiding rules would ordinarily be occasioned by the emergence of a problem or difficulty in the relations among men, difficulties for which the rules would provide a solution. As regards precept-type rules, rules that are not passed or promulgated by an authority, this is pretty clearly the case. Repeated experience with a particular type of conduct leads individuals to generalizations concerning it, and over time the generalizations are abbreviated into rules that have social standing. In the absence of such experience, even if it is only vicarious, there would be no occasion to generalize about the conduct or to form rules concerning it.[5]

---

5. Once rules develop they can be transmitted, taught, independent of specific occasions to apply them. Rules of etiquette, fair play, and good sportsmanship are taught in primary schools. This practice, however, would make little sense if it were not assumed that the pupils would have an abundance of occasions on which to apply the rules, that the rules cover types of conduct common in the lives of the members of the society. Primary schools do not teach codes of rules special to such professions as law or medicine—a task that, if performed at all, is left to schools of law and medicine.

III. HARE'S ACCOUNT OF RULE FORMATION

IT IS in connection with the points just discussed that we can see most clearly the peculiarities and the significance of Hare's treatment of rules. Hare aims to dissolve the controversy between rule-utilitarians and act-utilitarians in moral philosophy.[6] He argues that it is impossible to arrive at judgments about what ought to be done without describing the act that ought to be done. To describe an act is always to describe a kind or class of acts. Further, both rule- and act-utilitarians must (in Hare's view this is a logical must) accept the principle that all judgments about what ought to be done must be universalizable. Thus "X ought to be done" is necessarily a judgment that the class of actions X ought to be done, and to make this judgment is to accept the *rule* "The class of actions X ought to be done." In Hare's words: "Once the universalizability of moral judgments about individual acts is granted, the two theories collapse into each other . . . in nearly all cases.[7]

The difficulty with this argument concerns Hare's account of the proper way to delineate the class of action to be universalized (and thus to provide the subject matter of the rule). He discusses the well-worn example of a promise, made in private by B to a dying man A, to dispose of A's estate in manner X. After A has died it emerges that some other disposition would have a higher utility than X. In deciding how to describe X, the rule-utilitarian (as Hare interprets him) focuses on the fact that B has promised to do X and treats the class of actions to be universalized or not as "Doing what one has

6. The best discussion of this controversy is David Lyons, *Forms and Limits of Utilitarianism* (London: Oxford University Press, 1965). Several of the important papers in the controversy, together with an extensive bibliography concerning it, are available in Michael D. Bayles, ed., *Contemporary Utilitarianism* (Garden City, N.Y.: Doubleday and Company, 1968).

7. R. M. Hare, *Freedom and Reason*, p. 135. (London: Oxford University Press, 1963.)

promised to do or not." Thus for the rule-utilitarian there emerges a rule "Promises should be kept." But Hare insists that this is not the proper way to formulate the rule. In counseling B to consider whether he would be willing to universalize his action Hare does not mean that B should ask (to quote Hare again) "Is he prepared to prescribe universally that promises should be broken? No such general question is required. I mean, is he prepared to prescribe universally that in situations *precisely like this* the promise should be broken. . . ?" [8] Thus Hare would have B work more detail into his action description-cum-rule formulation, thereby limiting the scope of the resultant rule. According to Hare this is what the act-utilitarian does—and what he must do—and thus, contrary to his claims, he is formulating and applying a rule.

The question is whether it is helpful or even plausible to treat statements such as "Don't break promises in situations of precisely this kind" as the formulation of a rule. A rule is something that is expected to have continuing application over an unspecified period of time. As Fredrick Waismann put the point in distinguishing rules from commands:

> I say to someone 'Do this,' and wave a flag. This may be a command. But what if he is learning that in signalling he must in certain circumstances wave the flag in such and such a manner? In that case we should speak of a rule. What is the difference? The command says that a person should wave the flag only this time; it refers to an isolated event. It lies in the nature of a rule that it should be *repeatedly* used in an indefinite number of cases. [9]

If we take Hare's phrase "situations of precisely this kind" at all literally, action-descriptions of the kind he recommends exclude the possibility of a rule developing. "Precisely of this

8. Ibid., p. 134.
9. Friedrich Waismann, *The Principles of Linguistic Philosophy* (London: Macmillan and Co., 1965), p. 141. See also Wittgenstein, *Philosophical Investigations*, I, 197–202, (pp. 80–81).

kind" might include unrepeatable aspects of the situation such as *the* time of *the* day in which the situation occurred. Since Hare is a proponent of universalizability we are presumably not to take "precisely" quite so literally. But how exactly are we to understand "precisely" and its relationship to the notion of a "kind of action"? Hare needs the notion of a kind of action if "rule" and the universalizability principle are to have significant application; but any very forceful insistence upon "precisely," upon describing the action in question in terms of the features peculiar to it, will inevitably be in tension with the notion of a kind of action and with the notion of a rule. Even if unrepeatable features of the action are avoided, as greater detail is worked into the description of X the probability will diminish that an action that has the characteristics of X will recur. X will be a kind of action in the sense that it is logically possible for it to recur, but the probability of its recurrence will be low.

There is also a problem about whether "rules" of the kind Hare describes *ought* to be followed if an occasion on which to do so in fact presents itself. For reasons discussed in the previous chapter, for me to say that there is a rule requiring that I do X is ordinarily to say that I think there are good reasons for thinking that I should do X.[10] But the presumption of good reasons does not, or does not often, rest on the mere fact that on some relevantly comparable previous occasion I judged, with due attention to the universalizability principle, that I should do X. To decide I should not do X when I had previously decided that I should might be said to involve a kind of inconsistency. But if I am now convinced that it would be better to do X′ than to do X, it would be curious to tax me with inconsistency. Presumably I did X on the first occasion because I thought that there were good reasons for thinking that X was the thing to do. Hopefully I made that

10. There is no such presumption of good reasons if I am speaking as an observer of the society or social group in which the rule has standing. And even if I am a member of the society I can state that there is a rule and yet challenge the reasons that are thought to support following it.

judgment on the basis of an assessment of the possibilities available to me and the consequences of acting on them. But human affairs are complex and human beings are fallible. Perhaps I now see dimensions of the situation that I did not appreciate before. Experience with the situation and with X convinces me that it would have been better to have done X′ on the first occasion and better to do it now. To do X′ now would be consistent in that I would be acting on the same principle in both cases, namely "Do the action that reason and experience indicates is the right action." To do X would be consistent only in the sense of doing the same action in both cases.[11]

These points apply with greatest force to precepts, to rules that have standing in society such that the individual is "bound" to follow them unless he can justify or excuse his refusal to do so. These rules should not achieve standing as rules on the basis of one action by one individual. Experience with the type of action in question must be widespread before a case can be made that it would be appropriate to have a rule requiring it of large numbers of people. Moreover, it is unlikely that such a rule would be accepted before such experience had accumulated. The point of the remarks, of course, is not that rules have no proper place in morals or in other aspects of social life, it is that Hare's account of them is unsatisfactory.

There is, however, one type of rule, namely regulations promulgated by authorities, that has a number of the features of the rules that Hare describes and in connection with which his account is more plausible. Such rules, and particularly legal rules, are adopted and promulgated by individuals or comparatively small groups of individuals, they often cover quite specific kinds or classes of action, they are universal in the sense that they apply to all members of the society who fall into the class of citizens covered by the rule, and promulgating

11. There is a helpful discussion of these points in Julius Kovesi, op. cit., pp. 72–91.

them is intended to settle the question whether there is a rule and whether there is an obligation to obey it. Centralists such as Plato and Hobbes have tended to think that authority structures and the regulations they promulgate possess many of the advantages that "rules" of the sort Hare describes would have, namely that they abbreviate and perhaps rationalize the slow, uncontrolled, and sometimes uncertain processes by which precept-type rules evolve and achieve standing in a society. Questions of what counts as proper conduct can be settled despite disagreement among the members of society and despite the fact that the latter lack the information or the perspective necessary to reaching a defensible conclusion. Specific, complicated, and urgent questions can be dealt with that would be difficult to resolve through a decentralized decision-making process.

It is important, however, not to exaggerate the differences between regulations and precepts or instructions. Recall once again that authority structures cannot be understood in terms of regulations promulgated by an authority. Men may obey the law because it has authority behind it, but they do not regard law as authoritative because there is an authoritative rule that they do so. Secondly, legislatures cannot legislate without using language. Hence legislative processes and the laws they generate presuppose social arrangements in the sense in which all activity that takes place in language is social. Thirdly, we expect legislators to have reason to believe that the rules they promulgate will, if obeyed, serve the purposes they have in view. These reasons must rest on experience, however circumscribed or vicarious. Legislators who persistently supported laws having no relation to the experience of anyone but themselves would certainly be bad legislators (and with luck would not be legislators at all for very long). Centralized, authoritative rule-making processes no doubt reduce, to varying degrees in varying circumstances, the interaction that is necessary to the development and acceptance of precepts. They also lend great significance to the choices of individuals. It does not follow that they are asocial or supersocial processes uninfluenced by social life or understandable in terms of the choices of individuals acting in splendid isolation. Hare's account of rules is more plausible in the case of regulations than of precepts, but it is not a satisfactory account of either.

IV. SOCIAL RULES AND SOCIAL CHANGE

IT IS NOW appropriate to recall our earlier arguments that it is logically possible to question, in a categorical manner, established social rules and arrangements. We argued that the idea of questioning all such rules at one time is nonsensical, but that any one of them can be questioned categorically at any time and that such questioning is important. To deny this possibility is to render inexplicable some of the most familiar and important features of social life.

One of Hare's examples of such questioning is especially relevant to present concerns. We are familiar with the act of denying the authority of governments that are firmly established and veritable paradigms of legitimacy. The Scottish Nationalist and Black Nationalist denies that the present regimes in Great Britain and the United States have authority over him. He categorically questions rules that are so firmly established in the societies in question that it would be difficult for him to make his position understood without explicitly announcing his intention to reject them. The initial response to the man who simply blurted out, without any preparation of explanation, the view that all legislation passed by the British Parliament or the American Congress was not authoritative would almost certainly be puzzlement. "How can you say that? If the Parliament has no authority to legislate in this country, who on earth does?" To this the Nationalist might reply: "I recognize that the Parliament is generally thought to have authority in this country, but I deny (for the following reasons) that it should have authority over anyone and I refuse to accept its claim of authority over me." Such a reply would almost certainly dispel the puzzlement. Puzzlement would give way to agreement or disagreement, irritation or delight, contempt or admiration, depending on, among other things, the audience's estimate of the cogency and strength of the reasons the Nationalist gave in defense of his position.[12]

The Nationalist's position can first arouse puzzlement and then be understood only because there are established institutions and usages which he can question and reject. There are no rebels where no government is accepted as authoritative. (Colonial governments are a complication here because they may not be accepted by a significant number of the members of the society they govern.) Thus the Nationalist's position is dependent upon, we might even say parasitic upon, social rules and practices. It would make no sense in their absence. The thought of rebellion is his thought, but he can have the thought only because he is a part of a society the language and practices of which are governed by rules and conventions that have a social standing. The fact remains, however, that he can rebel, and that we cannot understand how it is possible for him to do so if we deny the possibility of questioning rules and conventions deeply embedded in the language and practices of the society. His act of rebellion is not independent of or logically incompatible with the social rules against which he rebels, it is logically dependent upon them.[13]

The Scottish Nationalists and the Black Nationalists want to change established rules in very fundamental ways. Their continued lack of success actually serves to dramatize both the possibility of questioning fundamental social rules and practices and the necessity of established practices and ways of speaking to activities such as theirs. It is also worth reminding ourselves

12. The Nationalist might also challenge the institution or practice of authority; the whole practice of according authority to agents or agencies. But then he would become some species of anarchist.
13. For Hare's discussion of this example see his "The Lawful Government," *Philosophy, Politics and Society*, Third Series, eds. Peter Laslett and W. G. Runciman (Oxford: Basil Blackwell, 1967).

of the obvious fact that groups with similar aims have sometimes been successful. The concepts "authority," "law," and
"obligation" are used of the Soviet regime as well as the Tsarist
one, of the Spanish Republic as well as the monarchy it re-
placed and the Franquist (Nationalist) regime that followed
it, and of the entire sequence of French regimes from the
Ancien Régime to the present. But the meaning of these concepts in each of these cases, and the things that were or are
said to justify their use, varies across a considerable range. A
man who understood only what was common to the institutions
and practices in all these regimes, and what was common
among the uses of "authority," "law," and "obligation" in
them, would have a woefully circumscribed understanding of
them. A man who knew only what was common to the notion
of authority in Russia in 1870 and in 1920 would be in a poor
position to understand the way authority worked in that country at those two junctures in its history. Radical change does
take place and sometimes it cannot be understood without attention to activities of individuals and groups who question,
criticize, and seek to alter social rules, arrangements, and ways
of thinking and speaking. Deliberate change would be impossible if we could not question and seek to change social practices
and the concepts in which we think about them. Our actions
might in fact change those practices, but we could not act to
change them.[14]

Of course not all social change begins with deliberate, pur-
posive questioning and criticism by individuals or groups. Nor
is such questioning and criticism sufficient to alter practices
that have wide social standing. The criticisms and suggestions
of initiating individuals must be accepted by or work an in-

14. The role of the individual in social change is emphasized in an
especially interesting way in the works of Bertrand de Jouvenel. See esp.
his *Sovereignty* (Chicago: University of Chicago Press, 1957). See also
the sensitive treatment of conceptual change in Michael Walzer's *The
Revolution of the Saints* (Cambridge: Harvard University Press, 1965).
Walzer typically speaks of what I have been calling conceptual change
as changes in symbolism.

fluence on the thought and activity of many other men and upon the institutions and arrangements shared among men. Understanding the rebel or critic requires understanding the beliefs, attitudes, and practices against which he rebels or which he criticizes; understanding successful and unsuccessful rebellion or criticism requires an understanding of the reaction to the rebel or critic on the part of those who hold the attitudes or beliefs and who are influenced by the practices to which the rebel or critic objects. Interaction between rebels or critics and the rest of society takes a great variety of forms. Without investigations of a kind we have not made we can say little about them. But just as there are logical points involved in the question of whether criticism and rebellion are possible, so it is a logical point that the notions of successful and unsuccessful criticisms and rebellion have reference to more than the thought and action of the rebel or critic. It is no better to treat rebellion against social practices as an action understandable entirely in terms of individual choice than it is to deny that the individual can make the sorts of choices that rebels make.

V. CONCLUDING REMARKS

THE RELATIONSHIP between social conditions and arrangements on the one hand and individual judgment and choice on the other is one of interdependence—in some respects logical interdependence, not mutual independence or logical incompatibility. To divorce the two is to render the former inexplicable and to give an incomplete and distorted picture of the latter. Of course the specific character of the relationship varies from one aspect of social life to another and even from individual to individual and circumstance to circumstance. In those aspects of social life covered by social rules the social dimension has greater significance for individual conduct than it does in, say, the realm of ideals. Within the realm of rule-governed conduct, instruction-type rules influence and structure the situation in which individuals act minimally (or with maximum flexibility); precepts and regulations in connection with which "obligation" is used structure and influence conduct to the greatest degree. But it is both a logical and a practical point that any instruction-, precept-, or regulation-type rule can be disobeyed, questioned, and rejected and thus cannot *determine* the conduct of any person.

With these conclusions in mind we will try to bring the foregoing discussion more directly to bear on political obligation by considering, from the perspective of this chapter, the similarities and differences among instruction-, precept-, and regulation-type rules.

Instruction-type rules are based in part on experience, experience in society at least in respect to the language in which they are formulated and usually in additional respects. But owing to their "hypothetical" character instructions need not, qua substantive instruction, have any standing in society. If they do have such standing in the sense of being widely accepted, this fact about them does not itself make them binding upon individuals. (Of course individuals especially desirous to conform to the beliefs and preferences of their fellows might feel bound to accept them.) Thus instructions and action guided by instructions can be very much the product of an individual's own reflection about his experience. Equally, individuals can reject or dismiss them without presenting justifications for doing so, and notions such as enforcement or punishment have no application to them. Thus any restricting, stabilizing, or unifying effect they have upon society is a consequence of the coincidence of individual attitudes and judgments. These attitudes and judgments are no doubt influenced and reinforced by interaction with others in a shared environment but the influence and reinforcement has no more normative character than the individual allows or grants it.

Precept-type rules are also based in part on experience, and the experience is social in character in respects over and above those in which instructions are based on experience in society.

They may be formulated by an individual. But their standing as rules depends upon their being accepted by a substantial number of the members of the society. Once accepted they have a kind of standing, that is normative standing, that instructions do not have. Individual members cannot reject, dismiss, or refuse to conform with them without justifying their decision, and such notions as enforcement by second parties and sanctions—though not punishment except in a metaphorical sense—are applicable. The formulation, acceptance, and enforcement processes, however, are not formalized or institutionalized as they are in the case of regulations. They consist of (usually) slow and difficult-to-predict processes of informal, decentralized social interaction.

It is a truism that such rules are widely accepted. There are no precept-type rules until putative rules are accepted by a substantial percentage of the members of the society. For reasons discussed above the development of such acceptance usually takes place in the course of widespread experience with the form of conduct. Thus it is likely that such acceptance as does develop will be firmly based in experience and not easily upset by exceptional events or developments. For these reasons evidence of the presence of precept-type rules is evidence of some degree of unity in the society in which they have standing as rules.[15] It is also evidence of forces at work to maintain the society in its present condition. Deviation from firmly grounded rules is likely to be forcefully disapproved. It can also be argued, and we so argued in the previous chapter, that the presence of precept-type rules in a society is evidence that evaluation and judgments about conduct have been arrived at in a rational manner. The development of precept-type rules presupposes that a substantial number of the members of the society have been convinced that there are good reasons for accepting those rules as a basis for proper conduct. (Of course it is possible for agreement to develop despite the fact that in

15. This point is a main concern of the following chapter.

the view of observers the discussion and exchange was anything but rational in character. If so the observer would have to hold that no precept-type moral rule should have developed.) For these reasons there is a good deal to be said, from both a moral and political standpoint, for precept-type rules and the processes that produce them. They contribute to both rationality and social unity and stability. Theorists such as Aristotle, Montesquieu, Hume, and Burke, as well as contemporary decentralists such as Lindblom, have in effect drawn attention to these points.

The theorists with whom we contrasted those just mentioned, for example Plato and Hobbes, have argued that it is these very features of precepts that render them unsatisfactory. In their view the formulation and acceptance processes involved are too much subject to the uncertainties and whimsicalities of the judgment of incompetent persons. Thus they conclude that matters involving the interests of society should be controlled by centralized authoritative agencies that have the intellectual and other resources necessary to rational decision-making and the power necessary to obtain conformity to those decisions. In the terms we have been using, just as Hare has preferred personal decision as a means of dealing with moral problems, they have judged regulations superior to precepts as a means of resolving social difficulties.

The striking fact about regulations, and hence about most rules that define the content of political obligations, is that they combine some of the characteristics of instructions with some of the characteristics of precepts.

In the case of a system of law, most particular legal rules are formulated, promulgated and applied and interpreted by comparatively small groups of individuals who hold executive, legislative, and judicial offices. A variety of devices have been employed to maintain communication between the officeholders and the larger population, and the latter often influence rule formulation. The judgments of those who hold office are nevertheless of paramount importance and they are properly held responsible for the content of the rules they promulgate. In this respect regulations are more akin to instructions than to precepts. Unlike instructions, however, regulations are binding upon all of the members of the society, binding from the moment of their promulgation.

Centralizing and institutionalizing the rule-formulation process serves to intensify and abbreviate it as compared with the formulation and development of precepts. There are also important respects in which centralization can discipline and rationalize that process. Decisions are made by fewer people and through procedures which allow opposing views and arguments to confront one another effectively. Conclusions can be reached on the weight of evidence and argument rather than mere distribution or accumulation of opinion. Centralization can also contribute to the clarity of rule formulation thought to be essential if the rules are to be enforced by the application of sanctions. In this way the virtues of an authoritative rule-formulation process carry over to and support the virtues of a centralized rule-enforcement process.

The defects and deficiencies of regulations are a mirror image of their virtues. By limiting, as compared with the process by which precepts develop, the number of people who participate in the rule-formulation process, a danger is created of excluding sources of information and judgment that might contribute to discovering the regularities that are no less important to good regulations than to good precepts. This danger is greatest as regards information concerning the views of those who will be expected to obey and support the rules and hence as regards whether the rules will be accepted and enforceable. The arguments for a particular rule might be very strong and yet be unpersuasive to men who have not had experience with the problems to which the rule is addressed or who have views that lead them to see the problem differently than do the legislators. If the legislators are unaware of these facts about their constituents the rules they pass may prove to be ineffective or worse.

These considerations bring us back to the relationship between particular regulations and the general rule "Obey the law." From our present perspective we see that the latter serves to undergird regulations with a rule that has the strengths and advantages of precepts. The regulation-making process can offer the brevity, finality, and rationality most readily available where decisions are made by individuals or small groups, but each regulation has the support of a rule grounded in public acceptance in a manner difficult to achieve apart from the slower, more decentralized processes characteristic of the development of precepts. This deserves to be called an ingenious arrangement (though not the product of any one person's ingenuity) and it has worked remarkably well in some countries. But neither the ingenuity nor the success of the arrangement can alter the fact that the two kinds of rules are very different and that they sometimes conflict with one another. Attaching the general rule to all regulations has the effect of making it applicable to a large number of types of conduct while shortcutting the processes by which precepts are ordinarily accepted and the range of their application worked out. It would be surprising if this did not, on the one hand, strain and weaken the commitment to the general rule. At the same time, commitment to the general rule may corrupt the processes by which regulations are formulated, promulgated, and accepted. If those in authority rely on the general rule to justify and win obedience to particular regulations, or if members of the public treat their commitment to the general rule as a sufficient basis for obeying particular regulations, the intensive, disciplined examination of particular rules that the regulation-making process can facilitate may deteriorate. In the first case regulations tend to lose the support of the general rule and one of the unifying and stabilizing forces in the society is weakened. In the second, badly conceived and iniquitous laws may be passed and accepted.

The moral to be drawn is not that regulations are an untenable type of rules that political societies either could or should do without. It is rather that we must understand the several aspects of their logic and the subtle ways in which they relate to one another and to other social processes and conditions. Political theorists have too often attempted to reduce the phenomenon of political obligation rules to one of the types of rules of which it is an amalgam, thereby concealing or distorting both its unique strengths and the special problems that arise in connection with it.

The implications of the foregoing discussion for consent theories of political obligation cannot be fully explored until we have looked more closely at the notion of consenting and the ways it has been used in consent theories. Doing so will be one of our objectives in Chapter Seven. It is evident, however, that a person can consent to an obligation rule only if a number of the types of social conditions and arrangements we have discussed are available to him. There must be a language in which "consent" and other concepts necessary to consenting are established; there must be relationships among the members of society such that there can be the sort of shared experience out of which rules can develop; notions analogous to the idea of precept- or regulation-type rules, and of conduct guided by such rules, must be part of the language and the social practice of society. Moreover each rule to which a person consents itself presupposes social arrangements and conditions such that the rule has significant application. Consenting to rules of political obligation, for example, presupposes the idea if not the existence of political and legal arrangements. And consenting to such rules in a going political society presupposes an understanding of the elaborate network of beliefs and practices that surround all the sets of political and legal arrangements we know about. Whatever other merits or demerits consent and consent theories of political obligation may have, it is evident that, as Hume argued, they are built on top of practices and understandings that do not themselves involve consent.

(5)

Obligation, Stability, and Change: Praise, Blame, and Disinclination

THE PREVIOUS CHAPTERS can be viewed as an exploration of some of the bases of political community, stability, and change. Wide and firm acceptance of rules that generate and define political obligations is one indication of a stable community. Roughly, the deeper and more widespread the commitment to such rules as there are, the more stable the community; the more rules to which there is commitment, the more inclusive and intensive the community. Thus one way to test the degree and stability of community would be to look for the sort of conduct we have called rule-governed. At the same time, the fact that "obligation" and "rule" are tied to "good reasons" can be viewed as one basis of the possibility of community change. When the rules change the character of the community changes. And the tie between rules and good reasons renders the community susceptible to change insofar as it consists of a structure or pattern of rules. When the members become convinced that the reasons for the rules are not good reasons, the way is prepared for changing them and thus changing the community.[1]

In the present chapter we will explore these matters further by examining two additional semantic conventions that govern most conduct-guiding uses of "obligation." The first is that use of "obligation" to guide conduct implies that it is appropriate to hold blameworthy those who do not discharge their obligations, inappropriate (apart from special circumstances) to praise those who discharge them. The second is that use of "obligation" to guide conduct presupposes that the person to whom the guidance is directed has given evidence that he is disinclined to discharge the obligation. In brief, " 'Obligation' implies blame, not praise" and " 'Obligation' implies evidence of disinclination."

I. " 'OBLIGATION' IMPLIES BLAME, NOT PRAISE"

THE FIRST CONVENTION has been formulated in a useful manner by Hart. Compliance with rules of obligation is not only within the capacity of those to whom they apply, it is "taken as a matter of course, so that while breach attracts serious censure, conformity to moral obligation . . . is not a matter for praise except when marked by exceptional conscientiousness, endurance, or resistance to special temptation." [2] To take what for present purposes is the most salient example, in such countries as Great Britain, the United States, and Canada, failure to abide by the law is blamed and punished, but conformity to the law is rarely praised and praise is rarely expected. Similarly,

1. It should be stressed at the outset that we are not offering anything like an exhaustive treatment of the bases and dynamics of community, stability, and change. Our primary aim is to continue to explore features of the practice of political obligation and their significance. We will take up questions about community, stability, and change only insofar as doing so furthers that purpose.

2. H. L. A. Hart, *The Concept of Law,* op. cit., pp. 166–67.

breaking promises ordinarily occasions blame, but keeping them is seldom praised.

A. Basis and Conditions of Application

From a conceptual standpoint that part of the convention which concerns praise can be understood in terms of the relationships between "rule" on the one hand and such notions as "merit," "distinction," and "achievement" on the other. The latter concepts must be applicable if an action is to be praiseworthy, and they are applicable only where the action is exceptional, either in the context of the larger pattern of actions by the person in question or by comparison with other persons similarly situated. As we noted in Chapter Three, to say that there is an established rule requiring X is ordinarily to imply that most of the persons to whom the rule applies in fact do X. Hence B's doing X is not a source of distinction or special merit such that his action can be praiseworthy. (Once again, this statement has to be qualified to allow for rules that demand exceptional sacrifice—for example conscription laws—and for special circumstances in which following a rule becomes unusually dangerous or onerous.) Similarly, if conforming to a rule is a matter of course for an individual, conformity to it in a single case will not distinguish that action from his usual conduct and praise will not be appropriate. More speculatively, insofar as praise is given in order to affect future conduct, it will be pointless in cases in which the individual's actions are already up to the desired standard.[3] By contrast, the occasional breach stands out and to blame or punish it provides a forceful reminder of the rule and the obligation to obey it.

If we treat the convention " 'Obligation' implies blame, not praise" as a descriptive generalization, there is reason to believe that the generalization will require the least qualification in societies or groups in which the rules that define obligations are

3. That praise (and reward) are often used in the hope of affecting future conduct is beyond question. Whether it is appropriate to use them for that purpose is a more difficult question that we will pass over.

widely accepted. Wide acceptance of rules brings about patterns or regularities in conduct against which nonconformity stands out as exceptional. If we treat wide acceptance of such rules as an indicator of stable community, we can say that the generalization holds best where there is a stable community. Owing to the connections between rule-guided conduct and good reasons, it also follows that "obligation" is typically used to guide conduct in circumstances in which most of the members of the society or group ordinarily conform to the rules for reasons other than fear of the blame or sanctions accorded to nonconformity. Persons who act in the manner required by a rule because of fear of sanctions may be guided by an instruction-type rule along the lines of "Act to avoid sanctions." An observer might note that their conduct also meets the requirements of a precept or regulation. But they have not accepted the latter and are not guided by it. It follows that such statements as "I was discharging an obligation" are not properly available to them in characterizing their own conduct and "You have an obligation to do X" is not available to them (except as a report of what others in the society might think) in guiding conduct of others. Moreover, if A knows that he is one of a very few people in his society who has accepted a rule, he will realize that talk of obligations is not likely to be an effective means of influencing the conduct of other members of his society.

Of course the threat of sanctions *is* a part of the use of "obligation" in a society in which there is wide acceptance of obligation rules. But the threat is usually unnecessary to bring about the desired conduct. As Hart points out, in a context of wide acceptance of obligation (and other kinds of social rules) one does not so much threaten others with sanctions as point out that their conduct falls or will fall under a rule and remind them of their acceptance of that rule.[4] Moreover, where the threat of sanctions proves to be necessary to influence conduct, it is issued in a context in which the application of sanctions to

4. See Hart, op. cit., esp. pp. 54–60, 79–88.

deviant individuals will have the support of most of the members of the society; it will have the kind of support that is forthcoming when those of whom it is requested believe that the rule which has been disobeyed is a good rule and that obedience to it is important to society.

Indeed the foregoing considerations might suggest that "obligation" is not widely used to guide conduct in a stable society and is not used with much success in any other kind of society. If the conduct required by obligation rules is "matter-of-course" for most members, there will be few occasions on which to remind individuals that they have obligations. If it is not matter-of-course, the appeal to reasoned acceptance of a rule which is implicit in use of "obligation" will be unavailing—as will be the appeal for the support of sanctions. We will explore these last implications more fully below. We can note immediately that there is enough merit in them to allow us to see one of the difficulties with theories that lay great stress on threats of blame and punishment in analyzing "obligation," in explaining why men conform to obligation rules, and in accounting for the stability of political societies in which there is evidence of wide acceptance of obligation rules.

B. Exceptions

We will begin to explore the larger implications of the foregoing remarks by examining a few of the exceptions to the convention that excludes praising an action which one has said to be obligatory. The first exception that comes to mind concerns the processes by which children are taught obligation rules and are led to accept and act upon them. Children learning the obligation rules in stable societies receive praise for conduct that is simply expected from adults. There is nothing odd or inappropriate about praising a child who makes and keeps a promise or an adolescent who shows an awareness of and a desire to abide by the law. This situation continues until those responsible for teaching the child or adolescent have reason to believe that he understands and has accepted (or rejected) the basic rules of society. Until this has happened conduct that conforms to the rules may be exceptional among his peers and among his own activities. If it is distinctive in these ways it may merit praise. Again, since the conduct has not become matter of course for the child, if praise aids or stimulates learning, administering praise might speed the process of the conduct's becoming a matter of course.

A second exception is provided by adults who consistently fail to consider social rules when deciding what to do and who are unable to defend their decisions in terms that meet the arguments that support the rules. We must say "consider the rules" and "defend conduct in terms relevant to them" rather than "follow the rules" and "justify conduct in terms of them" to distinguish people who are fully aware of social rules, recognize the need for them, but reject and disobey many existing rules in order to hasten changes in the content of the rules. Thoreau provides an example of the latter position. He considers rules and can defend his actions, but he often does not follow rules and does not justify his actions in terms of the rules. It would no more be appropriate to praise Thoreau when he obeyed a rule than to praise the most scrupulously rule-abiding member of his society. Thoreau disobeyed legal rules not because of underdeveloped capacities that might have been stimulated by praise, but out of considered rejection of the rules he disobeyed (and perhaps from skepticism about the value of rules qua rules). Obedience could have been won from him only by presenting reasoned arguments in justification of the rules that he had rejected (and perhaps of the social and political practice of forming and guiding conduct by rules). Of course within limits he could be coerced.

Persistent criminals are the best example of the exception we have in mind. They have not accepted social rules and their capacity to do so and to act upon rules despite competing temptations is judged to be latent at best. Society indicates that it takes this view of them in various ways, one of which is that when in jail they are given "time off for good behavior" and other special privileges. This policy involves praising and rewarding them for conduct no more than in accord with basic rules. Such treatment continues as long as they remain in the special category that society has developed for adults who evidence inability to accept and act upon fundamental social rules. When they are removed from that category special treatment is no longer deemed appropriate.[5]

The foregoing exceptions to the generalization occur in societies in which rule formulation and acceptance are well-developed; such societies make exceptions for classes of people distinct from the general population, exceptions that show up in the use of conduct-guiding concepts. A rather different set of exceptions occurs when society has few developed and accepted rules or when large numbers of people reject or doubt the justifiability of a major rule or set of rules. The former situation is exemplified by societies (and groups within a society) that are newly formed or have recently passed through a period of serious crisis or revolution. In such societies few things are "a matter of course" (or many things that once were a matter of course are no longer so) and there are comparatively few regularities or patterns against which individual conduct loses distinctiveness. Rules must be formulated and their acceptance must be consciously fostered. Blame or punishment is difficult to administer in the absence of consensus concerning the value of the violated rule, but praise can be applied without the latter. Praise is politically and probably economically cheap.[6] Thus it is not surprising that a characteristic of unsettled societies is a proliferation of honors, medals, and distinctions of all kinds, honors that are awarded for conduct that does no more

5. Note that both adolescents and ex-convicts are often sensitive about receiving special treatment and guidance. To praise and reward them for conduct unexceptional in the general adult population is to insult them.

6. Praise is not as cheap in societies with well-settled rule structures. To praise a man in such a context is ordinarily to recommend his conduct to others. Since praise is accorded exceptional conduct, issuing it will appear to be a step toward changes in the standards of conduct. (Academics might recall in this connection the controversies that are sometimes occasioned by the decision to award honorary degrees.)

than conform to (what are intended to be) basic rules in the society. For example, some of the newly independent states of Africa issue awards for payment of taxes.[7] Just as the decline of praise for conduct in conformity with social rules indicates a belief that a child has matured, the decline of such practices might provide an index of the "development" of "developing nations"—perhaps of development toward stability and greater community. Conversely, an increase in the incidence of praise for performance of obligations would certainly be an indication of instability and the breakdown of community.[8]

Yet a different type of exception arises where there is disagreement and conflict concerning social rules but where the rules continue to be accepted by many members of the society. This type of exception is exemplified by the rules, both legal and otherwise, that governed the position, activities, and treatment of the black citizen in the South in the United States. The so-called Jim Crow rules and laws were elaborately developed and they formed an important part of the system of moral (as opposed to nonmoral, not immoral), legal, and social rules that obtained in the region. For considerable periods there were only sporadic and isolated instances of overt challenge to them. Yet conduct that conformed to them, whether by whites or blacks, was regularly praised. White citizens could gain social and political recognition, prestige, and even power by scrupulous and insistent conformity to the rules; unswerving conformity was a path of advancement for blacks (preferential treatment for "Uncle Toms"). How are we to understand this exception to our generalization?

Blacks generally conformed with the rules and there was apparently substantial verbal assent to them, at least in exchange with whites. There is even some evidence that some blacks came to accept the rules in the strong sense of thinking that it

7. We owe this information to Professor Aristide Zolberg.
8. In the aftermath of the rioting in the Watts district of Los Angeles in the summer of 1965 an official observed a man pull his car to the curb when an emergency vehicle approached from the rear. The official took the man's name and he was later publicly praised.

was right and proper that blacks be treated as they were. Whites also conformed to the rules and regularly testified to their belief in the rightness of them. Despite these facts praise and reward were widely used. Their use suggests that there was widespread doubt that the acceptance of the rules was genuine and apprehension that the rules would be broken and over-thrown. The doubt and fear seems to have been too great to be explained by the incidence of overt challenge to the rules.

Perhaps the most straightforward explanation for this fact is also the most satisfactory: members of the white community did not believe that any group of people could accept so dis-criminatory and oppressive a set of social and legal rules. (Wit-ness the oft-repeated refrain that the blacks really liked it in the South and that relations between the races were really very harmonious.) In slightly more neutral language, the conflict between the rules concerning the blacks and the other social, moral, and legal rules obtaining in the South and in the larger society of which the South was part was simply too great. The tensions within the rule structure produced a number of anoma-lies, including a departure from that aspect of the logic of "obligation" that we are discussing.

The type of exception exemplified by the Jim Crow rules and laws is instructive concerning the practical significance of the relationship between "obligation," various types of rules, and good reasons. There were regularities in behavior; large numbers of people conducted themselves in the required manner a large part of the time. There were also precepts at work. Some of the members of the society accepted the rules in the sense that they regarded them as good, right, and a source of obligations. There were also regulations, both laws and rules of private associations possessed of authoritative governing bodies. Moreover many felt that the precepts and regulations concerning the place and treatment of the blacks were of fundamental importance to the society.

As with any set of precepts and regulations some of the peo-ple to whom they applied met their requirements out of habit or fear. They were brought up in an environment in which people behaved in certain ways and, perhaps without ever thinking of their behavior as falling under a rule, and without ever evaluating the behaviors in question, they behaved in that way. More likely, they realized that people who did not behave in the expected ways were not only disapproved of but often severely punished or injured. Thus they came to look upon the rules as what we have called instructions. "Do X and do not do Y if you want to stay in the good graces of those about you." "Do X and do not do Y if you want to avoid punishment or injury." This is the way hardened criminals and other immoral men view precepts and regulations. But they take this attitude not to challenge the reasons that support the rules but because reasons for the rules are irrelevant to them. They conform to rules or not on the basis of a judgment—when there is a judgment involved—whether doing so serves narrowly personal objectives. This attitude creates serious practical problems for a society but it does not involve a challenge to the judgment that the rules are good or defensible, that they ought to be obeyed, and that society is justified in applying sanctions to those who do not obey them.

In the case of the Jim Crow rules, by contrast, large numbers of people rejected the rules because they regarded the reasoning behind them as patently unsatisfactory. They treated these rules as hypotheticals not because they were uninterested in the reasons that led some members of the society to accept them as precepts and regulations but because the reasons were bad reasons or no reasons at all. The practical problem this created was the same as the problem created by ordinary criminality in that society could not rely upon acceptance of the rules to bring about conformity to them; it could not expect that most people would obey the rules because they believed that they had an obligation to do so. Thus the rules were heavily reinforced with threats of disapproval and with punishment. But because it was perceived that the disobedience could not be understood as mere criminality, devices not used in the case of criminals, namely praise and reward for obedience, were also employed by white society.[9] To put the matter somewhat crudely, it was as though those who accepted the rules tried to buy a measure of obedience over and above what they could obtain by a combination of persuasion, disapproval, and punishment.

To this extent white society went outside of the practice of political obligation. Fear of sanctions can play a supporting role in bringing about obedience to a rule or set of rules (assuming that those involved accept the rules according to which and under which the sanctions are applied) without taking it out of the practice of political obligation. Insofar as normal adults obey rules because they expect to be praised or rewarded for doing so the concept "obligation" can play no part in describing and understanding their action. As with the person who obeys solely out of fear of punishment, their conduct may be rule-guided, but the rule is an instruction not a precept or regulation.

Thus the "blame not praise" rule helps us to identify the boundaries of the practice and it reinforces and extends our earlier argument concerning the connections among "obligation," "rule," and "good reasons." It is also of practical importance, although here we must be somewhat more speculative. The most obvious and unspeculative point is that the use of praise indicates the unavailability of the conduct-guiding efficacy "obligation" may have in a stable society. The question is whether praise and reward are likely to be an effective substitute for it. We are all familiar with *individuals* who, despite finding a set of rules unacceptable, obey them in order to obtain praise and reward—especially when disobedience brings disapproval and punishment. But can praise and reward provide a society with an effective means of bringing about a satisfactory response to its rules from a substantial part of its population? (We must bear in mind that some of the rules will require conduct con-

9. Praise and reward are used in trying to rehabilitate particular criminals after they have been apprehended and put under supervision. They are not used as an inducement to obedience on the part of criminals generally or an indeterminate number of people with supposed criminal tendencies.

trary to the perceived interests of those from whom it is demanded.) To state the point more directly, we find it difficult to imagine a society in which praise and reward for conformity to basic rules is of more than marginal significance in maintaining social stability. Thus we are inclined to treat widespread use of praise and reward as indicative not only of the absence of the practice of political obligation but of the instability of the society.

Events in the South in recent years offer support for the above analysis of earlier developments in that region and for our more general speculations concerning the efficacy of praise and reward in maintaining stability. Unthinking conformity by both blacks and whites has been rendered difficult by strident agitation concerning the rules. The publicity, the increasing involvement of the federal government, and greater legal and political skill and power among blacks and their supporters, although they have not entirely destroyed the force of the threats mentioned above, have made them more difficult to carry out. More important, substantial numbers of people have demonstrated that they are prepared to pay the price attached to nonconformity. The result is that the long-standing fear of rejection of the rules has been widely realized.

As rejection of the rules spread, the attempt to shore them up by the use of praise and reward continued. Membership in the White Citizens' Councils and other groups dedicated to maintaining the traditional rules concerning blacks remains a source of praise and reward in those parts of the white community that continue to think the old rules fundamental to their society. Blacks who abide by the traditional rules and do not take part in the agitation against them continue to receive praise and preferential treatment. In at least some parts of the South, however, rejection of the rules has gone so far that the use of praise has taken on a new significance. Until roughly the Second World War conformity to the rules was sufficiently widespread among the politically efficacious segments of the community to support vigorous enforcement of the rules. Thus praise and reward served as supplementary forms of support for a rule structure that continued to have substantial grounding in societal acceptance and could be supported by the use of blame and punishment. Both of the latter have declined to the point that it may no longer be meaningful to describe the old rules as rules. Persons offering praise and reward are not so much supporting rules as attempting to establish (or reestablish) them. In this respect they are in a position analogous to leadership groups in "new states." We suggest that to the degree that they must rely upon praise and reward, neither is likely to achieve much success.

To summarize our discussion of praise and blame thus far, the exceptions to the convention concerning them indicate some of the implications of our earlier statement that the convention holds primarily in the context of widely accepted rules. When the concept is used in the absence of these conditions its logic is altered in ways indicative of the state of the society (or, in the case of children and criminals, of the person to whom the obligation is assigned) and predictive of the likelihood that the assigned obligation will be accepted or discharged. To praise for discharging obligations, unless it is simply a case of misunderstanding, is to indicate apprehension that the conduct is not thought obligatory or that it was not and in the future will not be performed *because* it is obligatory. This testifies to an unsettled or conflict-ridden rule structure and it involves an attempt to stretch or extend "obligation" to a context in which it is not appropriate—perhaps in the hope of benefiting from the force attached to the word in its ordinary uses. Insofar as "obligation" is stretched to build upon a solid structure of widely accepted obligation rules it poses no serious problem. Use of praise is unusual, temporary, and governed by restraints that are consistent with the general logic of the concept. Where little or no stable structure exists, the "matter of course" background of obligation is not present to make the usage forceful and the stretching is more likely to distort the concept than to bring about the desired behavior.

C. Some Normative Implications

The points just summarized are relevant to two more explicitly normative issues in the theory of political obligation. First, they call attention again to the features of the general rule "Obey the law." We argued earlier that the efficacy of the general rule is apt to be affected by attitudes toward the content of the particular rules that it supports. As agreement concerning the importance and the value of particular rules diminishes, an increasing burden is placed upon the arguments for the general rule. (Witness in this connection the fact that it is now commonly argued that the South must choose between a lawful society and the traditional rules concerning blacks.) If the strain reaches sufficient proportions, it generates departures from the usual logic of "obligation" such as praising and rewarding for obedience. But this is at best a temporary expedient and neither it nor appeals to the general rule are likely to eliminate or solve the problem. The solution to the problem lies in part with the particular rules and the capacity to communicate and win acceptance of the view that the rules are good and defensible rules. It also helps if the laws are not "savage commands" and the lawmakers are genuinely open to persuasion that they should be changed.[10]

Second, community has often been used as a ground for assigning obligations, the argument having taken two major forms. Where a well-developed political community exists it is possible to justify assigning and enforcing political obligations in terms of the importance of maintaining community. Socrates' position in the *Crito* rests in part on this kind of argument. The command that he take the hemlock is unjust, but it should be obeyed because disobedience would undermine the law and the law is an essential part of the community that benefits all of the citizenry. This view is also important in the thought of Edmund Burke. As used by Socrates and Burke, arguments for obedience grounded in community are closely related to arguments grounded upon benefits received.

10. Cf. Plato, *Crito*, 51–52.

It can also be argued that a law ought to be obeyed, despite disagreement with its content, because obedience under such conditions is the only way to *develop* a moral and political community, a community that will reduce the likelihood that improper or unjust laws will be passed as well as confer other benefits upon its members. This argument is most cogent in developing states or in the case of previously disadvantaged groups in well-developed states. It is an argument that is likely to be made when "obligation" is being stretched in the manner described above, and it is apt to appear in association with the promise of more personal and tangible rewards.

II. OBLIGATION AND DISINCLINATION

" 'OBLIGATION' implies blame, not praise" concerns the conditions that obtain consequent upon most uses of "obligation" in guiding conduct. For A to say that B has an obligation to do X it must ordinarily be the case that A be prepared to hold B blameworthy if B fails to do X and that he not be prepared to praise B for doing X. The rule has to do with what A ordinarily can and cannot say and do after having said that B has an obligation to do X. In turning to " 'Obligation' implies evidence that B is disinclined to do X" we return to the conditions that ordinarily must be satisfied antecedent to saying that B has an obligation to do X. Just as A must be able to say that B is able to do X and that there is a rule requiring B to do X in order to say that B has an obligation to do X, so A can *say* the latter only if he has evidence that B is disinclined to do X.

From what might be called a sociological standpoint this thesis is important as a corrective to what might seem to be an implication of the previous three chapters, namely that a society with a well-established structure of obligation rules is not only a stable society marked by considerable community but a static society. It might appear that such rules betoken a society in which human action is governed by strict and inflexible rules that "must" be and in fact generally are obeyed and in which the individual members are subordinated to social rules and the social fabric. The argument that obligation rules presuppose good reasons supporting the rules is of course a bar to drawing this inference in an extreme form. But if, as we argued in Chapter Four, the reasons and the reasoning presuppose and are heavily influenced by social conditions, these requirements could be satisfied in very static societies marked by considerable subordination of the individual. More important, if conformity to obligation rules is "matter-of-course" for most members, it might seem that a society in which "obligation" plays an important role would to that degree have to be a static society. Contrary to our earlier arguments, in other words, it might seem that theorists such as Plato, Hobbes, and Bergson are our best guides to understanding the practice of political obligation. The convention that "obligation" implies evidence of disinclination shows these interpretations to be mistaken.

A. *Basis and Conditions of Application*

There is an obligation rule that citizens must submit tax returns to the government. But we would not *say* "You have an obligation to submit a tax return" to a citizen poised before the letterbox with his completed return in hand. To do so would be superfluous if not insulting (or perhaps a joke). Nor would we tell a person of known good character that he has an obligation to keep his promises or to honor and respect his parents. There *is* an obligation to do these things, but there being an obligation that B is under is not sufficient warrant for telling B that he has such an obligation. Similarly, a person would not ordinarily use "obligation" or "obligatory" to describe an action that he was about to take but for which he had no disinclination whatever. (He might so describe it if he was trying to teach himself or others a lesson to be applied in a future circumstance.) In such a situation he would simply do the action.[11]

11. For some finer points on this matter, see P. H. Nowell-Smith, *Ethics* (Baltimore: Penguin Books, 1954), pp. 208–9; David Gauthier, op. cit., pp. 177–79.

This convention applies in a quite straightforward manner to a great many cases. But disinclination is shown in many ways and under various circumstances, the application and significance of the convention is correspondingly diverse, and there are numerous exceptions to it. The standard type of case in which the convention applies involves four elements: (1) the obligation rule in question is settled and widely accepted in society, (2) the agent in question (B) has himself accepted the rule in the sense that he thinks it right or proper to conform to it (it is a precept or regulation for him), (3) B's conviction that he should conform to the rules comes into conflict with some other conviction, interest, impulse, or purpose that inclines him to disobey the rule, disinclines him to conform to it, and (4) evidence of B's disinclination to perform prompts A (who accepts the rule) to remind B that he has an obligation. Adapting the example used above: (1) the rule that citizens are obligated to submit tax returns is settled and widely accepted, (2) B accepts it in the sense that he believes that it is ordinarily proper to conform to it, (3) opposition to the government's policy vis-à-vis Vietnam or perhaps merely a somewhat straitened financial circumstance inclines B to refuse to submit a tax return in a particular year, and (4) evidence of B's disinclination to submit a return prompts A to advise B that he is under an obligation to do so.

B. Exceptions

The main exceptions to the generalization, which are closely related to the exceptions to " 'obligation' implies blame, not praise," occur when one of the first two elements is missing. Exceptions arising out of the absence of the first element, the settled and widely accepted standing of rules, are common in newly independent states and they occur when there is conflict or disagreement concerning rules or a certain set of rules in an otherwise settled and stable society (as in the example of the Jim Crow rules used above). In the first case there may be few obligation rules for an individual to accept and hence little possibility of either inclination or disinclination to conform to rules. Of course, A might think that there should be rules or a particular rule, and he might campaign for their acceptance. He might use "obligation" in doing so. A would presumably have evidence that the other members of his society were disinclined to act in the manner he thought desirable. If this were not the case it is not likely that A would think it important to have a rule requiring the action. But the disinclination in question could not be disinclination to obey a rule or to discharge an obligation because as yet there is no rule and no obligation. A could be using "obligation" as a means of trying to win acceptance of rules and an obligation to conform to them. He would hope to make use of the forceful connotations of the word, connotations that it has because it is ordinarily used where there is a widely accepted rule covering types of conduct thought to be of great importance to society.[12]

The second element, acceptance of the rule by the person whose conduct is in question, is often missing in the case of adolescents and perhaps persistent criminals, and its absence results in the use of "obligation" without specific evidence of what could properly be called disinclination. Not having accepted a rule, it is a logical point that the adolescent cannot be disinclined to conform to it. But he is likely to be inclined to actions and behaviors that are prohibited by the rule. Absence of indications of acceptance and evidence of tendencies to behave in prohibited ways makes it appropriate for A to use "obligation" in discourse not only with B but with the class,

12. We might recall in this connection the extraordinary prominence of the concept "obligation" in Hobbes's political theory, a theory that provides abundant grounds for assuming disinclination but that also assumes away virtually all social rules and seeks to create them anew on a more rational basis. Interestingly, the concept is also extremely prominent in the speeches of at least two leaders in African states, Leopold Senghor and Sekou Touré, both of whom, and especially Touré, were faced with the task of building a system of politically relevant obligation rules where practically none existed. (See Nancy McMillin, "Reconversion and Political Obligation Theory in Guinea and Senegal," Masters Thesis, University of Chicago, 1967.)

adolescents, of which B is a member. It continues to be appropriate until there is evidence that B has accepted (or rejected) the rule. After such evidence is available it would be appropriate for A to use "obligation" only given specific evidence that B was disinclined to conform to a particular rule.

The third element mentioned above, conflict between the conviction that one should obey and other convictions, interests, and impulses, is the least interesting for present purposes. It can take an enormous variety of forms. A man can be disinclined to pay his taxes from high-minded concern to protest an indefensible war or out of purely adventitious and parasitical motives. The specific nature of the disinclination will of course have a bearing on the arguments that it would be best for A to use. But if B accepts the rule, and if he gives A reason to think he is disinclined to obey it in the circumstances, it will be appropriate for A to use "obligation," which is all that is relevant here.

(Two other exceptions can be noted in passing. First, no evidence of disinclination is necessary for "obligation" to be used for descriptive purposes—for example by an observer giving an account of the obligation rules of a society. Second, the conventions governing the use of "obligation," as with the conventions governing most concepts, can be deliberately and successfully violated to achieve a special effect. The preacher sermonizing the faithful few on the obligation to attend church or the party leader haranguing the regulars concerning their obligation to vote may be simply violating the logic of "obligation." But it is also possible that they are twisting that logic for rhetorical purposes. Their audience may find it pleasant to be reminded that they are in fact fulfilling or fully intending to fulfill their obligations, and reminding them may aid the speaker in stirring the audience to efforts above and beyond their obligations. But first, to twist the logic of a concept in this way is a risky rhetorical strategy. The faithful few are apt to be bored if not insulted. [It is no accident that the type of sermon referred to is the basis of a standard joke concerning preachers.]

Owing to the matter-of-course, blame-not-praise character of "obligation" the risk is particularly great with this concept. Rhetorically speaking, while obligation is a strong word, it is also a comparatively cold one. Secondly, twisting the logic of a concept can be successful only if that logic is well established so that the audience is able to perceive the departure from ordinary usage clearly enough to grasp the speaker's meaning. For this reason "twists" of the kind under discussion would lose their point in the absence of the standard uses of the word.)

C. Implications as Regards the Scope and Significance of Political Obligation

Taken together with the accepted, matter-of-course, blame-not-praise character of obligation rules, our discussion of disinclination may suggest that in stable political societies "obligation" is used primarily in discourse with people who are not fully incorporated into the political community—with children, criminals, perhaps aliens, and others who have yet to accept the basic rules. If full-fledged members conform to the obligation rules as a matter of course they would rarely if ever evidence disinclination to conform to them and hence there would rarely be an occasion to use "obligation" in guiding their conduct. This suggests that "obligation," aside from its uses in discourse with children and the like, is very much a philosopher's concept, a concept that is little used in ordinary discourse and that has gained such currency as it has largely as the result of its use by philosophers.

These apparent linguistic or metaethical implications of the foregoing discussion correspond to sociological and political implications of some potential interest. Contrary to our earlier remarks, the discussion might suggest yet once again that in settled societies "obligation" works much the way that thinkers such as Plato wanted it to work. Men discharge their obligations out of habit, habit so strong that it approaches the force of instinct. Discussion and deliberation are so rarely necessary that it is difficult to engage in them without straining ordinary language. In this respect it may seem that our analysis requires conclusions similar to those Bergson reached through a very different mode of investigation. Recall the argument of his *The Two Sources of Morality and Religion* that we noticed in the Introduction:

> We are thus being perpetually brought back to the same comparison, defective though it be in many ways, yet appropriate enough to the point with which we are dealing. The members of a civic community hold together like the cells of an organism. Habit, served by intelligence and imagination, introduces among them a discipline resembling, in the interdependence it establishes between separate individuals, the unity of an organism of anastomotic cells.

> Everything, yet again, conspires to make social order an imitation of the order observed in nature. It is evident that each of us, thinking of himself alone, feels at liberty to follow his bent, his desire or his fancy, and not consider his fellow-men. But this inclination has no sooner taken shape than it comes up against a force composed of the accumulation of all social forces: unlike individual motives, each pulling its own way, this force would result in an order not without analogy to that of natural phenomena. The component cell of an organism, on becoming momentarily conscious, would barely have outlived the wish to emancipate itself when it would be recaptured by necessity. An individual forming part of a community may bend or even break a necessity of the same kind, which to some extent he has helped to create, but to which, still more, he has to yield; the sense of this necessity, together with the consciousness of being able to evade

it, is none the less what he calls an obligation. From this point of view, and taken in its most usual meaning, obligation is to necessity what habit is to nature.[13]

It would be foolish to deny that there is a measure of truth in these conclusions—truth about matters linguistic and otherwise. "Obligation," "obligatory," and "obligated" are not the stuff of which day-to-day moral and political discourse consist. Or at least they are not the stuff of day-to-day conversation in a stable society. Certainly Bergson was right to reject the view that all action that meets the requirements of obligation rules is the result of the victory of a rationally based sense of obligation over lawless passion, instinct, or even mild disinclination. He was also correct in thinking that much of the behavior that meets the requirements of obligation rules is best characterized as habitual behavior.

Admitting this much, we must insist that conclusions such as Bergson drew go well beyond the actual implications of the theses we have been examining.[14] The key to the difficulties of Bergson's position lies in the fact that "obligation" is a rule-dependent concept. To see the significance of this fact in the present context we must keep separate statements about a society and its rules on the one hand and statements about the individual members of the society and their attitudes toward those rules on the other.

The main point is that there would be no need for a society to have a rule requiring a type of conduct unless there was evidence of substantial and continuing disinclination to act in the manner prescribed by the rule. (There would of course be a regularity.) Such a rule would be as superfluous as A's use of "obligation" before the letterbox in our original example. At

13. Garden City, N.Y.: Doubleday and Co., 1935, pp. 13–14.
14. In fairness it must be said that Bergson recognizes the possibility of disinclination to conform to social rules. He thinks that acting in accord with such rules is best understood by analogy to habitual or instinctual behavior, not that it is equivalent to habitual or instinctual behavior.

the same time, it would be misleading to say that there was a social rule unless it were the case that the rule was accepted by most of the members of the society and that society was generally successful in countering and overcoming the disinclination. If the rule were rarely if ever obeyed it would cease to be a rule in the sense that it would not in fact *rule* conduct. Thus if disinclination disappears *or* if the disinclination is rarely countered it becomes misleading to talk of the existence of a social rule. On the level of statements about society the logic of "rule" requires a continuing tension between conflicting inclinations. Theories that analyze conduct out of a conviction of obligation in terms of habitual or somnambulistic (Bergson) behavior go wrong in that they fasten on the importance of general acceptance and conformity and ignore the fact that the logic of "rule" requires evidence of continuing disinclination in the society.

In practice it is sometimes difficult to decide whether to say that a rule exists at a particular moment in time. For example it is now difficult to decide which of the traditional rules concerning the behavior and treatment of blacks in the American South are still properly characterized as social rules. Disinclination to conform with them is sufficiently evident, but it very regularly triumphs over any remaining belief that they should be obeyed. This is even more clearly the case as regards a number of once very firmly established rules concerning sexual behavior. Can we say, without ambiguity, that there is a social rule prohibiting extramarital sexual intercourse in this country? On the other side of the equation, there are indications that rules prohibiting discrimination against some minority groups are now of doubtful status owing to the decline of disinclination to conform to them. Would an observer of the United States in the 1960's be likely to find evidence that people of Irish and German descent were treated with respect out of a sense of obligation to do so? Would people of English or Scandinavian extraction be found *saying* that it would be "wrong" or "unfair" if people of Irish or German descent could not hold certain jobs, live in certain neighborhoods, etc.? (In the last two cases there are regularities.)

The main point of these examples is simply that both acceptance and disinclination have to be considered in deciding whether to say that there is a rule. The first two examples are borderline cases and, as analysts at least, it would be less important for us to decide whether to say that there is a rule than to survey the considerations for and against such a statement. Only the passage of time would allow us to make a decision with confidence.

The foregoing generalizations about social rules need not hold for all of the members of a society. Some members of a settled society may never experience disinclination to behave in a manner that accords with undoubted social rules. They may have internalized the rules so completely that the question of conforming to them never arises for them.[15] Or they may conduct themselves in a manner that satisfies the rule for reasons that have nothing to do with the rule. Their behavior could be fully explained without reference to the rule. It might be part of some other practice, arrangement, or pattern of conduct that is independent of the practice of political obligation. Bergson's theory best fits such people, and we might suppose that such people would be regarded as ideal subjects in the republic Plato described. It is difficult to say abstractly how widespread habitual behavior could be before it would become misleading to describe a society as governed by obligation rules. We presume that really widespread behavior of this kind would eventually lead to the disappearance (or substantial modification) of at least the conduct-guiding uses of "obligation" from the active language of the society. But before this had happened there would be a diminution and finally a disappearance of the kinds of talk characteristically engaged in by people conforming to rules. We suspect that there would also be a very substantial reduction in the elaborate machinery of coercive en-

15. For a pertinent analysis of the notion "the question arises" see R. M. Hare, *Freedom and Reason*, pp. 56–60.

forcement found in even the most stable of the societies we know.

If the foregoing arguments are cogent, the abundant evidence that there are obligation rules in societies such as Great Britain and the United States is also evidence that conduct associated with "obligation" in those societies cannot be explained in terms of habit or on any other mechanical model. Such a model would be an appropriate explanatory device in societies such as those projected in Aldous Huxley's *Brave New World*, George Orwell's *1984*, and perhaps Plato's *Republic*. The subjects in these societies are conditioned, both genetically and psychologically, so that all of their motives and inclinations lead to conduct in conformity with what in such a society would be the only thing called rules. The citizen could not be disinclined to conform because he would be unable to have any inclination other than to conform and hence he could not give evidence of disinclination to others. In such a society rule-governed behavior and the conduct-guiding uses of "obligation" as we know them would disappear, as would the practice of political obligation.

Whatever we may think of this conception of society as an ideal, there are a number of aspects of social life that work against its realization. We will mention only two. Rule-governed conduct differs from habitual behavior in that it involves a conviction that it is proper or right or obligatory to conform to the rule. If asked why he submitted his tax return B could say that he did so because a legal rule demanded it; if questioned further he could go on to indicate that he thought it right or proper to obey the rule. A person acting habitually, by contrast, would be puzzled or upset by such questions. Now after a person has submitted his tax return year after year doing so may become much like a habit. But even if B himself is never inclined to violate the rule—or never sufficiently so inclined as to make it evident to others—his awareness of it as a basis for conduct is not apt to disappear unless evidence of disinclination to conform to the rule vanishes among the other members of his society as well as in himself. If those about him violate the rule or display an inclination to do so, B will have occasion to evaluate their conduct and perhaps to remind them of the rule. In doing so his own awareness of the rule will be sharpened.

The transformation of rule-governed conduct into habitual behavior is also hampered by conflicts between the conduct required by two or more rules. If perceived, resolution of such conflicts would be difficult without reevaluating the rules in question, and thereby sharpening awareness of them. Since it would be difficult even to imagine a system of rules that made no conflicting demands, it is difficult to imagine a society in which rule-governed conduct gave way entirely to habitual behavior.

III. OBLIGATION, STASIS, AND STABILITY

To CONCLUDE, our earlier emphasis upon the settled and accepted character of obligation rules and the matter-of-course conformity to them may have suggested that there can be an effective system of obligations only in a static society or only in relatively static periods in the history of a society. It is now evident that we require a distinction between stasis and stability. In terms of the present discussion stasis should be associated with reduction or elimination of inclinations—perhaps through manipulation or through uncritical and unchallenged habit. Citizens would become incapable of adapting to, perhaps even of perceiving, changed conditions that create problems for accepted procedures and patterns of behavior. *Action* once governed by obligation rules would degenerate into habitual *behavior*. The conflict of inclinations characteristic of "obligation" as we know it would disappear along with the distinction between rules in the sense of precepts or regulations and rules in the sense of descriptive regularities.[16]

16. In this connection we should note that it is not surprising that thinkers such as Plato who have favored the elimination of conflicting

In a stable society, by contrast, awareness of and distinctive attitudes toward rules remain. Obligation rules are settled and accepted and violations are ordinarily disapproved. But there is resistance to the transformation of rules into descriptions of regularities in behavior produced by habitual or conditioned responses. Deviant inclinations exist and evidence of them provides occasions for assessment of settled rules in the light of changed conditions. Ideally, the rules are also discussed and evaluated at a general level, that is outside of the context of specific decisions, and critical discussion creates inclinations to deviance.

It is worth emphasizing that these remarks do not imply that none of the members of a society in which the practice of political obligation operates conform to rules in a merely habitual or uncritical manner. Nor do they imply that all members are constantly engaged in critical reflection concerning the rules. The foregoing remarks are consistent not only with great variations in the conduct of individuals but with the possibility that reflection concerning social rules is largely confined to limited segments of the population. The practice of political obligation can and does exist along with other practices which make similar requirements but which have a different structure or form and different (or no) justification. How widespread reflection must be in order for it to be appropriate to describe a society as rule-governed and as containing the practice of

---

inclinations (and activities and influences productive of such conflicts) have identified change with decay. When conduct governed by the basic rules of society degenerates into habits, change renders existing behavior patterns ineffective, adaptation to change is difficult, and the society may be unable to solve its problems and hence decay. If we may be allowed one more digression, aspects of Marx's theory can be understood in these terms. Only the rising class, which achieves a critical awareness of social rules, can rescue a society by changing the rules so as to adapt them to changed conditions. It is a question, of course, whether Marx has any solution to these problems for communist society. With the removal of the dynamic element, that is the differing perspective produced by differences in class position and the class conflict generated thereby, it is not apparent what will prevent a condition of stasis followed by decay. But perhaps there are to be no rules in the communist "society"!

political obligation would be difficult if not impossible to say abstractly. (Consider the case of the republic Plato describes. We might say that the practice of political obligation operates among the philosopher-kings and perhaps among the guardians but not among the brass. Or we might say that the defining features of the practice are found among so few members of the society that we should not speak of the practice at all in connection with the society. Once again, the important question is not how we classify borderline cases but that we are aware of what is implied in classifying them one way rather than another.)

We might summarize these remarks, and underline their relationship to arguments of earlier chapters, by saying that inclinations to conduct that deviates from basic rules, and even deviant conduct itself, is valuable in that it contributes to the maintenance of critical attitudes toward those rules and hence to maintaining the adaptability of society. Less paradoxical but to the same point, activities that sometimes prompt deviant inclinations and actions, especially critical examination of established rules, are valuable and must be preserved if stultification is to be avoided.

A system of obligation rules is a tough and useful device in the continuing human endeavor to achieve and maintain an orderly and stable society. But the virtues of such a system that have been most emphasized in writing concerning it, the settled standing of the rules and their stabilizing effect on human *action*, must not be confused with the dangerous rigidity of habitual or mechanical *behavior*. The tension between conflicting convictions and inclinations that is an integral part of the logic of "rule" and of "obligation" is a manifestation of the subtle, tense, and crucially important relationship between stability and change in the workings of a political society.

(6)

Obligation, Political Freedom, and Coercion

W E CAN BEST FRAME the issues that will concern us in this chapter by summarizing the main features of the account of "obligation" that we have given to this point. "Obligation" is used to guide conduct where there are precept or regulation-type rules that require or prohibit specified forms of conduct that are thought to be of fundamental importance in the society or social group. These rules have social standing. It is not open to B to reject or refuse to conform to them without excusing or justifying his decision to other members of the society. If he does so, or if his excuse or justification is judged to be inadequate, he is subject to blame and perhaps to sanctions.

"Obligation" can ordinarily be used to guide B's conduct only if B is able to do X, only if he shows disinclination to do X in the circumstances at hand, and only if A accepts the rule requiring X because he thinks there are good reasons supporting the rule. B can be said to have discharged an obligation only if he has done X because he has accepted the rule requiring X when "accepted" means that he thinks there are good reasons for the rule. Even if his conduct meets the requirements of an obligation rule, it cannot be characterized as the discharge of an obligation if he has done it because of compulsion or out of fear or habit.

The set of features summarized in the first paragraph suggest that society can properly bind B to do X despite his disinclination to do it. Their import is expressed by the dictionary entries according to which "obligation" means "must be performed" and to say that B has an obligation is to say that he is "bound" or "constrained" to do X (*Oxford English Dictionary*). The second set of features might be summarized by saying that use of "obligation" requires that it be possible for B to choose to do X or not, that he be free not to do X.

Juxtaposing the two summary statements we obtain the apparently paradoxical result that to tell B that he has an obligation to do X is to tell him both that he must do X and that he not only can but may or is free to choose not to do X. The main conceptual issue that we will be exploring in this chapter is whether, and if so how, these features of the use of "obligation" can be reconciled.

Exploring this conceptual question will involve further development of some of the main themes we have been discussing. The conceptual question is a species of the generic question concerning the distinction between action and behavior as it applies to and within the practice of political obligation. If the fact that obligations "must be performed" means that we literally have no choice but to discharge our obligations, doing so would be a species of behavior, not of action.

It is evident that coercion, sanctions and the threat of sanctions, and other means of influencing conduct that eliminate or restrict freedom are used to bring about conformity to obligation rules. This being the case, it is not implausible to think of the discharge of obligations as a species of behavior not of action. It is even more plausible to treat it as an example of prudential conduct (conduct guided by an instruction-type rule) in which men obey laws and other rules to avoid the sanctions applied to disobedience.

Granting as we must that coercion and threats play a role in bringing about obedience, we will try to show that the logic of "obligation," "rule," and "must be performed" as it is used in connection with the first two concepts require distinctions among various kinds and degrees of obedience, some of which are compatible with "freedom not to do" in an important sense. Thus we will distinguish among various grounds on which men obey and disobey and various circumstances under which they do so, and among criminal conduct, civil disobedience, and revolution. We will also consider such questions as whether it is self-defeating to attempt to "legislate morality."

I. ACCEPTED OBLIGATION RULES AND FREEDOM OF POLITICAL ACTION

THE CONCEPTUAL ISSUE turns largely on the question we have had before us through much of this study, namely what is involved in being under and in being guided by the types of rules that we have found to be a part of the practice of political obligation. Our attempt to resolve the issue will consist in large part of bringing arguments we have already presented together so as to bear explicitly on it.

A. Excuses and Open Texture

Our previous discussions have uncovered respects in which the logic of fully developed and established rules allows individuals who accept them a degree of judgment concerning what conformity with a rule involves or requires. The most obvious of these is excuses, particularly excuses based upon lack of capacity or ability. However firmly established and well-justified a rule might be, the individual for whom it is genuinely impossible or unusually difficult will be completely or partially excused. This is relevant to the question of individual choice in three ways. Excuses are temporary and personal in nature, and as J. L. Austin has written, they rarely "get us out of it completely." [1] "Excuses" that were permanent or general in the population would be exemptions or exceptions, not excuses. These facts make it difficult to generalize about excuses because examples of the phenomenon are closely tied to particular circumstances. But owing to this very difficulty it is impossible to work all of the allowable excuses into the rules themselves; it is impossible to formulate rules that will fully indicate to the individual whether, or to what degree, his condition will excuse him for not conforming to the rule. Hence the problem, at least in the first instance, is necessarily thrown into the hands of the agent himself. He must decide whether he is genuinely able to act according to the rule. His judgment will be subject to review by others—for example in a court of law if the rule is a legal one. But this does not alter the fact that the rule does not cover his case completely and hence cannot dictate his conduct completely. Further, the personal character of excusing disabilities means that the individual's testimony will be relevant when his action is reviewed by others. His judges need not accept his testimony as conclusive, but it will be difficult for them to do without it. Hence the individual agent, acting on his understanding of himself and his situation, will have to make important judgments in applying rules to the situations in which he must act. Thus the possibility of excuses indicates one respect in which conduct guided by obligation rules involves reason and hence is a species of action not of behavior.

The topic of excuses calls attention to only one of the kinds of difficulties that arise in applying general rules to particular cases. Since Aristotle it has been clear that even the best developed rules cannot be reduced to a list of conditions that are necessary and sufficient to their proper application to all the

---

1. J. L. Austin, "A Plea for Excuses," *Philosophical Papers*, p. 125.

cases that might arise under them. As with linguistic rules, rules of conduct have an element of what has been called "open texture" which can be "filled in" only in applying them to particular cases (hence the importance of the perfectly honorable practice of casuistry). When it is not clear from the rule itself (including in the rule the established exceptions to it) it again falls to the agent to decide what to do. In such cases the rule does not bind him to a specific mode of conduct. We might say the rule leaves the agent free to choose the conduct he thinks best in the circumstances. But such a formulation, which has been imputed to if not actually used by act-utilitarians, would suggest that he is free to act according to the rule or not. It would be less misleading to say that the rule limits the range of allowable choices but the agent must make a judgment as to how to act within that range.

In such cases, then, the rule will not fully specify the proper conduct and *cannot* bind the individual to a particular action. But the exceptions that are a part of the rule and, more important, the considerations that support the rule and exceptions to it will provide guidance in deciding what to do. For his action to count as rule-governed, the agent's justification for the conduct he chooses must take account of the reasoning that supports the rule and must indicate in what respects his conduct serves the purposes that the rule serves or is thought to serve. Attempts to provide such justifications are evidence that the agent's conduct is rule-governed, and demands for such justifications on the part of others is evidence that they accept the rules in question. If he chooses to break a promise he must show that his breach would not have the consequences that support a general prohibition against breaking promises and/or that keeping the promise would not have produced the beneficial effects expected from promise keeping generally. Hence while the details of his conduct are not specified by the rule, neither is his conduct independent of the rule. But from the fact that it is not entirely specified by the rule it follows that to understand or assess his conduct it is necessary to understand and assess his deliberations concerning the alternatives; deliberations that take place in the light of the rationale behind the rule and the values on which it is based.[2]

B. *Explanations and Justifications*

Having emphasized the scope for judgment and choice in rule-governed conduct we must not lose sight of the fact that the realm of obligation, and especially obligations defined by law, is the realm in which "universal propositions"[3] predominate and are the least open-ended or open-textured. Concern with that "must be performed" does not mean must not be allowed to obscure the facts emphasized in our contrast between obligations and ideals in Chapter One, namely that obligation rules are content-specific to a degree unique among precepts and regulations and that owing to their basic or fundamental character fewer exceptions are found to them than is true of other types of conduct-guiding rules. Hence the points we have been discussing do not themselves adequately reconcile "must be performed" and "freedom not to do." There are cases in which rules clearly cover the situation before the agent and in which it is obligatory in the strongest sense for him to do the action required by the rule.

The foregoing discussion does not fully resolve the problem but it does carry implications that point the way to a more adequate resolution. To pursue these implications we must distinguish between two kinds of answers to the question: "Why did B do X in circumstances Z?," namely between explanations for doing X, and justifications for doing X. When we deal with exceptions to obligation rules we are sometimes describing and explaining features of rules, not justifying these features. We

2. Cf. Wittgenstein's remark: "What one acquires here is not a technique; one learns correct judgments. There are also rules, but they do not form a system, and only experienced people can apply them right. Unlike calculation rules." (*Philosophical Investigations*, II, xi [p. 227e]. See also I, 242.)

3. Aristotle, *Politics*, 1286.

could of course go on to attempt to justify the fact that rules have exceptions or to justify the exceptions we discover, but these would be additional steps. The same is true of discussions of excuses; we could try to justify the place of excuses in a system of rules, and we could attempt to justify allowing particular excuses. But here again we would be taking on a distinct task. Similarly, if the student of social or moral psychology is asked why the members of population A regularly do X under circumstances Z, he might explain that the members of A have a rule "do X in Z." Or he might explain that the members of A, or particular members, are especially sensitive to sanctions such as disapproval or legal penalties and regularly do X in Z to avoid the sanctions imposed on those who fail to do so. Again, he might explain that the members of A habitually do X in Z. His statements would be true or false depending (to oversimplify for purposes of sharpening a contrast) upon the evidence available concerning the members of A.

Of course persons concerned with justification regularly perform explanatory tasks akin to those just described. If someone should ask such an agent: "Why didn't you go through the red light?," he would be apt to explain that going through red lights is against the law (and he is likely to be puzzled by the question unless it comes from a child, a foreigner, or some other category of person not likely to understand fully the institutions and conventions of his society). If challenged as to why he went through a red light while taking a person in critical condition to a hospital, he is likely to explain the circumstances and assume that the interrogator will know that such circumstances are covered by a recognized exception to the rule against going through red lights. If the interrogator were puzzled by these responses he might go on to explain further what he meant by a rule, an exception to a rule, etc. Only when it was clear that the interrogator understood his explanation would he go on to offer a justification for the rule or for conforming to it in the case at hand. The fact that explanation typically precedes justification is another important indication that the agent's conduct is rule-governed.

Nor are such explanations irrelevant to justifying conduct. Some explanations will ordinarily rule out the possibility of a satisfactory justification; they are sufficient to show that the conduct was unjustified and unjustifiable: "Why did you decide for the plaintiff?" "Because he paid me $100." Others are sufficient to justify conduct: "Why did you keep me waiting so long?" "Because there was an injured man and I was the only one there to help." To show that conduct violates or accords with an established rule is, at one level, to justify it.

As we tried to show earlier this is not because further justification is impossible but because the reasons of which a further justification would consist are known to be widely accepted, thus rendering it unnecessary or worse to present them. But the very notions "rule" and "rule-governed conduct" require that a request for a justification be appropriate and that the person be able to provide a response other than those discussed thus far. Rules and rule-governed conduct are distinguished from habits and responses motivated by fear in that they are based upon an assessment of experience supporting a judgment as to the best form of conduct in a situation of a certain type. Ideally, at least, this judgment prevails over other possible judgments (attains the status of a rule) because the arguments for it are more cogent than those for alternative judgments.

For the same reasons that make it logically possible, it is sometimes absolutely essential to defend rules. If a justification is demanded or an argument is offered against the rule, failure to offer a defense will cast doubt on the claim that the individual's conduct was rule-governed. If such failure is widespread in connection with a rule, suspicion of the standing of the rule will be appropriate.

We have repeated these points because they are of the utmost relevance to understanding the relationship between obligation rules and individual choice in the realm of obligation. They indicate that the agent cannot fully be said to have been guided by obligation rules unless he accepts as valid the reasons that support and justify those rules. The rules may have been developed and supported by others in the first instance—indeed this will be the case most of the time in a society or group with a well-established body of precepts and regulations. Hence the individual agent will not be the creator of the rule and the reasons for the rule will rarely be original with him. But just as the scientist adopts or accepts principles, laws, and rules of scientific procedure that he did not originate, so moral and political agents adopt or accept principles and rules of morality, politics, and law. Just as we would not say that the rules of science had been "imposed upon" the scientist, that his "scientific will" had been "heteronomized," or that he was not responsible for the use he made of the rule, so we would not say that the moral or legal rules had been imposed upon an agent, or that he could not be held responsible for conforming to those rules. Acting according to rules on the basis of the reasons that support them is one of the things that is meant by free, that is uncoerced, *action* for which the agent is fully responsible.

In the class of cases we have considered thus far, to summarize, the "must be performed" associated with "obligation" is best analyzed as follows: persons who accept obligation rules are bound to obey them by the cogency of the reasons that support the rules defining the obligation. Accepting a rule involves deliberation about the reasons for and against it, and applying the rules involves a determination whether those reasons warrant obedience in the case at hand. These are conceptual points. If the analysis of "obligation" and "rule" on which they rest is correct, they show that "must be performed" and "free not to do" are compatible in cases in which the person accepts the rule that applies to his action. It would be a misuse of language to say that a person was coerced, imposed upon, or otherwise unfree when he discharged an obligation under such circumstances. And if he could show that he did not do what the rules required because the reasons for the rules did not hold in the case in question, he would have shown that his action was not only consistent with his general position but justified.[4]

The more difficult class of cases remains to be dealt with. These are cases in which a person rejects, on reasoned grounds, the arguments that other members of the society, for example those in positions of authority, think support a rule and require obedience to it. We will take up some of the salient members of this more difficult class of cases in the next section. Before doing so we must consider the relationship between the conceptual points we have been discussing and some facts about political societies that might be thought to render the conceptual points insignificant or worse.

II. OBLIGATION RULES, POLITICAL FREEDOM, AND THE USE OF SANCTIONS

IT IS MANIFEST that political societies do not rely entirely on reasoned argument to win obedience from their citizens or subjects. They attach severe sanctions to disobedience and they maintain elaborate institutions and employ large numbers of officials to detect disobedience and to apprehend and punish those who disobey. This being the case, persons considering actions that fall under (obligation-creating) legal rules are in a situation in which they can decide to obey in order to avoid the sanctions applied to disobedients (or to disobey and "pay the price" of having sanctions applied to them). It thus appears that all cases of obedience and disobedience could be analyzed in terms of fear of sanctions. If so our discussion of accepting rules because there are good reasons for them would, at best, be an instance of tracing the contours of a conceptual heaven having little or no relation to the real world of government and poli-

4. We might even say that he had discharged his obligation. We think that using this expression in such cases is an extension of the ordinary use of "obligation"; it seems more natural to say that the person was right or justified in disobeying. But it is this kind of situation that renders the notion of an obligation to disobey a plausible notion.

tics. Moreover, while doing X out of fear of punishment involves a decision to do X (recall the discussion in Chapter Three of the distinction between threats and coercion), it is hardly the paradigm case of an action (as opposed to a behavior) that the agent chooses to take and for which he assumes full responsibility. The man who calls attention to the sanctions he would have undergone if he had not done X may sufficiently explain his having done X and he may even excuse his having done X. He does not justify his having done X.

A. Acting to Discharge Obligations versus Behaving Out of Fear of Sanctions

We have argued that "obligation" is tied to "rule" and through it to "good reasons" in the sense both of evidence for thinking that doing X will serve a purpose or objective and in the sense that the objective is defensible in the light of the consequences of pursuing it. Thus it seems best to say that the person who meets the requirements of a rule out of fear of punishment should not be described as discharging an obligation. He may be obeying or conforming to a law but he is not discharging an obligation and in this sense he is not participating in the practice of political obligation. Once again, the reasons why a person does something affect the question of the ways in which it is appropriate to characterize what he has done. (Whether we use the term or marker "obligation" is of course of little significance. What is important is the differences in the analysis of the two phenomena.)

Strictly speaking it would not upset this analysis if most or even all of the empirical cases of obedience to law in any political society were cases of behaving out of fear of punishment not cases of discharging obligations. If this proved to be the case it would be more plausible to argue that the practice of promulgating authoritative rules, together with the methods used to win conformity with such rules, had the effect of inhibiting freedom of choice as a basis of conduct in that society. The "must be performed" associated with authoritative rules would be consistent with "free not to do" only in the attenuated sense in which a person can be said to be free to choose to accept disagreeable consequences rather than do what he is ordered to do.

B. Legislating Morality

The significance of the issues here can be accented if we examine the question of whether it is self-defeating to attempt to "legislate morality." To legislate morality is presumably to enact laws requiring conduct that, independent of the fact that it is required by law, is thought to be morally obligatory. It is an attempt to use the institution of law to bring about conduct that is morally requisite. The argument against attempting it involves two premises: first, that a person can be said to be acting in a moral (as opposed to immoral and nonmoral) way only if his action is done freely and out of morally good motives; second, that obedience to law does not meet these criteria because it is done out of fear of sanctions. Simply accepting the first premise for present purposes, it is evident that the objection does not hold insofar as obedience to law satisfies the criteria that we have argued *must* be satisfied in order to describe an action as discharging an obligation. If the reasons for a legal rule are moral reasons, the person who accepts and acts upon them is acting morally. On the other hand, if empirically speaking all or most obedience to law is best analyzed as behavior motivated by fear of sanctions, it would indeed be plausible to argue that attempts to "legislate morality" will be self-defeating.

C. Conceptual and Empirical Questions About Obedience

Once we have clarified the concepts involved, the question whether any particular case of obedience or disobedience is a case of discharging an obligation or one of behavior out of fear of sanctions (or of habit, of impulse, or of some mixture of the various possibilities) becomes an empirical question that can be decided only by inquiring into what the person said and did in the circumstances. We have not made investigations of this sort. There are, however, considerations that cast doubt on the view that all or even a substantial proportion of the cases of obedience to law in moderately stable political societies are explainable in terms of fear of sanctions. Although the empirical question is not our major concern, rehearsing a few of these considerations will put the foregoing discussion in a larger perspective and will prove helpful in dealing with cases in which persons reject the arguments for obligation rules.

D. Some Limits on the Use of Threats and Coercion in Obtaining Obedience

Regulation-type rules are promulgated by authoritative bodies and are legally binding from the moment of their promulgation. Such rules and the authoritative mechanisms through which they are promulgated supplement the slower, less uniform evolution of precepts through social consensus. For these reasons sanctions undoubtedly play a more prominent role in efforts to win conformity to them than in the case of precepts. Perhaps this is the reason it has been widely thought that the use of the sanctions is the most important factor accounting for obedience to them.

1. THE SOVEREIGN'S ASSISTANTS

The distinctions between explanation and justification and between the logic of obligation rules and the reasons that people act in the manner required by obligation rules, must be borne in mind in sorting out this question. In addition we must distinguish again between obeying particular legal rules and conforming to the general rule "Obey the law." If we artificially isolate the former for a moment we need only recall the arguments of Hobbes and Hume to see that it is most improbable that obedience to particular rules could be explained entirely in terms of fear of sanctions. Such an explanation calls up the image of men obeying rules out of fear that the person or persons who promulgated the rule would punish them if they did not. The practical limits of such an arrangement mean that the rule promulgator(s) or "sovereign" must have assistants or supporters who will aid him (them) in applying sanctions to others. If these assistants act in concert they may be able to coerce or frighten many others into obeying the sovereign. But the assistants will see that they could overwhelm the sovereign as easily as they could overwhelm those that the sovereign seeks to command. Hence an explanation of their continued cooperation with the sovereign that is cast in terms of fear of him will not be believable. If the sovereign cannot win some cooperation on grounds other than fear, he cannot use fear as a basis of rule. For this reason alone obedience to law cannot be fully explained in terms of fear of sanctions.

We know that cohesive minorities, especially given the weapons made available by modern technology, have sometimes been able to control bodies of men much larger than themselves—at least as long as the latter remain unorganized and untrained. And there is little doubt that there have been political societies or at least periods in the history of political societies in which much of the obedience to law could best be explained in this way. Nor can it be doubted that some of the obedience that obtains in all systems at all times is best explained in this way. If this were not the case the resources that regimes give to maintaining the machinery of coercive enforcement would have to be regarded as wasted.[5]

2. THE GENERAL RULE

However practicable it might be to win widespread obedience through threatened sanctions, the expenditure of resources required by sole reliance upon this method would obviously be enormous. Note also that the need for obedient assistants grows as the reliance upon sanctions or threatened sanctions increases. These assistants are unified to a degree by the mere fact that

5. On the last points see especially Hume's discussion in "Of the First Principles of Government" and "Whether the British Monarchy Inclines More to Absolute Monarchy or to a Republic," *Essays: Moral, Political, and Literary,* op. cit.

they have been given a common role, and the weapons of enforcement are necessarily placed in their hands. Hence the heavier the reliance upon fear as a basis of rule, the greater the need to win cooperation and support on grounds other than fear—cooperation that must come from those segments of the population most likely to be successful in refusing cooperation with impunity. For these reasons it is of great importance to develop other means of winning obedience, to extend the willingness to obey for reasons other than fear of sanctions from the assistants to the population generally. (In the comparatively stable societies of the modern western world, noncoerced obedience by the bulk of the population has tended to be taken for granted for long periods while the obedience of the sovereign's assistants has often been regarded as more problematical.)

We have stressed that the most effective and defensible way to do this is to convince the bulk of the citizenry of the value, or at least the importance, of the particular rules they are expected to obey. Given the diversity and conflict characteristic of political societies, however, it is unrealistic to expect any regime to achieve complete success in this respect; in fact all regimes make use of, or at least benefit from, many other techniques and influences. From the perspective of present concerns the most interesting of these, and the one most closely related to the "ideal" method just mentioned, is to foster acceptance of the general rule "Obey the law." The most interesting aspect of this rule in the present context is that, as a rule and as distinct from particular legal rules, it is not supported by sanctions. Where the rule is accepted and acted upon particular rules are, by hypothesis, obeyed; when it is rejected in its application to a particular rule that is also rejected, *the particular rule* is disobeyed and the sanctions are applied for disobeying the particular rule, not for disobeying the general rule. Legal systems do not punish for violation of the general rule. It is true that citizens who have been punished for violating laws X, Y, and Z might draw the prudential generalization (instruction-type rule) that laws should be obeyed in order to avoid punishment. But accepting this generalization would not be equivalent to accepting the general rule. The punishment that had followed violations of X, Y, and Z would have been punishments for the violations of the latter rules not the general rule, and the justification that supports punishing violations of particular laws is not the same as the justification that supports the general rule "Obey the law." Hence obedience to laws X, Y, and Z out of fear of punishment would not be evidence that the general rule was obeyed out of fear of punishment and would not be evidence that the practice of supporting particular rules X, Y, and Z with sanctions conduced, as an empirical matter, to fear-inspired conformity to the general rule. To the extent, then, that there is evidence that the conduct of citizens is genuinely governed by the rule "Obey the law," their conduct cannot be explained by fear of sanctions.

These arguments, of course, do not prove anything concerning the empirical incidence of rule-governed conduct of the kind in question. They do counter an important argument for thinking that such conduct is empirically rare. Knowing that the general rule is not supported by sanctions, the considerable evidence concerning the acceptance of that rule in stable societies is evidence against the charge that, empirically speaking, the practice of promulgating legal rules fosters behavior motivated by fear of sanctions. Thus such features of political life as the part played by the general rule in political discourse, the continuity of obedience through a succession of political authorities, and the small number of enforcement agents in proportion to citizens, all testify that the use of obligation rules does not obviate individual freedom in the areas of conduct covered by such rules. To repeat, the practice of political obligation may coexist with a number of other practices and arrangements which may impose substantively similar requirements and which may even contribute to the achievement of the same social objectives—for example an orderly society. If we are to understand political obligation and political societies in which it plays a part we must understand its relationships to those other arrangements and practices. We do not understand political obligation if we deny its distinctive features and their significance by assimilating it to related practices.

III. REJECTED RULES, POLITICAL FREEDOM, AND COERCION

WE NOW TURN to the class of cases deferred above, those in which men reject, on reasoned grounds, the arguments that are widely thought to support a rule or rules. It is commonplace that reasoning, whether about rules or other matters of conduct, does not obviate well-grounded disagreement.[6] The presence of well-founded disagreement, however, does not prevent societies from holding that men have obligations to conform to rules with which they disagree. Nor does it prevent them from thinking they are justified in applying sanctions against men who refuse to conform to such rules. It is the fact that there are reasons supporting a rule that makes such justifications possible. Thus the very features of obligation rules

6. See my *The Public Interest* (New York: John Wiley, 1966), especially Part Two and passim. I now think, however, that my argument there accepts too readily the view that, in Philippa Foot's words, "moral arguments can always break down." As Foot has argued, and as I have tried to indicate in Chapter Three above, there are cases in morals and politics in which there is one and only one judgment or conclusion that is rationally warranted in a set of circumstances. Or rather there is one and only one warranted conclusion so long as the persons involved do not question the established rules governing the concepts they are using or the practice they are engaged in. But there are numerous cases in which there is room for well-grounded disagreement as to which of the several concepts and rules that could properly be applied should or ought to be applied. Secondly, it is possible to question concepts and rules categorically. When this is done the possibility of intractable disagreements is increased. For Foot's views see especially her articles "Moral Beliefs," loc. cit., "Moral Arguments," loc. cit., "Goodness and Choice," *Proceedings of the Aristotelian Society, Supplementary* Vol. 35 (1961).

that make it possible to accept and conform to them freely create a basis for conflicts that may be resolvable only by forceful imposition.

Once again, a genuine conceptual issue arises only when disagreement over a rule takes the form of reasoned differences concerning the grounds on which the rule rests. Where assigned obligations have no reasoned basis, or where they are not discharged due to ignorance, rejected on the basis of emotional impulses or on purely self-serving or adventitious grounds, no attempt has been made to reconcile obligation and individual freedom and no conceptual issue arises concerning their relationship. Ordinary criminal behavior (as opposed, for example, to civil disobedience) usually falls into these categories. Since the preponderance of the use of sanctions in stable systems is occasioned by ordinary criminal behavior, most uses of sanctions do not raise the questions before us.

A. Selective Rejection of Legal Rules

Assuming controversy over the reasons that support the rule or rules, numerous types or levels of disagreement and rejection are common. We will discuss a few of the main species. The first involves the now familiar distinction between rejecting a particular legal rule and rejecting the general rule "Obey the law." A person might disagree with a particular law but accept the general rule. If so, his acceptance of the latter provides a basis for obeying the particular rule despite his objections to it. Hence the combination of the obligatory status of the particular rule and his objection to it need not lead to his being forced to obey. His obedience can be governed by a rule that he has accepted because of the reasons that support it. The possibility of alternative reasons for and hence alternative descriptions of the same act makes it possible to decide to do under one description what one would be unwilling to do under another description taken alone. In cases in which obedience is so understood, rejection of obligation rules is compatible both with obedience and with personal freedom.

B. Selective Disobedience of the General Rule: The Posture of Civil Disobedience

Secondly, a person might reject a particular rule, accept the general rule as generally well supported, but claim that he is justified in selectively disobeying the general rule in its application to particular rules that he finds especially obnoxious. This is the position of civil disobedience. People disobey a particular rule because they reject the reasons for it,[7] and they reject the rule "Obey the law" as it applies to the particular rule in question. But they submit, as a matter of principle, to the penalties assigned for disobeying the particular rule, thereby accepting the law establishing the punishment and the general rule in its application to the law establishing the punishment. In addition, they often justify their obedience to the law assigning the punishment in terms of their commitment to the general rule "Obey the law" and the regime or system of authority that rule supports in the case at hand.[8]

7. This is not always the case. There have been instances of disobedience of laws perfectly acceptable to the disobedient. He disobeys them in order to dramatize his disagreement with other laws or policies. Few civil disobedients, for example, quarrel with trespass laws, but they have regularly disobeyed them in order to give force to their objections to other laws or policies.

8. For representative statements by advocates, critics, and students of civil disobedience, see: Hugo Bedau, "On Civil Disobedience," *The Journal of Philosophy*, 58: 653 ff; Harrop A. Freeman, et al., *Civil Disobedience* (Center for the Study of Democratic Institutions, 1966); M. Gandhi, *Non-Violent Resistance* (New York: Schocken Books, 1961); Norman Jacobson, *Law Enforcement and Racial and Cultural Tensions* (Berkeley: University of California Press, 1964); Martin Luther King, Jr., *Why We Can't Wait* (New York: Signet, 1964); Irving Kristol and Robert Penn Warren, "On Civil Disobedience and the Algerian War," *Yale Review* 50: 470 ff; Bertrand Russell, "Civil Disobedience," *New Statesman* 61: 245 ff; Mulford Q. Sibley, ed. *The Quiet Battle* (Garden City, N.Y.: Anchor, 1963); William L. Taylor, "Civil Disobedience," in Donald B. King and Charles W. Quick, eds. *Legal Aspects of the Civil Rights Movement* (Detroit: Wayne State University Press, 1965). Many of the important statements concerning civil disobedience are usefully collected in Hugo Bedau, ed. *Civil Disobedience: Theory and Practice* (New York: Pegasus Books, 1969) and in Robert A. Goldwin, ed., *On Civil Disobedience* (Chicago: Rand McNally, 1968).

A significant element of individual choice and freedom is present in this type of case. The particular rule does not deter the agent from acting in the manner that he thinks right in the situation—for example commiting a trespass, and the penalty —for example going to jail or paying a fine—is accepted by him. The rules establishing and assigning the penalty restrict him in the sense that he must do what they require. But "must" means that he thinks highly of the reasons that support the penalties and the general rule that he should submit to the penalties. Hence reason requires that he obey the rules. By accepting the restrictions imposed by an obligation rule, in other words, the agent disarms the charge that he did not choose to obey. He also makes it difficult to argue that in his case the use of coercion or threats is the distinctive feature of law, the state, or the tie between him and the state.

We have emphasized the degree to which the posture of the civil disobedient depends upon his acceptance of the rule "Obey the law." Viewed from a different perspective, the civil disobedient, whatever else one might think of his position or his conduct, has not completely abandoned reasoned discourse as the basis of social and political interaction. His tactics bring a unique form of pressure to bear upon authority; they face the authority with choices, for example the choice whether to arrest citizens engaged in what is often high-minded, public-spirited political action, that are rarely posed, or rarely posed in so public a manner, by other forms of political activity. But his insistent acceptance of the penalties attached to his disobedience distinguishes him from the revolutionary, from the nihilist, and from anyone else who has concluded that rational discourse is of no avail (in the society in question or generally).[9]

9. Peaceful submission to penalties might be interpreted as, and in some cases might be, no more than a prudent or tactical recognition of the distribution of power in the community. But the true civil disobedient claims more than this; he claims that he accepts the imposition of penalties as justified. This point, incidently, also distinguishes civil disobedience from action taken to test laws alleged to be nonauthoritative

C. Categorical Rejection of Particular Rules and the General Rule: The Revolutionary Posture

Stating the matter as we have just done is important to understanding the next type of case in which the question of obedience arises, namely where there is disagreement with and rejection of the rule "Obey the law" as it applies in the regime in question—whether in a single case or generally. Continuing to assume a reasoned basis for the rejection of both particular and general rules, a man in this situation is unable to find a basis on which to accept (at least some of) the obligation rules of the system. Given the line of argument we have been pursuing, this situation seems to allow no resolution whatever between "free not to do" and "must be performed." Either the regime will impose its requirement upon the man through coercion, threat, or some other means not dependent for its efficacy on his acceptance or the man will successfully resist such imposition and the rule will, to that degree, be rendered inoperative.

To this point our attempted resolution of the apparent conflict between "must be performed" and "free not to do" has relied upon analysis of "obligation" and "rule." We have tried to show that obeying an obligation rule involves choosing to accept it as rationally defensible. If this analysis is correct it resolves, on a conceptual level, the apparent conflict we have been examining. The agent is at once free not to discharge the obligation and bound to discharge it.

Unfortunately the problem is not resolved by this analysis in the type of case we have now reached. Rather, our argument suggests that there is no resolution—that either "must be performed" or "free not to do" must give way. If so it would seem

---

—for example, unconstitutional. If a law is unconstitutional, penalties cannot be properly assigned for violating it, and the person who disobeys must protest the penalties as well as the law itself—even if he decides against resisting those penalties. The civil disobedient neither resists nor protests.

to follow from our analysis that in such cases the practice of political obligation breaks down. The person who is compelled to obey (or to go to jail) does not think there are good reasons for any of the obligation rules under which his conduct falls and hence he cannot be described as acting to discharge an obligation. If he successfully violates the rules by resisting attempts to coerce him, the rules do not govern his conduct. The implication of this conclusion, of course, is that such justifications as there are for the practice of political obligation as a way of ordering human interaction are not available to the actors in the situation.

Before drawing this conclusion in an unqualified manner we should at least notice that there are dimensions of recurrent thought concerning freedom, or interpretations of "freedom," which if accepted would allow us to avoid or at least to modify it.

The most salient of these interpretations stresses what Franz Neumann called the "cognitive element" or dimension of freedom.[10] Briefly, the man who understands, who has *intellectual* control over the forces that impose upon him is said to retain freedom despite the fact that he is unable to resist those forces or effectively choose or decide to act contrary to them. A citizen may be compelled to obey a rule he rejects, but he knows why he rejects the rule and why it is wrong for him to be compelled to conform to it. The fact that he is compelled does not affect his knowledge or understanding, and the latter are the loci of his freedom.

This use of "freedom" is common in statements such as: "We kept the drinking water free of contamination by keeping the canteen tightly closed as we waded through the swamp." To be free in this sense is to be free of or free from something, not to be free to do something. A part of the self is preserved against the encroachments of alien and irrational forces. Al-

10. See Franz Neumann, "The Concept of Political Freedom," *The Democratic and the Authoritarian State* (Glencoe: Ill.: The Free Press, 1957).

though the individual cannot act as he thinks best, he is able to limit the extent to which other men and other things act on or affect him. Of course this sort of protection or preservation of self may be extremely important in maintaining the personal resources necessary to effective action at such time as the forces imposing upon the individual weaken or otherwise change. And even before such change takes place the self-knowledge and composure of men who we say are free in this sense may work an important influence on others. Thus freedom in this sense may have interpersonal significance, including political significance, as well as the personal, self-sustaining, and self-consolatory significance attached to it in the writings of the Stoics.

Freedom in this sense, however, does not provide more than a verbal solution to the "bound to do"–"free not to do" problem. To say that a person is free only in the "cognitive" sense is to admit that he cannot effectively choose not to conform to the requirements of the rule. His deliberations concerning the rule will affect his beliefs and judgments but his public behavior will be the result of threats or coercion by others. (Thus "cognitive freedom" is not the same as what Sir Isaiah Berlin and others have called "negative freedom." Negative freedom involves protection of the freedom of action by avoiding or preventing outside interferences with it.) In such a case the person may behave in a manner that meets the requirements of a rule that others in the society regard as defining an obligation, but his behavior is not a case of action governed by that rule. Thus to rely on the notion of cognitive freedom is to evade, not to resolve the problem of reconciling "must be performed" and "free not to do." The same conclusion holds for so-called subjective conceptions of freedom, conceptions that leave out the cognitive dimensions stressed by Neumann but that nevertheless treat freedom as a condition internal to the individual.[11]

Of course the agent himself might insist that there is no

11. See Felix Oppenheim, *Dimensions of Freedom* (New York: St. Martin's Press, 1961), pp. 143–48.

conceptual or theoretical problem here. It is not a case of rule-governed action and there is no tension between rule-governed action and freedom not to do. The problem with resolving (or dismissing) the matter in this way is that other members of the society think that there is a well-supported rule that generates an obligation; thus they regard the individual's unwillingness to accept and act according to the rule as blameworthy, and they think they are quite justified in imposing sanctions against him. The individual might want to treat the matter as a case of mere compulsion or imposition of which he remains cognitively free, but others in the society will not accept this analysis.

Has the practice of political obligation ceased to operate in such cases? We now see that the answer to this question is more complex than we allowed when we first discussed it (see above, p. 191). It has broken down for the individual in that his conduct, although it might meet the requirements of an obligation rule, cannot be described as discharging an obligation. It has broken down from a societal standpoint in that society has been unsuccessful, in the case at hand, in winning obedience through the workings of the practice of political obligation. But the practice continues in society in that there are still rules that are accepted by some members. Moreover the reasons for these rules provide those who accept them with a justification not only for following the rules themselves but for blaming and perhaps punishing those who do not. The practice continues for the individual who rejects the rules because others in the society continue to accept them, to expect him to do so, and to feel justified in taking various steps to get him to do so. Depending on how many (and perhaps which) members of the society continue to accept how many of the obligation rules, and how strong are their convictions and the convictions of those who reject the rules, these features of the practice will be more or less effective, more or less salient in the lives and activities of the members of the society. Aside from the extreme cases (that is, "everyone accepts all rules," "no one accepts any rules"), which almost certainly are not instantiated empirically, we cannot decide whether to say the practice has broken down or not; we cannot decide because we have no criterion by which to make the decision. What we can do is look for the marks and the consequences of the practice in social and political processes and interactions.

IV. OBLIGATION, FREEDOM, AND REASON

ON A CONCEPTUAL LEVEL, then, we find that there is no way to resolve the conflict between "must be performed" and "free not to do" when it takes the last of the forms we have discussed. Either the requirements of the rule and of the practice are maintained against the will of the agent to whom they apply or the agent successfully resists them and to that extent the rule is subverted. This conclusion is scarcely surprising. Moral and political issues and conflicts arise when men live together so as to become interdependent, so that their actions affect one another in serious ways. Such interdependence is workable if there are at least some standards or rules of conduct that apply to all or most of those involved and are typically conformed with by them. But such rules are compatible with personal freedom of action only when they are grounded in considerations that have public or interpersonal standing, considerations accepted on the basis of antecedently identified criteria of evidence and logic. The generic name for such considerations is "reasons." Each man's reasons are his own, and the decisions and judgments he reaches by reasoning are *his* decisions and judgments; but the reasons he develops in reaching decisions are available to all other men who possess the requisite faculties, who know the criteria, and who speak his language. Those men are able to examine his reasons and to accept or reject them (make them "theirs") on the basis of reasons or grounds that they can in turn exchange with others. Through this process it is possible for otherwise very diverse men to reach agreements, accept decisions, and live together without giving themselves over to other men in the sense of becoming subject to impulses, desires, or purposes peculiar to those other men.

But reason must compete with other forces and agencies for control of human conduct. And even when it wins control it is by no means a perfect or infallible instrument. When it is defeated or ignored, or when careful use of it fails to produce a basis for agreement, human affairs will be controlled by forces that lack, except for contingent coincidences, the interpersonal standing characteristic of reasoning. To the degree that this is the case the basis on which to combine shared rules and individual decisions and choices is obviated and one or the other must give way. From the standpoint of resolving the problem before us, then, the "trick" or "secret" is to build institutions and arrangements and above all to educate men so as to maximize the likelihood that reason will prevail to the greatest possible degree. Doing so will not eliminate the problem but it will reduce it to the minimal possible proportions.[12]

Two points remain to be stated, one of a practical nature, the other conceptual. The practical point can be introduced by recurring to the question whether cognitive or subjective concepts of freedom might provide the basis for resolving the tension between "freedom not to" and "must be performed." Although inadequate from a conceptual standpoint, this argument is of great practical importance because it directs attention to the fact that where B has a sense of freedom the conceptual problem does not arise for him. If B thinks of himself as free he

12. It should be emphasized that the above remarks about reason and reasoning are conceptual not psychological. They are remarks concerning some of the uses of the concepts "reason" and "reasons," not remarks about mental events or nonlinguistic phenomena of any other kind. With Wittgenstein we neither affirm nor deny the existence of mental or other events or states that correspond or stand in any other relation to various uses of the concepts. Also, we are concerned with "reason" and "reasons" in the sense of considerations offered in justification of or for an action, and not in the sense of an explanation for an action except insofar as the two senses sometimes coincide. Cf. R. S. Peters, *The Concept of Motivation* (London: Routledge and Kegan Paul, 1958), esp. Ch. 1.

will not raise the question of how he can be said to be free in the circumstances. This is indicated to others by the fact that he does not use the concept of freedom in discussing his situation. To *use* the word freedom ordinarily implies that the agent perceives a restraint that threatens to prevent him from doing what he wishes to do.[13] Perceiving no such restraint, the individual simply describes himself as doing or not doing those things he wants or does not want to do.

Testimony of this kind is of course subject to criticism and evaluation by others. Learning that many of the citizens of Nazi Germany thought themselves to be free, we might want to criticize the concept of "freedom" we discovered in use among them.[14] We might have to concede that the use in question was well established in their language, that they were not making any conceptual or linguistic mistakes. We could nevertheless argue that the usage testified to an unsatisfactory conception of freedom and of the relationship between freedom and other aspects of social and political life. The fact that a number of uses of a concept are well established does not preclude criticism of any one of them.

But we would have to concede that the citizens had achieved a kind of solution to the social and political problem of living together. The rules are enforced and the citizens do not think themselves unduly imposed upon. The explanation for the practical resolution would not satisfy the requirements of the conceptual criteria we have been developing, but it would show how it was that the society was able to maintain itself.

We selected the Nazi regime as an example in order to eliminate doubts concerning the distinction between practical and conceptual solutions; practically speaking the Nazi regime was effective for a time, but it hardly gives us an example of a satisfactory solution to the problem of reconciling "must be performed" and "free not to do." But it is difficult to imagine a system in which the conceptual problem is actually resolved

13. Cf. J. L. Austin, loc. cit., p. 128.
14. Cf. Jean-Jacques Rousseau, *Social Contract*, Book I, Chapters 1–4.

in a manner that fully satisfies our criteria. As Hume and many others have emphasized, it would be exceedingly difficult to achieve or sustain a stable society if obedience to rules could rest only on the sort of rational grounds we have been emphasizing. Habit, impulse, mindless acceptance of the status quo, narrow self-interest, and various mixtures of these factors all serve to bring about obedience without a sense of being imposed upon; yet additional obedience is brought about by fear and by outright coercion. Hence whatever else may be wrong with the foregoing argument it should not be thought of as an excessively rationalistic account of the manner in which societies do or realistically could be expected to resolve the tension between obligation and freedom. The argument is an attempt to show that there is nothing in the logic of obligation rules that prevents a resolution of most (but not all) of the aspects of this ancient problem. The extent to which the problem is actually resolved in this way is an independent question. If its independence is not recognized, our attempt at a conceptual solution will blind us to aspects of the manner in which political societies actually operate; it will hamper our attempts to understand how political societies are able to maintain themselves despite tensions of the type we have been examining.

It must also be recognized, however, and this is the final point, that from perspectives other than "must be performed"– "free not to do" the distinction between conceptual and practical solutions to that problem can be misleading. The fact that there is no solution to the conceptual problem in the case of the revolutionary does not allow us to treat the problem of the revolutionary as merely a practical problem. Even if we conclude that "freedom not to do" of a conceptually satisfactory kind cannot be preserved, there remains the question whether imposition and coercion are justified. Freedom of decision and action is one of the highest of human values. But it is not the only one and the fact that it is disserved in certain circumstances does not settle the question of how we should evaluate those circumstances or the decisions and actions that have brought them about. The fact that imposition is inescapable in revolutionary circumstances is relevant to evaluation of such circumstances in that the sacrifice of freedom of choice is a disvalue that revolution or rejection of the demands that lead to revolution produces; hence it is a ground for avoiding situations in which revolution is likely. (This is one reason why lovers of freedom, as well as lovers of order and stability, have often been skeptical concerning the desirability of revolution.) But loss of freedom for some does not *settle* the question whether imposition and coercion, by established authorities or by revolutionaries, is justified. Maintenance or subversion of a given body of requirements serves and disserves a variety of values; evaluation of action to maintain or subvert those requirements must take account of the full range of the consequences of doing so. Or to put it another way, an answer to the question: "Can individual freedom and the binding quality of rules be reconciled in the case of rule X?" is not a sufficient answer to the question: "Is it right or wrong to try to sustain X and its requirements?" (To translate rightness into freedom as Rousseau did when he wrote of being "forced to be free" serves only to generate fruitless paradoxes.)

The importance of this point is not limited to revolutionary situations. Although the tension between "must be performed" and "freedom not to do" is resolvable in nonrevolutionary situations, in practice much obedience can be explained only in a manner inconsistent with that resolution. Men are imposed upon, threatened, and coerced in the day-to-day politics that we know. Recognizing this to be a fact raises the question of whether imposition can be justified, whether, given a commitment to the value of individual freedom, we can justify the existence of political societies that, as a practical matter, subvert or disserve that value in important respects. This and other questions of a more explicitly normative sort will be our concern below.

(7)

Obligation, Consent, and Utility

T HUS FAR we have dealt only indirectly with the questions that figure most prominently in discussions of political obligation in the tradition of political philosophy. We have limited ourselves to certain logical points concerning the justification of the practice of political obligation qua practice, and we have said very little concerning the time-honored questions of whether, when, and why citizens should (as opposed to can or can be said to) accept and discharge political obligations. Of course our attempts to identify and analyze features of the practice are relevant to answering questions that are more explicitly normative. The latter arise within and concerning the practice and cannot be resolved or even understood apart from an understanding of the practice. It is for this reason that we have been able to suggest, in passing, reasons for thinking that certain influential normative arguments are unsatisfactory. They are unsatisfactory because they are based on misunderstandings and misinterpretations of the practice.

We will now move toward a more direct and sustained discussion of normative questions. More specifically, we will develop and defend a broadly utilitarian treatment of these questions. But just as the foregoing analysis of the features of the practice could not avoid normative questions altogether, so our discussion of normative issues will be concerned with descriptive and analytic questions. Indeed in the present chapter the latter will continue to be a primary concern. Neither a utilitarian nor any other kind of argument for obedience or disobedience will get off the ground if there are unrecognized logical or conceptual disjunctions between the concepts distinctive of utilitarianism (or whatever theory) and the concepts internal to the practice of political obligation. Even a person who wishes to alter the practice in fundamental respects must know what it is he is trying to alter and must concern himself with the conceptual relations between his argument and the concepts internal to the practice. Thus our first task is to dispose of the widely held view that utilitarianism is inconsistent with the practice of obligation and that if accepted as a normative position it would undercut that practice. Having done this, we will be in a position to take up more explicitly normative issues in the next chapter.

Our main strategy in this chapter will be to examine the relationships between utilitarianism and what seems to us to be its main competitor, namely consent or (more broadly) past-assent theories. We will try to show that the conceptual advantages commonly claimed for consent theory are either spurious or are equally available to a utilitarian position. We will also argue that utilitarianism does not suffer from a number of serious difficulties created by consent arguments.[1]

1. Consent theories are a species of the genus known in moral philosophy as "deontological" or "formalist" theories; utilitarianism is a species of "teleological" or "consequentialist" theories. Thus this chapter could be viewed, was originally viewed by the author, as a case study bearing on the general controversy concerning deontological and teleological theories. While the specific issues between consent and utilitarian theories of obligation continue to seem real and important, we have found it increasingly difficult to achieve a meaningful formulation of the differences between deontological and teleological positions when viewed as general and conflicting accounts of moral practice. Because we have not

Since we will be criticizing consent theory in much of the chapter, it is well to emphasize at the outset that there is a great deal of common ground between the argument we have been developing in earlier chapters and major versions of consent theory. Stated in terms of the general themes we have been discussing, most consent theorists have emphasized reason, freedom of choice, the abundant basis for disinclination to obey, the importance of continuing critical scrutiny of political practices, and the need for mechanisms of change if a justifiable and even a stable political order is to be maintained. A large part of their point in insisting on consent has been to counter attempts to base political obligation, or at least obedience, on force, habit, unquestioning acceptance of tradition, and other nonrational or irrational grounds. (Locke's polemic against Filmer is a good example.) In the most general of the terms we have used, their aim was to put political obligation into the realm of human action. For these reasons, much of our discussion in this chapter will serve to detail positions already taken.[2]

I. THE ALLEGED MONISM OF UTILITARIANISM

SOME OF THE POINTS we have made concerning "obligation" also apply to (though they don't necessarily carry the same

arrived at a satisfactory alternative to the general conceptualization of the issues with which we began, remnants of our original understanding remain in this and the following chapter. We can only say that we are uncomfortable with them. (The work that seems to us to hold the greatest promise for putting the controversies that have gone on under the deontological-teleological labels on a sounder basis is not in moral philosophy but in the theory of language and meaning more generally. Salient examples would be John Searle's *Speech Acts* (Cambridge: Cambridge University Press, 1965) and Julius Kovesi's *Moral Notions*.

2. The one major exception to the above remarks about our agreements with consent theory concerns the question of the relationship between the individual and his society. As we noted in Chapter Four, consent theorists have tended to isolate the individual and his actions. From this perspective, our discussion below will specify respects in which consenting presupposes social relationships and conditions not based on consent.

implications for) other concepts typically used to guide conduct. Thus " 'Obligation' implies ability" closely parallels " 'Ought' implies can." Again, all *action*-guiding concepts presuppose freedom not to do the prescribed act. It has nevertheless been our assumption that the logic of "obligation" is distinct from the logic of "good," "right," "ought," "duty," etc. To say that B has an obligation to do X is not the same as to say that he ought to do X, that it would be right for him to do X, or even that he has a duty to do X.[3] The initial and most general objection to utilitarianism is that it is inconsistent with this assumption in that it claims to account for all moral guidance, for the logic of all moral concepts, in terms of one consideration, the utility of acting on the guidance supplied by the use of those concepts. Utilitarianism is a monistic theory which, in its normative formulation, posits one measure of value and disvalue, namely utility, and claims that all decisions as to what to do ought to be based upon that measure. In its meta-ethical formulation it contends that all defensible decisions and guidance are (at least tacitly) based upon it, and that the uses of all moral concepts are to be explained or accounted for in terms of that measure.

The first point to be noted here is that one principle or test can have numerous applications each of which is distinct in important respects. For example the fact that all laws are promulgated by an authoritative agent or agency by no means eliminates or reduces the importance of the numerous distinctions among types or kinds of laws. The fact, if it is a fact, that all processes in the physical universe can be subsumed under certain general laws such as the laws of thermodynamics does not (would not) reduce the significance of the manifold distinctions to be drawn for other purposes and at other levels

3. The general thesis underlying this view is expressed in the tag phrase "Language does not proliferate forms without functions." If ordinary language contains both "obligation" and "duty," there is a presumption—but only a presumption—that the two terms usually, or at least sometimes, do different jobs, that the concepts are differentiated in order to mark distinctions that people have thought important to them.

of analysis. The argument that a monistic theory such as utilitarianism must obliterate all distinctions among action-guiding concepts is sometimes formulated as though, say, Aristotle had never distinguished among four causes. The utilitarian must display the internal complexity of the principle of utility and he must show that the fundamental questions that arise about action-guiding concepts are best answered in utilitarian terms. We have been working at this task in the previous chapters and will try to carry it forward as regards "obligation" in this and the final chapter.[4]

II. UTILITARIANISM AND RULES

SHORT OF THE CHARGE based on the alleged reductionist monism of utilitarianism, the most influential objection to a utilitarian account of "obligation" focuses on the antipathy to *rules* of conduct that has long been alleged to be intrinsic to utilitarianism. If the utilitarian cannot accept the notion of a rule of conduct, and if "obligation" is a rule-dependent concept, then utilitarianism can only provide a basis for criticizing or attacking the notion of obligation, not for explaining it or contributing to judgments that are made under its rubric. The seriousness with which this objection to utilitarianism has been taken is indicated by the fact that some utilitarians have reformulated their theory in order to meet it. Thus recent years have seen the emergence of rule-utilitarianism. According to this theory the question whether an act is right, wrong, or obligatory is (at any rate very often) to be decided exclusively by applying a preestablished rule, not by applying the principle of utility directly to the act. On this view the principle of utility

4. It should be stressed that this work is not intended to be a systematic treatise concerning utilitarianism, and many important questions concerning it will not be taken up. For a recent attempt at a systematic treatise on the subject that meets a number of standard objections to utilitarianism, see Jan Narveson, *Morality and Utility* (Baltimore: The Johns Hopkins Press, 1967).

is appropriate only when deciding whether the rule qua rule is good or defensible. Thus the element of formalism or recognition of the independent significance of rules, thought necessary to bring the theory into accord with moral practice, is added to utilitarianism.

We discussed a number of the issues that arise in connection with formalism—whether of the rule-utilitarian variety or some other—in earlier chapters and no purpose would be served by repeating in any detail points already made. Aside from recalling the importance of distinguishing among different types of rules, there are two points to be stressed in the present context. The first is that rule-utilitarianism can give a correct account of some part of moral and related practices but it is not a utilitarian account. The second is that rule-utilitarianism is mistaken as regards what we can and cannot do (as opposed to what some of us do in fact do some of the time). It is beyond question that people regard themselves as having an obligation to keep promises, contracts, and agreements to do X because they have promised, contracted and agreed to do X, and it is equally beyond question that people obey laws simply because they are laws. Nor is there any reason to deny that such actions are sometimes rule-governed in a highly formalistic sense, i.e., are done out of awareness of a rule that the person thinks is applicable to him and out of a sense that one should do the action simply because the rule requires it. In some cases persons who act this way may think that the rules are binding because, as rules, they satisfy utilitarian tests. But even if this is the case, we take David Lyons's recent work to have demonstrated that if these persons think it inappropriate to apply the utilitarian test to particular actions (not if they simply do not do so in some or even all cases) they are not utilitarians and their actions cannot be explained or accounted for (though of course they might be criticized) in utilitarian terms.[5]

5. See David Lyons, op. cit., esp. Chap. 4.

To admit these points is to concede (to make these points is to insist) that not all common and widely approved forms and processes of moral judgment and action are compatible with, can be accounted for by, utilitarian theory. But it is not to admit to the additional, and crucial, point that it would be logically or in some other way inappropriate to apply the utilitarian test to the actions in question. Put another way, it is not to admit that it would be inappropriate to regard the rules in question either as being of the "summary" ("rule of thumb") type, firmly (or not so firmly) supported by utilitarian considerations or as a convention properly subject to examination and criticism from a utilitarian perspective. In the first case there is simply no problem for utilitarianism.[6] The second case involves stepping outside the practice or rule and perhaps even the language in which discourse involving the practice or rule usually takes place, and subjecting it to critical examination. This might lead to logical disjunctions—for example if one began to use concepts inappropriate to the discussion of human action—but there is no reason to think that it must do so. Nor is there any reason to think that it will undercut acceptance of and willingness to act according to the rule or rules in question. If the rule is defensible examining it will presumably strengthen acceptance of it and, insofar as the decision is made on reasoned grounds, willingness to act according to it. If the rule or practice proves to be indefensible, the rule will indeed be "undercut" and "weakened"—except that these are not the verbs we ordinarily use when speaking of net improvements in human affairs.

III. ANTECEDENT ASSENT AND UTILITY

A THIRD and closely related objection to a utilitarian treatment of "obligation" rests on what we might call the past or antecedent assent interpretation of "obligation." According to this

6. See Flathman, op. cit., Chap. 9.

view, of which consent theories of political obligation are examples, "obligation" is appropriately used only when there is a particular kind of event in the past by which the agent or agents in question have undertaken to do or refrain from doing an action. However good the results of the action might have been or might be expected to be, that action is not appropriately called obligatory unless there is an assent, for example a promise, a commitment, an act of consent, an oath, or perhaps a kindness or benefit accepted, that provides an "obliging factor."[7] In Kurt Baier's words: ". . . Obligations . . . can arise only on account of what has already happened or been done. The future is indeed morally relevant, but it does not create obligations."[8] Similarly, Alexander Sesonske, who has devoted much of a book to distinguishing between "oughts" resting on evaluations of goodness and badness ("$ought_e$") and "oughts" assigning obligations ("$ought_o$"), says: "I do not intend to deny that we ever have obligations to perform acts productive of good, but only to deny that the obligation stems merely from the goodness to be produced."[9] On this thesis, especially as argued by Gauthier and Sesonske, if A says to B: "You have an obligation to do X," B sufficiently disposes of A's statement by showing that he never undertook to do X by promising, consenting, or any other form of undertaking. It may be that B ought to do X, that it would be good or right for him to do X, wrong for him not to do X, but it is not the case that B has an obligation to do X.

A. Similarities Between Antecedent Assent Theories and Utilitarianism

From the perspectives developed in this work the appeal of this thesis (or set of theses) about obligation (whether argued as a conceptual thesis or on some other grounds) lies in part

7. See David Gauthier, op. cit., pp. 175 ff.
8. Kurt Baier, The Moral Point of View (Ithaca: Cornell University Press, 1958), p. 218.
9. Alexander Sesonske, op cit., p. 73.

in the fact that it puts "obligation" squarely and surely in the realm of human action. Consenting, promising, agreeing, and contracting are all actions that we take as opposed to events that happen to us or that we suffer. They are things that we do intentionally, after deliberating, and for reasons, not habitually or because of the operation of some set of causally sufficient forces upon us. Thus to show that "political obligation" is logically tied to one of these forms of assent is to take it out of the realm of phenomena that can be sufficiently understood or explained in terms of fear, coercion, habit, or mindless conformity. Merely to recite the contrasting lists of appropriate concepts is to do much to explain the attractiveness of the thesis.

The past-assent interpretation also bears some more particular similarities to the argument we have been developing here. First, both theories argue that use of "obligation" presupposes an event in the past. For Sesonske and Gauthier the event is the expression of consent, agreement, etc., to do or refrain from doing X. On the present theory the past "event" is the development and acceptance, in the society, of a rule requiring or forbidding X. We agree with Baier at least to the extent of holding that the future, taken alone, does not generate obligations. Moreover, the use of most of the devices to which Sesonske and Gauthier point as instruments by which obligations can be undertaken is governed by rules, including a rule according to which proper use of the instrument places the agent under an obligation. Promising and contracting are the clearest cases because the rules governing them are quite well worked out, but the point holds for most cases of consenting and agreeing as well. Indeed, as Hume pointed out some time ago, it is only because there is a rule that lays down that to promise (or to agree or contract) is to undertake an obligation that the theory has such cogency as it enjoys.[10] Thirdly, we have

10. Benefits received or accepted is a more complicated case, but in many societies bestowing and receiving gifts is governed by very elaborate rules, including rules that generate obligations. See for example the classic

stressed the point that B's conduct is genuinely governed by an obligation rule only if he has accepted the rule under which it falls in the sense that he thinks there are good reasons for it and hence that it deserves to be followed. Since "accepting" a rule bears more than a little relationship to consenting to it, it might even appear that there is no significant difference between our thesis and the consent interpretation; it might appear that we not only should and do find the thesis attractive but that we should and do accept it.

Finally, the thesis is attractive because it is quite clearly a correct account of at least a part of the logic of a number of prominent uses of obligation. It is beyond question that we do undertake obligations by promising, contracting, giving consent, accepting benefits, etc. It is equally beyond question that utilitarian calculations often play little or no immediate or direct role in these actions. In some classes of cases some form of assent is a sufficient condition of having an obligation (assuming, of course, that the "form of assent" is well established in the society or social group). There may even be cases in which it is necessary condition. (The latter point, however, is probably true only in a trivial way. Thus having made a promise is a necessary condition of having an obligation to keep a promise.)

Thus it is hardly surprising that the past-assent interpretation of obligation has had, and continues to have, many adherents and supporters. It is, nevertheless, an unsatisfactory interpretation and we must reject it as a complete account of "obligation" and qualify, amend, and supplement it in far-reaching ways before we can incorporate it into our own analysis. Our first task will be to show that not all uses of "obligation," including not all political uses, involve a past assent or undertaking by the person who has the obligation. (Because of

---

study by Marcel Mauss, *The Gift*, tr. Ian Cunnison (Glencoe, Ill.: The Free Press, 1954). Concerning contemporary western societies see Peter Blau, *Exchange and Power in Social Life* (New York: John Wiley & Sons, 1964).

its traditional place in the theory of political obligation we will concentrate on consent among the forms of past assent.) The reasons that this is the case, together with arguments presented above, will do much to establish the second major point, namely that even in cases that do involve past assent utilitarian considerations are relevant and important.

B. Criticism of Past-Assent Theories

1. PAUCITY OF CONSENTORS

One of the standard embarrassments of consent and contractarian theories of political obligation is that accepting them seems to lead to the conclusion that very few people have or have ever had political obligations. It is asserted that having consented to obey the law is a necessary condition of having an obligation to do so, but it has proven difficult to find a sufficient number of warm-bodied human beings who have actually consented or contracted to give the theory plausibility as an account of political practice. Thus a theory that aims to distinguish between legitimate and illegitimate government and to put one's obligation to obey government in the category of something he undertakes or chooses to do rather than something imposed upon him—a theory with these aims has the consequence of rendering virtually all known governments illegitimate and of turning known cases of obedience into cases of behavior imposed upon the individual.

2. NORMATIVE AND METAETHICAL RESPONSES TO THE PAUCITY OF CONSENTORS

There are various ways in which a person attracted to the consent theory can respond to this difficulty. Two of these are of particular interest here. The first is to concede that few known societies have been based on consent, few governments have been legitimate, but to put the consent theory forward as a recommendation as to how authority and obligation ought to be established and maintained. This is certainly Rousseau's stance in *The Social Contract*, and it is explicitly the position of Joseph Tussman in his recent *Obligation and the Body*

Politic.[11] It may be the best way to understand Hobbes and Locke as well, although Locke in particular often gives way to the temptation to write as if things are and even must be the way he thinks they should be.[12] The problem for the consent theorist who takes this position is to show how the obstacles to a government based on consent could be overcome and to show that there would be genuine advantages in doing so.[13]

A second response is to assert that appearances to the contrary notwithstanding, large numbers of people have consented to the authority of their government and hence do have obligations to it; that the appearance that few if any have considered is created by an unduly narrow understanding of what counts as consent. This move, which virtually all of the consent

11. New York: Oxford University Press, 1960.

12. For some provocative remarks on the last-mentioned theme, see Bertrand de Jouvenel, "On the Nature of Political Science," *The American Political Science Review* 55 (December 1961): 773 ff.

13. Tussman's essay calls attention to some of the *conceptual* problems that can arise when a theorist takes to the way of conceptual stipulation. Although he nowhere argues that "authority," "legitimacy," and "obligation" in fact work only where there is agreement or consent, he does say that they are "built into" the notion of a voluntary group and that they "relate . . . more easily to agreement" than to other notions that have been put forward as a basis for them. He then says: "This is sometimes expressed as the view that obligations are, or even must be, voluntarily assumed" (Tussmann, op. cit., p. 8). Now if it is stipulated that consent is a necessary condition of authority and obligation, and if there is no consent, then there is, quite obviously, no authority and obligation. But the conceptual implications do not stop here. To mention only the most obvious points, if there is no authority or obligation there can be no law, no crime, and no punishment (in the legal sense). Nor can there be any legal rights or duties. If one is going to stipulate a new definition of one member of a family of concepts, one must follow the implications of that action through the elaborate conceptual web of which it is a part and with which it has intricate relationships. Despite the remarks just quoted Tussman wants to talk of law and crime and punishment in the case of people who haven't consented. But if consent is a necessary condition of authority, it is illegitimate for him to talk in this way within his system. Talk about law, crime, and punishment ceases to be a concession to an unpleasant reality and becomes a logical impossibility. Or rather it becomes a logical impossibility unless new rules for the use of "law," "punishment," etc., are stipulated as well. Thus Tussman is either trying to say things he cannot say or using two conflicting conceptual schemes at the same time. The way of stipulation is a long and a hard way.

theorists make at some point, usually involves the introduction of some variant of the notion of "tacit" consent; for example, Hobbes's notion of "signs of contract by inference," [14] and of obligations "derived" from "the end of the institution of sovereignty," [15] of Sesonske's "implicit" consent and commitments "we make, or are held to have made, merely by our continuing membership in a community." [16] The problem here is to show that the concept of tacit consent that is advanced is consistent with established uses of the concept such that the moves permitted by the ordinary-language concept are in fact available to the theorists. In the absence of such a showing, one might try to establish that the stipulated concept of consent allows the desired inferences consistent with the other concepts, stipulated or not, that the theorist employs.

3. METAETHICAL RESPONSES: THE LOGIC OF "CONSENT"

The past-assent thesis about "obligation" advanced by Sesonske and Gauthier is an example of the second type of response to the problem. Their thesis is a metaethical thesis that rests on evidence about the way concepts are used in ordinary discourse. Since "obligation" is used in political and legal contexts, either a past assent can always be discovered in such contexts or the thesis is false.[17] To get at this question,

14. Hobbes, *Leviathan*, Chap. 14.   15. Ibid., Chap. 21.
16. Sesonske, op. cit., pp. 80–94. The quoted passage is on p. 82.
17. Actually these are not the only conceivable alternatives. A proponent of the thesis might hold that all uses of "obligation" that are modified by "political" or "legal" and which do not involve consent or some other form of past assent are misuses. But of course if it was argued that all such uses are misuses *because* there is no evidence of a past assent the argument would be circular. For a more general discussion of the problems involved in declaring the notion of political obligation to be categorically inapposite or meaningless, see the discussion of John Ladd's argument to this effect in Chapter Two above.
We should note that the most ardent defender of the past-event thesis about "obligation," Sesonske, does not apply it to political and legal obligation. He gives a footnote to the topic and simply asserts that "the act of making a commitment is not, in general, a necessary condition of legal obligation. We may have a legal obligation to obey the laws of any nation . . . we happen to be in . . . no matter what the circumstances of our arrival there and no matter what commitments we may have made" (op. cit., p. 80 n.).

as well as to assess the first response we identified, we must examine the concept of "consent."

The rules governing the use of "consent" include few if any restrictions on what, substantively speaking, we can consent to do. But they do restrict the circumstances under which we can consent (and, of course, the moves we can make after we have consented or refused to consent). Similarly, many forms of speech and action are suitable means of expressing or giving consent and they constitute evidence that second parties use in deciding whether consent has been given. But the criteria of whether a person has consented, whether expressly or tacitly, are quite specific and exacting. Without attempting an exhaustive analysis of the concept we will try: (a) to identify some of the main types of circumstances in which the question of consenting or not can properly arise, and (b) to state the criteria by which to judge whether consent has been given in such circumstances. In doing so we will be carrying forward the discussion of Chapter Four by identifying some of the social conditions presupposed by consenting and hence some of the ways in which individuals who consent to something depend upon and in other ways relate to the society in which they act.

a. Conditions under which consent is appropriate   In order for the question of consent to arise for B there ordinarily must be a claim, proposal, or request advanced by A which, if consented to by B, commits him to acting in a manner appropriate to satisfying the claim, proposal, or request. A clear case would be if A claimed the right to or requested to be allowed to represent B in a negotiation or to cast B's vote at a meeting which B could not attend.

A part of the point here is that we do not consent to our own actions. We consent to the claims, requests, etc., of others, and the consent carries with it a commitment to do or refrain from doing a certain action. Since there was no such claim or request it would make no sense to say that I consented to come to my office this morning, to eat lunch with Smith yesterday, or to write these words. Nor would it make sense to say that I refused to consent to stay home today, to have lunch with Jones yesterday, or to refrain from writing these words. The concept of consent has no application in these circumstances. I simply came to my office, had lunch with Smith, and wrote. To put this part of the point another way, it makes sense to consent only when there is a second party who would be warranted in holding me to the consequences of my act of consenting. In this respect the notion of consenting to my own actions suffers from the same difficulty that attends the notions of a duty to oneself or an obligation to oneself.

Not all claims, requests, or proposals create the conditions that make consent appropriate. The most important point here is that the claim, request, etc., must be such that its validity, or the justification for it, must depend on the consent of the person to whom it is addressed. We return to this point immediately below. It is tempting to say that the question of consent arises when the person to whom the claim is addressed is known to be disinclined to do the action to which acceptance of the claim would commit him. This move has been particularly attractive in the context of political theories that stress the natural freedom and equality of men and hence emphasize how much man gives up when he consents to the proposal that he enter a political order. But whether this is the way most men do, or should, view their political ties is of course controversial—controversial even among those who argue for consent. Moreover it is clear that there are many cases in which people consent to claims, requests, etc., with great enthusiasm. For example I might consent to my daughter's marrying Smith when I am enthusiastic about her doing so.

It would be closer to the mark to say that the question of consent arises where consenting or not to the claim or request is thought to carry serious—as opposed to trivial—consequences for both or all of the parties involved. The person who consents to the claim may be enthusiastic about doing so or exceedingly reluctant to do so, but he (and the person who advances the claim) believes that it is a serious step that carries significant consequences. When a claim is not thought to be serious in this sense A's request for B's consent is perfunctory or even a nuisance; [18] likewise B's insistence that A not go ahead without obtaining B's consent would be picayune, unreasonable, and perhaps even overbearing or imperious. If consent were given to trivial or inconsequential claims or proposals it would be difficult to sustain the view that the person who consents is bound or has an obligation to do what he consented to do. A man must be a devoted formalist indeed to invest much energy in holding people to commitments that all concerned regard as trivial in substance. (That there are such formalists, unfortunately, is quite impossible to deny.)

We now return to the question when the validity or justification of a claim, request, or instruction depends upon the consent of the person to whom it is addressed such that the question of consent must arise. According to the past-assent theory, the question of consent (or some other form of assent) must arise in order that a claim, request, or instruction generate an obligation for the person to whom it is addressed. But this is obviously false. If I instruct or request my six-year-old to go to bed when the usual hour arrives, the legitimacy of my instruction or request does not depend upon her consent. Again, if the seriously injured A instructs B (a perfect stranger but the only person about) to call an ambulance for him, neither the legitimacy of A's request nor B's obligation to comply with it depend upon B's consent. In both cases the claim or request is justified and the obligation binds independent of the consent of the person to whom the claim is addressed and who is obligated by it.

There are also numerous cases in which the legitimacy or justifiability of a claim or request depends upon consent but not upon the consent of any of the particular persons for whom the claim creates an obligation. Thus when claims and di-

18. For example the subordinate or student who wants the consent of the boss or teacher to minor, inconsequential changes in his work.

rectives are addressed to organizations or groups it may be that the organization must consent, but this might be done by a single person, or small number of persons, authorized to act on behalf of the organization, by a majority vote, or in some other manner not requiring the consent of all or any particular one of the individual members. But from the fact that an individual member does not consent, that he or she expressly dissents, it does not follow that he or she has no obligation in connection with the claim. In some but by no means all organizations the individual can avoid the obligation by severing his relationship with the organization. A soldier in the army often, indeed usually in modern conscripted armies, cannot opt out of the organization if he doesn't consent to the claims directed to it and accepted by those authorized to speak for the army.

The issues here, of course, are precisely the issues on which seventeenth- and eighteenth-century contractarian political theorists dissented from the views of earlier political theorists. Numerous political philosophers had argued that the claim to political authority, and the claims made by political authorities, did not require the consent of those to whom they were addressed. They derived their legitimacy, and hence their capacity to generate obligations, from the distinctive wisdom or other attributes of those who advanced them, from God, from tradition, or from some other source having nothing to do with consent. Other theorists argued that political authority and political obligation do depend upon consent, but upon the consent of the society or community, for whom authority was thought to act, not the consent of discrete individuals.

Hobbes, Locke, and Rousseau insisted, each in his own way, that political authority must rest on consent, and that, since authority acted on behalf of—"represented," as Hobbes put it—discrete individuals, it must be the consent of those individuals. Leaving to later the various qualifications they entered as regards what would count as consent, these theories provide systematic statements of the position that the past-assent theory asserts to be established. Indeed, the metaethical version of the past-assent theory asserts that it is now impossible to formulate any other view, for example a utilitarian view, without misusing language. Perhaps the influence of the consent theorists upon modern political thinking and practice accounts in part for the plausibility of the past-assent theory—at least as regards politics. But it is manifest that neither political nor other aspects of the practice of obligation accord entirely with the views of these thinkers. The consent theorists hardly won the agreement of all or even most of the political thinkers that followed them. To assert that all claims that generate obligations—political or otherwise—require the consent of those to whom the claim is directed is all too obviously to employ what H. L. A. Hart has called the definitional stop; and to employ it where substantive arguments are urgently required.

The points just discussed bring out one of the important differences between consent theories and the present argument concerning accepting obligation rules. The consent theorist makes B's having consented to X a necessary condition of his having an obligation to do X. Thus merely by refusing to consent, for whatever reason, B can render inapplicable the entire apparatus of concepts and of justification that is part of the practice of political obligation. On the present argument concerning acceptance, B cannot be said to be discharging (or rejecting) an obligation if he has not accepted (or rejected) the rule that defines the obligation. But from the fact that he is not *discharging* an obligation it does not follow that he does not *have* an obligation. To begin with a point noted in Chapter Six, if the other members of the society think there are good reasons for the rule that defines the obligation (and if the rule applies to B), they will think that B has an obligation under the rule. Hence they will think they are quite justified in taking various measures to induce B to do what they think he has an obligation to do.

But they are no more participating in the practice of political obligation than is B if they merely "think" B has an obligation.

They must present their reasons for thinking it, present them to B and to one another. By the same token, if B is to show that they are mistaken in these views, he must show that the reasons for the rule are not good reasons. If he does not do so he gives society no reason to doubt that they are justified in holding him blameworthy.

The advantages of the present view can be seen by examining Tussman's treatment of what he calls the problem of "shrinkage," the problem that arises from the fact that in any of the societies we have known there have been people who cannot be said to have consented to political obligations. Rather than stretching "consent" to "show" that they have in fact consented, Tussman says that such people are "like minors who are governed without their own consent. The period of tutelage and dependence is unduly prolonged." [19] Again, if having consented is a necessary condition of having an obligation to obey, such people cannot have obligations. Of course Tussman thinks they ought to obey, can be punished for not obeying, etc. Given his admission that on this view the "body politic [that is the body of those who are full members because they have consented] may shrink alarmingly," [20] the argument threatens to become markedly elitist and questions arise as to whether the "elite" who have consented will be able to govern the "political child-brides" who have not. But the practical problem of getting nonconsentors to obey is as much a difficulty for the present argument about accepting rules as it is for Tussman. If few people accept the obligation rules in a society it will be tough for the minority who do to get the nonacceptors to obey. What matters here is that on Tussman's argument the sort of reasoning about rules we have discussed is not only practically ineffective, it is logically out of place. The nonconsentor is not a part of the practice of political obligation, and the concepts, rules, and requirements of that practice do not apply to him. Nor do they apply to others as regards their treatment

19. Joseph Tussman, op. cit., p. 37.   20. **Ibid.**

of nonconsentors. The apparatus of reasoned justification which is the heart of the practice of political obligation is rendered irrelevant. This is a mistaken account of the practice and it hardly serves to encourage the kind of action on the part of the "elite" that would enlarge the number of participants in or increase the salience of the practice in the working of society. One of the central advantages of the present argument is that it can recognize the existence of "political child-brides" and yet avoid this outcome, an outcome to which Tussman's view inevitably leads.[21]

b. Criteria of having consented   The foregoing points about the conditions under which the question of consenting appropriately arises are enough to show that consent is not a necessary condition of all established conduct-guiding uses of "obligation." We now turn to the criteria by which to decide whether consent has been given in circumstances in which the question of giving it appropriately arises. We should note at once that it is only here that the problem of tacit or implicit consent arises; B can no more consent tacitly than he can consent explicitly or expressly if consenting is inappropriate in the circumstances in which he finds himself.

The best evidence that B consents or not to A's request that he (B) do X is that B says: "I consent to your request that I do X" or "I do not consent to. . . ." Given such a statement it would be cogent to ask whether B consented or not (assuming the circumstances were such that it was appropriate for B to consent) only if there is evidence that B deliberately deceived A, or that he was asleep, drugged, under hypnosis or extreme duress, or in some other abnormal state.[22] But the fact that

21. For related criticisms of Tussman's position, see Hanna Pitkin, "Obligation and Consent—I," op. cit., pp. 997–99.
22. The question of deception raises complex problems that we will not go into in detail here. Suffice to say that if B *says* "I consent to your request that I do X" he can often be held to have consented and to have undertaken any obligations attendant upon his consent. "I consent," as with "I promise," is a "performative" the utterance of which (in the appropriate circumstances and short of evidence of abnormality) constitutes the act of consenting. The complexities arise if there is reason to think that A or other affected parties knew that B intended to deceive.

these questions can arise calls attention to the distinction between the *evidence* that B consented and the *criteria* by which to judge whether he consented, a distinction of practical importance in the garden-variety cases of consent.

"I consent to" or "I hereby consent to" is a formal locution most often employed in legalistic or other highly structured circumstances. Even if my consent is required to validate your request, for me to say: "I hereby consent to your request that we have lunch together today" would be priggish—or a joke. This is also true of such expressions as: "You have my permission to . . . ," "Consider yourself authorized to . . ." and other locutions of an explicitly consenting character. Much more common than these formal locutions are expressions such as: "Okay," "Go ahead if you wish," "It's all right with me," "Good," and "I have no objection." Even the latter can be dispensed with in favor of a nod of the head, a handshake, an approving smile, or simply acting in a manner which, in the circumstances, would ordinarily be taken to be evidence of consent by persons who understand the form of life and know the language. As Hobbes put it, anything can be a sign of consent that "sufficiently argues the will" of the person consenting.[23]

The movement away from "I hereby consent" toward actions that can be interpreted as consent is a movement from express or explicit consent to tacit or implicit consent. But the difference between the two, as John Plamenatz wrote some years ago,[24] concerns the manner in which consent is expressed, not the conditions requisite to consenting, not what is consented to (what obligations are undertaken by consenting), and not the criteria of what counts as consent. B can no more tacitly than he can expressly consent to get the ambulance for A; B can ex-

---

23. *Leviathan,* Chap. 14, par. 13 and 14, p. 106. Unfortunately Hobbes says this about contract, where it is less plausible. Also, Hobbes makes little or no attempt to identify the criteria by which to judge whether "the will" has been "sufficiently argued."

24. See J. P. Plamenatz, *Consent, Freedom and Political Obligation,* 2nd Edition (London: Oxford University Press, 1968), p. 7.

pressly consent to anything to which he can tacitly consent and vice versa; most important B can be said to have tacitly consented only if the criteria of consenting, express or tacit, are satisfied.

Assuming the circumstances are right for the question of consent to arise, for B to consent he must: (a) know what he consents to, (b) intend to consent to it, (c) communicate his knowledge of what he is consenting to and his intention to consent (that is, communicate his consent) to the person or persons to whom the consent is given. (The communication can be either direct or indirect.) We will not discuss the third point independently except to note that the notion of consenting privately makes no sense. B might know that he intends to consent to X without communicating his consent to any other person, but he does not actually consent until he communicates his consent to other persons. By consenting one undertakes an obligation to do the thing he consents to do. If the consent is private it would be impossible for anyone else to know that B had undertaken an obligation and hence impossible for anyone else to know what the obligation is or whether B discharged it or not, and hence impossible for them to hold B to the obligation, to blame him for failure to discharge the obligation, etc. The notion of private consent, of consent only in "one's own mind or heart," shortcircuits the logic of "consent."

Points (a) and (b) are intimately connected. As Stuart Hampshire has stressed, intention is inseparable from, is even a kind of, knowledge. B cannot intend to do X without knowing it, and he cannot do X intentionally without knowing it.[25] Thus B cannot consent intentionally without knowing it. What B could do so far as intentionality is concerned is to consent to A's claim or request without knowing what his consent commits

25. Stuart Hampshire, *Thought and Action* (New York: The Viking Press, 1960), Chap. 2 and passim. G. E. M. Anscombe says that our intentional actions are a subclass of the things that we know without observation, *Intention*, 2nd Edition (Oxford: Basil Blackwell, 1963), p. 14 and passim. Hampshire says that intention is a source of "noninferential" knowledge (op. cit., p. 121).

him to do. This is a notion of consent that consent theorists of political obligation have been willing, indeed anxious, to put forward. The trouble with the notion stems from the fact that to consent is not just to act now, it is to commit oneself for the future. If B does not know to what his consent commits him, his consent (the statement by which, or the description of the action by which, he consents) provides no guidance as to what he should do or refrain from doing after he has consented. It provides no criteria by which he, or A, can determine what he is bound to do or not. Which is of course to say there is nothing that he is bound (by his consent) to do or not. The notion of consenting without knowing what one commits himself to in consenting (what *it is* that he is doing when he consents) suffers from the same difficulty that vitiates the notion of private consent. Hence in the case of consent we must treat "intentional" as including "knowing what I am committing myself to in consenting." [26] To give up this point would be to break the very connection between the individual and his obligations that has been thought to be a primary advantage of obligations undertaken by consent.[27]

In addition to clarifying what is involved in knowing and intentional consent, the foregoing discussion serves to recommend the position, which is pretty hard to deny in any case, that consent must be intentional. The difficulties with the notion "consenting without knowing to what" would be considerably compounded by "consenting without knowing that one consented." Since there is no such thing as acting intentionally but unknowingly the same considerations indicate why the notion

26. It does not follow that there must be an *intent with which* B consents in the sense of a further intention that he has in mind in committing himself, by consenting, to do X. (Of course if there was such a further intention B would know it.)

27. It does not follow that B must know, at the time he consents and in fine detail, every action that his consent commits him to take. He could, for example, commit himself to do whatever another person (e.g. Hobbes's sovereign) tells him to do. What is essential is that his consent provide criteria by which to decide whether a particular action falls within the scope of his commitment.

of unintentional consent bars the very moves that consent makes available to us.

The problem, then, is to determine what counts as knowing and intentional consent. In the case of express consent this is ordinarily no problem. If B says, in the appropriate circumstances: "I hereby consent to X and I understand that doing so commits me to do Y," A doesn't need a philosophical analysis of "knowledge" or "intention," to decide that B did in fact consent. In this respect determining express consent is no more a problem than determining that any other action is done intentionally. As G. E. M. Anscombe says: "The greater number of the things which you would say straight off a man did or was doing, will be things he intends. . . . What is more, if it is not an intention of his, this will for the most part be clear without asking him." [28] We know that B intentionally votes, pays taxes, etc., because we know two types of things: first, linguistic conventions—in this case the conventions governing the use of "votes," "pay taxes," and "intention"; second, that B acted in a manner such that these conventions are satisfied and the concepts apply to him. B reads of the election, discusses the candidates and issues with his wife, says he is going down to vote before supper, and drives to the voting place. Later he gives reasons for his choices in discussions with others. Moreover, there is no indication that he is in any abnormal condition. Even if the verb "to vote" does not enter into his discussions, he will readily accept its application to his actions if asked to do so. And if we should have reason to doubt that he acted intentionally we can, unless we have reason to doubt the sincerity of his response, settle the matter by asking him. Since he knows what he has been doing he will have no difficulty in telling us.

It is in the same way that we ordinarily know that B consented intentionally to A's claim. A advances the claim, B discusses it with him or with others, communicates with A, does what he committed himself to do or fails to do it, and tries to

28. Anscombe, op. cit., pp. 7–8. We might add that if it isn't clear without asking him, a question or two will usually settle the matter.

justify or excuse his failure, etc. The verb "to consent" may not enter into his discussions, but he will readily apply it himself or accept its application to his actions if asked. Or to consider a case of tacit consent, B comes to the auction house, examines the merchandise to be auctioned, takes his place on the floor, gives the conventional sign of a bid to the auctioneer, pays for the merchandise, goes home, and tries to justify his extravagant purchase to his wife. The verb "to consent" is never used, but (short of evidence that B is mentally ill, under hypnosis or drugs, or in some other abnormal condition) there is not the slightest doubt that B consented—knowingly and intentionally—to buy the merchandise at the price the auctioneer called.

Determining whether B consented intentionally is a *general* problem in consent theories of political obligation because of the suggestion that such actions as voting, other types of participation in the political process, "travelling on the highways," etc., in the discussion or description of which the verb "to consent" is ordinarily not used, are alleged to be indications, even criteria, of (tacit) consent. In this situation, while the marks of intention to vote, to participate, to travel, are present and leave us in no doubt, the marks by which we ordinarily decide that there is consent are not. Thus to the question "Did B consent or not?" we are inclined to respond: "Why raise that question? The issue here is whether B voted intelligently, whether a quorum will show up at the caucus, whether he took the best road or why he was out at all on such a wretched night. The question of whether he consented to something in doing these things is out of place." In the absence of the conventional landmarks we lose our way in trying to deal with questions about consent.

Of course there could be a society in which it was established that voting in elections, joining a political party, or even Locke's traveling on the highways constituted consent to, say, the authority of the government. If this was the case determining whether B intended to consent to the authority of the government by voting would not be problematical. If there were no indications of special circumstances, the fact that B discussed the election, went to the polling place, and voted would ordinarily indicate that he consented. If there were doubts the matter could be settled by asking B. The question would be meaningful to him and he could readily answer it. Because he could not not consent without knowing it, his answer would be conclusive unless we had reason to believe that he was deceiving us.[29]

Some of the cases we have considered thus far [30] involve express, some tacit, consent, but they share one crucial feature: the conventions governing the use of the verbs that describe the actions in question are tolerably clear in their application to the examples given and we can decide without difficulty if we can obtain the relevant evidence concerning the agent's actions. Indeed the conventions are so clear that B would not understand what he was doing in saying "I consent" or bidding or voting if he did not understand that in doing so he was giving his consent to something. (Of course he might challenge the conventions by which bidding or voting constitute consenting.) [31]

The task of identifying knowing and intentional consent becomes more difficult as we move to cases in which the relevant conventions are less clearly worked out. Such cases are common in consent theories of political obligation because the theorists in question are trying to stretch or extend the conventions in order to argue that obligations are in fact grounded in consent even though it would appear that no consent had been given. Sometimes they "stretch" them past the breaking point and it

29. B's testimony is not conclusive if the question whether he consented to X is put to him well after the time at which he was alleged to consent. This is because B might forget that he had consented. He could be proven wrong by, for example, producing a tape recording or motion picture of the circumstances in which it was thought that he had consented.

30. The express consent with which we began, the auction, the hypothetical case of the society in which it is established that to vote is to consent, and the case in which we do not know what to do with questions about consent.

31. Thus in such cases the distinction between explicit or express and tacit consent is of no theoretical interest.

is altogether obvious that the action put forward as an indicator of consent could not be treated as such unless the conventions changed substantially. Locke's suggestion that traveling on the highways indicates consent to political authority is a case in point. A more difficult type of case, which we can use to illustrate the characteristics of difficult cases generally, is the suggestion that participation in the activities of a group or society, particularly in the decision-making processes, indicates consent to some set of demands or claims that the group or society make upon the individual.

Assume that B attends a meeting called to organize a campaign against pornographic literature. At the meeting officers are elected, bylaws are adopted, and it is decided that each member will be assessed dues of $10. All of this is done by majority vote, with B participating in the voting. Nothing is said at the meeting to the effect that participation constitutes consent to paying the dues or to anything else. Afterwards the elected treasurer (A) seeks to collect $10 from B. When B displays unwillingness to pay up, A tells him that by participating in the decision-making process he tacitly consented to the decisions of the meeting and therefore has an obligation to pay his dues. How do we decide whether B consented to pay?

That participation is not a criterion of consent, and that it is sometimes not evidence or an indication of consent, is obvious from the following examples. Assume that B is an agent for the League for Freedom in Literature and is infiltrating the meeting. If so, the fact that he participated in it will not give A grounds to hold that B consented to pay his dues and is therefore bound to do so. B participated intentionally but he did not intend to consent to anything. We learn this by discovering what preceded his participation (discussions with the members of the League as to how to infiltrate the new organization and what to try to find out), what his reasons are for participating (to render the new organization ineffective), and what he does and says after he has participated (reports to the League on what happened at the meeting). We know that B intentionally participated but we also know that he did not intentionally consent.

Another clear case would be if B was a newcomer in the society and did not know that participation is sometimes thought to indicate consent. He had heard that X was a society that encouraged the widest and most active participation in all decision-making processes. He also knew that participation sometimes means to discuss and debate, make motions, vote, etc. But he did not know that participation is sometimes regarded as an indication of consent to the outcome of the process. We cannot say that he did not know how to use "participate" because "to participate" does not *mean* "to consent." Whereas the agent for the League for Freedom in Literature did not intend to consent (maybe even intended not to consent), the newcomer did not know that the question of consent had arisen and therefore could not know that he consented or what he would have consented to if he had consented. A would discover this when B expressed surprise or even incomprehension at the suggestion that he had consented to pay dues, but it could also be evidenced by what B said before coming to the meeting, while at it, and in discussing it later. Note that in both cases it could be argued that B had an obligation to pay his dues, and even that he had an obligation because he had participated. But it could not be argued that B had an obligation because he had undertaken one by consenting.

These special cases provide the key to the normal case in which B participates because he is sympathetic to the purposes for which the organization is being formed and knows that in the wider society participation of the sort in question is sometimes regarded as an indication of consent. If these conditions are satisfied B is in a position to be sensitive to less-than-explicit indications that a claim is being advanced to which consent would be appropriate—a claim, moreover, which B had not in effect rejected before coming to the meeting. We find out whether these conditions are satisfied by observing B's actions and statements before coming to the meeting. (Although if B is an adult member of the larger society we would ordinarily take the fact that he came to the meeting to be sufficient evidence on these points, evidence that would be conclusive in the absence of special indications to the contrary.) Of course the fact that B is in a position to be sensitive does not mean that he will be. If he expresses genuine surprise at A's assertion that he had consented to pay dues, his doing so will indicate that he did not realize that his participation had been interpreted as consent and thus that he did not consent knowingly. In order to show that B's expression of surprise was insincere, A would have to point to things that B did or said which indicated the requisite awareness.

We hasten to add, however, that B's awareness that his participation was being taken as an indication of consent is not sufficient to establish that he did consent by participating. It would be sufficient only if participating *meant* consent in the way that it would in the hypothetical society we discussed above or in the way that certain signs *mean* consent at an auction or in a betting shop. Since the conventions establish no more than that participation is a possible sign or indication of consent, B must provide A with a warrant for so interpreting his (B's) participation in the case at hand. The most satisfactory such warrant, which would be conclusive short of evidence that B was in an abnormal condition, would be for A *to say* that he intended his participation to indicate his consent. (One can imagine B doing this if C objected to A's interpreting B's participation as a sign of consent.) By the same token, if B explicitly denies that he consented, A can challenge his denial only if he can present evidence that B has now forgotten what he said at an earlier time or that he is lying. The former would ordinarily be plausible only if considerable time had elapsed between the participation and the denial; owing to the uncertainty of the conventions the latter would be extremely difficult to establish even if considerable time had elapsed.

One can imagine circumstances in which B's actions would go far to warrant A in imputing consent to him. If, for example,

A asserted that B had consented and B then paid the dues without protest. Or better, if C interpreted his participation as consent in B's presence and B then paid the dues. The possibilities are numerous and nothing would be gained by enumerating a large number of them. The one generalization that can and must be made, however, is that in all such cases A is in effect saying that B *would* (have) expressly consent(ed) *if* he was (had been) asked to do so and his assertion or imputation is contradicted and nullified if B denies that he consented. B is and must be the guardian of his own consent. He can express his intentions, including his intention to consent and his intentional consent, through action as well as words, and therefore he can consent "tacitly." But to use the notion of tacit consent to divest B of his guardianship of his consent would be to alter "consent" in ways that would make it impossible to draw the inferences which its use now allows and thus to defeat the purpose of imputing consent to B. To "save" the consent theory of obligation by taking away B's guardianship of his consent would be a verbal achievement in the worst possible sense.[32]

32. The above discussion of intention reflects our acceptance of the position that first person present- and future-tense statements concerning intention are ordinarily incorrigible. Unless there is reason to think that B is lying or in some abnormal condition his intentions are given by his statements concerning them. Without going into the complex questions that arise here in detail, we would qualify this view as follows: It can be appropriate for A to raise questions about B's statements even if he has no evidence of deceit or abnormality. As Hampshire argues, B may state his intentions badly, i.e., choose inappropriate language in describing them. This may be suggested by the clumsiness or lack of clarity in B's statement. Moreover B testifies to his intentions by his actions as well as his words, and conflicts among either or between the two may lead A to believe that B is not clear about his intentions. "If it was your intention to patch up the quarrel why did you say that?" Such questioning may prompt B to think more carefully about actions he has taken and statements he has made hurriedly or under pressure of circumstances and he may come to a clearer understanding of them. We are all familiar with the phenomenon of achieving a better understanding of our intentions in doing X after we have done it.

The danger of course is that our later understanding, especially when it is influenced by A's questioning, is not so much better as new. We agree with Hampshire that this is the best way to describe the results of psychoanalysis and other forms of therapy (Hampshire, op. cit., pp. 131–32.

But cf. 133 and 166–69). Awareness of this danger requires that we not dismiss or ignore B's original testimony simply because clearer, more consistent testimony becomes available. The present or future tense testimony must be given a preferred status because it was available to B when he acted; or rather, because it was a part of his action. B could not act on an understanding that was not available to him at the time he acted. Thus it is only insofar as the later testimony is consistent with but constitutes a clarification of the earlier testimony that it can be preferred as an account of B's *intentions* in doing the action. (So far as we can see it would be impossible to state any general criteria for deciding whether the later testimony is consistent with but a clarification of the earlier testimony. It is a matter of making a sensitive judgment in a set of circumstances.)

Of course a later account might be preferred as a nonintentional *explanation* of his action, an explanation in terms of forces at work upon B when he acted that B was not fully aware of at the time he acted. This is the best way to think about what is sometimes called unconscious intention. Developing the example mentioned above a bit further, B tells A that he is going to try to patch up the quarrel between C and D. But in talking with C and D he makes a remark (X) which could be predicted to, and which in fact does, deepen the quarrel between C and D. Afterwards A questions B in a manner designed to determine whether B possessed the information on the basis of which the consequences of saying X to C and D could have been predicted. It turns out that B did possess the information in the sense of having been told of it. But B claims, sincerely as far as A can tell, that he didn't think of it while he was talking to C and D and was genuinely surprised by the results of X. Further discussion between A and B reveals that B was fond of C, disliked D, and had seen more of C during the period of the quarrel between C and D. B now "sees" or "understands" that he said X "in order to" prolong the quarrel between C and D.

There is a strong temptation to say that B said X with the intention, perhaps the unconscious intention, of prolonging the quarrel. But we can say this only if we can show that B was dishonest in claiming that he had been surprised by the outcome. If we grant his sincerity and yet impute intention we are saying that a man can act intentionally without knowing what he is doing. Saying this would involve a change in the use of "intentionally." But changing the language in this one respect would not alter the difference between acting with awareness of and, to that extent control over what we do, on the one hand, and being caused to behave in a certain manner on the other. This distinction is crucial not only to questions of responsibility, praise and blame, and other modes of evaluating individuals and their conduct, but to our understanding of ourselves and one another. To speak of acting intentionally but unknowingly might have no more than the trivial consequence that we would be led to mark the distinction with some other terms. But it could also lead, has in fact led in some quarters, to a blurring of the distinction itself and all of the issues that depend upon clarity concerning the distinction. (See for example John R. Silber, "Being and Doing: A Study of Status Responsibility and Voluntary Responsibility," *The University of Chicago Law Review* 35: 1 [Autumn 1967].)

Thus if we accept B's claim to have been surprised by the consequences *c. Summary on the logic of "consent"* To summarize, the question of consent appropriately arises where A directs a serious claim, request, or instruction to B, a claim the validity or legitimacy of which depends upon B's consent. B consents to it if and only if he knows that the claim has been addressed to him, knows what consenting to it would commit him to do, intends to consent to it, and communicates his consent (directly or indirectly) to A. Knowing whether these conditions are satisfied in a particular case depends on (a) knowing the conventions governing the use of various concepts that must be applicable if the conditions are to be satisfied and (b) having evidence, from the words and actions of B and A, that the conventions are satisfied in a particular case. Less formally, B is the guardian of his own consent, and in all but very special circumstances his testimony is conclusive as to whether he has given it. To eliminate any of these requirements would be to break the very connection between consenting and having an obligation that constitutes the distinguishing feature of obligations undertaken by consenting.

This analysis of consent holds for tacit as well as express consent, the two being differentiated only by the manner in which B testifies that he is consenting to A's claim. If the analysis is correct, tacit consent is not a promising remedy for the difficulty in the past-assent theory of political obligation which

---

of saying X we do better to say that he intended to patch up the quarrel but that he was caused to act so as to deepen it by forces about the operation of which he did not come to know until later and which he could not control until later. We can then make such distinctions among types of causal forces as seem warranted and useful and we can act to increase the individual's sensitivity to the operation of forces of various types.

To summarize these skeletal and overly simplified remarks, it is sometimes appropriate for A to question B's sincere present- and future-tense testimony concerning his intentions and it is sometimes appropriate for A and B to prefer the revised testimony to the original. But the revised testimony can be accepted as an account of B's intentions in doing X only if it is consistent with the original testimony. In this sense B's sincere present- and future-tense testimony concerning his intentions is incorrigible.

(It follows from these remarks that notions such as "unconscious consent" are untenable.)

prompted us to examine "consent." That difficulty, it will be recalled, is that according to the theory consent is a necessary condition of having an obligation to obey, but it is difficult to find people who have consented. If the foregoing discussion of consent is correct, it will be no easier to find genuine cases of tacit than of express consent. If the consent theorist stipulates relaxed criteria of "consent," for example, by dropping the requirement that B know what he consents to do or by allowing A to impute consent when B does not accept the imputation, he blocks the very moves that genuine consent allows him to make and which led him to value it in the first place. Thus the notion of tacit consent will not help us to escape the dilemma we stated earlier: either there can be legitimate government and people with obligations to obey it without consent (and the past-assent theory is false as a complete account of "obligation"), or there are (and have been) few if any legitimate governments and few if any cases of citizens with an obligation to obey their governments. Whatever we may think would be the ideal arrangement or state of affairs, it is perfectly clear that the first alternative must be accepted by anyone who wishes to present an accurate account of actual practice. Since the past-assent theory of "obligation" is false as a complete account of "obligation" it cannot form the basis of an argument against any other account of the concept.

4. NORMATIVE RESPONSES

We now turn briefly to the argument that it would be better if all political obligations were undertaken by genuine consent. Socrates identified the fundamental normative difficulty with this view in a single phrase. He asked Crito: "Ought one to fulfill all one's agreements, *provided they are right*, or break them?" [33] Socrates' point is that there are fundamental objections to treating "having agreed" or "having consented" as the *criterion* of right action. The reason that it would be objectionable is indicated by noting one of the items that did not appear

33. *Crito*, 49e, emphasis added. Hugh Tredennick, translator. Plato, *The Last Days of Socrates* (Baltimore: Penguin Books, 1959, p. 89).

on our list of the criteria of a person's having consented, namely that he have good reasons for agreeing to or rejecting the claim or request to which he is asked to consent. B must know what he is doing in consenting, and this ordinarily means that he have a reason or reasons for consenting. But there is nothing in the notion of consent which requires that his reasons for consenting be good reasons in the sense of showing that the action is justifiable in the light of its consequences for other people. A man might agree or consent to do what would, by this standard, be wrong to do and he might refuse to agree or consent to what would be right to do. Socrates does not speak of obligation (although the issue before him is one in connection with which we would use that concept), but the same difficulty obtains in the case of the latter. "Obligation" is used where the conduct in question is thought to have or is expected to have substantial interpersonal consequences—where A as well as B is significantly affected by B's doing X. To say that B's consent or refusal to consent is a sufficient criterion of whether he has an obligation to do X would be to license any decision that B made irrespective of its consequences for A. To say that B's consent is a necessary condition of B's having an obligation to obey the laws of his government would be to say that, regardless of the consequences for other citizens, B has no obligation to do so if he does not undertake such an obligation by consent. To say that B's consent is a sufficient condition of his having an obligation to obey the laws of his government is to say that, regardless of the consequences of his doing so, B has an obligation to obey the laws.

Of course given a society of men who genuinely and thoughtfully concern themselves with the well-being of their fellows this position might lead to highly desirable results. But in such a circumstance the logical work leading us to approve the situation would be done by the descriptions of the men in question, not by "consent" or "agreement"—which is of course why political philosophers such as Rousseau, who clearly did not think that consent theory accurately described existing political practice, were insistent upon specifying what would count as acceptable consent.[34] As Pitkin has argued, examination of traditional consent theories reveals that obligation rests not on what men do or even would consent to do, but upon what they ought to consent to if they are rational and moral men.[35] But of course to make this move is to alter "consent" every bit as much as to say that men did consent when the usual criteria of the application of the concept are not satisfied.[36]

C. Consent and Utility

The one issue that remains is whether giving consent to do X renders utilitarian considerations inappropriate in deciding whether to in fact do X. Granting, as we have done from the outset, that in some circumstances giving consent is a means of undertaking an obligation, does it follow that doing so excludes, or limits the relevance or appropriateness of appeal to utilitarian considerations in making or justifying further decisions concerning X. Assuming that we have shown that not all uses of "obligation" are tied to consent or any other form of past assent, is it possible that consent and utilitarian considerations complement one another in cases in which consent is appropriate?

From a logical or conceptual standpoint the set of questions that arise here, and the answers to them, are identical to the questions we discussed and the conclusions we reached in connection with Pitkin's thesis about "authority" and "obligation" in Chapter Three. In the English language as we now have it, having consented to do X is always a reason to do X: a person

34. "The clauses of the contract are so determined by the nature of the act that the slightest modification would make them vain and ineffective" Rousseau, the Social Contract, I, VI, G.D.H., Cole, trans. (New York: Everymans, 1950).

35. Pitkin, loc. cit.

36. It does not follow that it would not be desirable for men to consent to what they should or ought to consent to or for them to refuse to consent to what they ought not to consent to. Their doing so might be psychologically significant to themselves or others and it might, as Pitkin suggests, be useful evidence concerning the regime to which they gave or refused their consent.

who does not understand this does not understand "consent." But it is not always clear what doing X would consist of, the reason provided by the fact of having consented may be outweighed by other reasons—may be a reason but not a good reason, and B might challenge the practice of consenting categorically. For the reasons discussed in Chapter Three, in all these cases the notion of reasons for doing X or not, reasons over and above the reason supplied by the fact of having consented, is a cogent notion.

Rather than working out these conceptual arguments in detail in respect to consent, we will probe the more explicitly political aspects of the question by considering the substantive position taken by Hobbes, a theorist who might be expected to argue a rigorously formalistic, antiutilitarian view. Hobbes is famous both as a consent or contract theorist and for his views concerning the scope of the authority that ought to be granted to the sovereign. "Authority" is the "right of doing any act," and it is created when A "authorizes," commissions, or licenses B to do acts that it is A's right to do.[37] Political authority is created when "a multitude of men do agree, and covenant, everyone, with everyone, that to whatsoever man, or assembly of men, shall be given by the major part, the right to present the person of them all, that is to say, to be their representative; everyone, as well as he that voted for it, as he that voted against it, shall authorize all the actions and judgments, of that man, or assembly of men, in the same manner, as if they were his own, to the end, to live peaceably amongst themselves, and be protected against other men." [38] Hobbes insists that "every subject is by this institution author of all the actions, and judgments of the sovereign instituted"; and for Hobbes "it follows, that whatsoever he [the sovereign] doth, it can be no injury to any of his subjects." [39]

37. *Leviathan*, Bk. I, Ch. 16, par. 4.
38. Ibid., Bk. II, Ch. 18, par. 1.
39. Ibid., par. 6. See also Bk. II, Ch. 21, par. 7, where Hobbes says that "a sovereign prince, that putteth to death an innocent subject 'does

It would appear, then, that any and all commands issued by the sovereign are authoritative. Thus if Hobbes accepted an unqualified version of the view that where there is authority resting on consent there is obligation, it would conclusively follow from the fact of authority that the citizen would have an obligation to obey all the commands the sovereign directed to him. For the subject to consider the utility of obeying a particular command, indeed for him to give attention to any consideration external to the fact that it is an authoritative command to which he had consented, would be a mistake. Hobbes does say that such thinking involves a conceptual or logical mistake that leads not only to wrongdoing but to "absurdity." [40] But in the chapter called "Of the Liberty of Subjects" we find Hobbes discussing "the particulars of the true liberty of a subject; that is to say, what are the things, which though commanded by the sovereign, he may nevertheless, without injustice, refuse to do"; [41] Hobbes finds several types of commands that the subject can sometimes refuse to obey, including "to kill, wound or maim himself; or not to resist those that assault him; or to abstain from the use of food . . . or any other thing, without which he cannot live"; to testify against himself without assurance of pardon, and, under some conditions, to fight in war.[42]

Perhaps these passages should be viewed as drawing the limits of authority, not as denying that where there is authority there

no injury to the subject.' When David killed Uriah, Uriah was not injured 'because the right to do what he [David] pleased was given him by Uriah himself.' "

40. See *Leviathan*, Bk. I, Ch. 14.

41. Ibid., Bk. II, Ch. 21, par. 10. It is important to note that Hobbes is using "liberty" in the special sense he calls "liberty of subjects" not in the general sense of "absence of opposition" with which he opens the chapter we are discussing. He aims to show not merely that it is physically possible for the subject to refuse to do certain of the things commanded by the sovereign, but that the subject has no obligation to do them. This is also clear from the words "without injustice." See especially Bk. I, Ch. 14, par. 7. For helpful discussions of Hobbes's views on liberty see the papers by J. R. Pennock and A. G. Wernham in Keith Brown, ed., *Hobbes Studies* (Oxford: Basil Blackwell, 1965).

42. *Leviathan*, Bk. I, Ch. 21, 14th par. from end.

is obligation. Perhaps Hobbes is saying, despite the passages we quoted above, that there *are* limits to the authority of the sovereign. Perhaps he is saying that there are some "commands" that the sovereign does not have the authority to issue and that, if made and enforced, would constitute an injury or injustice to the subject. This interpretation might be suggested by Hobbes's remark that "it is manifest, that every subject has liberty in all those things, the right whereof cannot by covenant be transferred. I have shown before in the fourteenth chapter, that covenants, not to defend a man's own body, are void." [43] There are a number of very specific difficulties with this interpretation. First, Hobbes does not call into question the status of the commands in question, does not say that the sovereign cannot properly issue these commands. Nor does he say that the subject would be injured if such commands were issued. What he says is that the individual is at liberty to refuse to obey without injustice. Moreover, it is hard to see how the sovereign could discharge what Hobbes believes to be his most basic duties without exercising his authority in ways that the subject would have to disobey under the doctrine we are considering. If the sovereign passes a law assigning the death penalty to murder, the murderer who does not resist the penalty foregoes his liberty. But this will hardly prevent Hobbes's sovereign from assigning the death penalty. Secondly, Hobbes makes it clear that commands of the types in question are the basis of obligations for all the other subjects. If the sovereign commanded A to submit to death, A would be "at liberty" to refuse. But if the sovereign commanded B to compel A to submit, B would have an obligation to do so. Now of course the command to B is not the same command as was addressed to A. But since Hobbes holds the view that "whosoever has the right to the end, has the right to the means," it is not implausible to assume (though we cannot prove) that he would accept the view that he who does not have the right to end X does not have the right to command Y

43. Ibid., 15th par. from end.

on the ground that Y would bring about X. If so, and if the sovereign could not command A to die, he could not command B to kill A. But Hobbes makes it abundantly clear that B can be so commanded and that he has an obligation to obey. Third and most important, Hobbes argues that there are cases when the subject *has* an obligation to act in ways that seriously endanger his life. Such an obligation "dependeth not on the words of our submission [I authorize, or take upon me, all his actions]; but on the intention which is to be understood by the end thereof. When therefore our refusal to obey, frustrates the end for which the sovereignty was ordained; then there is no liberty to refuse; otherwise there is." [44] Hobbes explicitly applies this doctrine to military service, saying that "when the defense of the commonwealth, requireth at once the help of all that are to bear arms, every one is obliged; because otherwise the institution of the commonwealth, which they have not the purpose, or courage to preserve, was in vain." [45] Because the commonwealth is in jeopardy, an action not obligatory under other circumstances becomes so. But the change in circumstances does not affect the sovereign's authority. When the commonwealth is not in jeopardy a subject may refuse to fight without injustice, "though his sovereign have right enough to punish his refusal with death." [46] Unless we are to assume that the sovereign has authority to punish actions or refusals to act that he does not have authority to prohibit or require, we must conclude that the change in circumstances affects the obligation of the subject but not the authority of the sovereign.[47]

44. Ibid., 11th par. from end.   45. Ibid., 10th par. from end.
46. Ibid.
47. Hobbes never applies this argument to the case of a command of actual self-destruction, but the argument could easily support an application. Consider the following hypothetical case. A sovereign trained in Hobbes's political philosophy is the ruler of Russia in October 1917. He knows that there is a strong revolutionary movement in the country, and he learns that Lenin is the supreme and unquestioned leader and inspiration of the movement. But the sovereign also knows that to capture and execute Lenin would be to set the revolution in motion. Hence he orders Lenin to come to Moscow, to disavow the revolution publicly, and to

For these reasons we must conclude that for Hobbes there is
sometimes authority based on consent but no actual or binding
(as opposed to prima facie) obligation. Or rather, that there are
cases in which there is authority based on consent but prima
facie or ordinarily or normally no obligation. In such cases an
actual obligation to obey develops only if disobedience threatens
extreme consequences.

From a conceptual standpoint the interesting aspect of
Hobbes's discussion is the way he brings concepts concerning
ends and purposes into reasoning concerning consent, authority,
and obligation. He wants to supply men with good reasons for
consenting to and obeying political authority; he clearly thinks
that we do not so much understand the latter—to say nothing
of being able to relate intelligently to them—if we do not understand the ends and purposes they serve and for which they
ought to be sustained. Of course Hobbes expressed sharp dis-
satisfaction with ordinary language as a vehicle for political
philosophy and he was quite willing to stipulate new uses for
key terms in his theory. Thus as interesting and suggestive as
these conceptual features of his argument are, there are strong
objections to using them as evidence concerning refined conceptual or metaethical disputes.

The substantive problems before him in the passages we have
been quoting, however, are urgent and recurrent political problems that are not special to his theory. As Richard Wasserstrom
has pointed out, most of the classic discussions of disobedience
have been concerned with revolution.[48] Writers on this subject
have, if you will, accepted the argument that where there is
authority there is obligation and hence have concluded that the

take his own life by drinking the hemlock on a platform in Red Square.
Since the sovereign has judged that Lenin's self-destruction is essential
to the purposes of the institution of sovereignty, Hobbes's argument requires the conclusion that Lenin is obligated to take the hemlock and
cannot resist doing so without injustice.

48. See Richard Wasserstrom, "The Obligation to Obey the Law,"
University of California at Los Angeles Law Review, Vol. 10 (1963),
p. 780.

possibility of justified disobedience arises only when authority is in question, that is, when men are prepared to withdraw their consent and revolt. But Hobbes, perhaps for the very reason that he was so vigorously opposed to revolution, saw that there could be a question of justifiable disobedience in situations in which authority based on consent was firmly established, in situations in which the withdrawal of consent and revolutionary behavior would not be seriously considered or would be clearly unjustifiable. Perhaps authority and law themselves, and the human purposes that authority and law serve, could sometimes be served better by *allowing* disobedience than by proscribing it entirely.

One way to see the persistence and importance of the issue Hobbes raises is to note the surprising parallels between Hobbes's arguments and the arguments of recent proponents of civil disobedience. Hobbes says that there are circumstances in which the subject can, without injustice, refuse to obey an authoritative command. But because the command is authoritative, the sovereign may, without injustice, punish the refusal. The civil disobedient also argues that it is sometimes justifiable to disobey admittedly authoritative commands and he too admits the sovereign's right to punish the disobedience. As with Hobbes, the civil disobedient hopes to avoid the undesirable consequences (he would usually say injustice) of particular laws or other authoritative commands without upsetting law generally or the authority structure that (logically) makes law possible. But the civil disobedient goes beyond Hobbes in insisting that the disobedient must willingly submit to the penalty that is assigned. Willing acceptance of penalties, Martin Luther King, Jr., argued, "distinguishes . . . civil disobedience from the 'uncivil disobedience' of the segregationist. In the face of laws they consider unjust, the racists seek to defy, evade and circumvent the law, and they are unwilling to accept the penalty. The end result of their defiance is anarchy and disrespect for the law. The . . . [civil disobedients], on the other hand, believe that he who openly disobeys a law, . . . and then willingly accepts the penalty, gives evidence thereby that he so respects that law that he belongs in jail until it is changed." [49] Hobbes, on the other hand, suggests that there are some penalties to which the subject is not obligated to submit. The subject resists without injustice, and then he and the sovereign do battle. (Again, resistance by the subject is apparently justified only if the sovereign determines that it will not destroy the institution of sovereignty —which presumably means that the subject is justified in fighting the sovereign only if the sovereign is sure beforehand that he [the sovereign] will win the fight, or perhaps that the subject will escape without destroying the sovereign. Hobbes in effect grants the subject the liberty to go out with a [small] bang instead of a whimper.)

The disagreement on this issue points to very fundamental differences between Hobbes and recent defenders of civil disobedience. But this disagreement should not be allowed to obscure the importance of the problem they both recognize. Stated very generally, the problem is as follows: most of us would agree that life in society would be difficult without authority and law and that authority and law would be ineffective if not meaningless if there were not ordinarily an obligation to obey them. The linguistic fact that "authority" ordinarily implies "obligation" might be viewed as a reflection of these beliefs. But we are also aware that the most carefully constituted systems of authority and law are sometimes used in a destructive or iniquitous manner. However necessary and justifiable it may sometimes be as a final resort, revolution is a crude and undiscriminating solution to this problem. Hobbes and the civil disobedients raise the question whether selective disobedience, disobedience that seeks to remedy particular iniquities or avoid certain ill consequences, without destroying authority and law, is sometimes a feasible and attractive solution to this problem. If a disjunction between authority and obligation serves the

49. Martin Luther King, Jr., "The Time for Freedom Has Come," *The Quiet Battle*, ed. Mulford Q. Sibley (Garden City, N.Y.: Anchor, 1963), p. 303.

purposes of law and authority, whether based on consent or something else, there can be no objection to it. If a relationship of covariance between the two disserves those purposes, the relationship must be modified. Authority and obligation ordinarily go hand in hand *because* the ends of establishing authority and obligation are ordinarily served by their doing so. They are sometimes disjoined *because* those ends or purposes require it. To use the fact that authority rests on consent as ground for insisting that there is and must be obligation wherever and as long as there is authority is to put an allegedly liberal doctrine to absolutist and authoritarian uses that not even Hobbes would condone. Thus the argument that consent to do X excludes or renders inappropriate consideration of the utility of doing X is conceptually unsound and politically objectionable. The fact that B has consented changes the situation in that it gives him a reason, ordinarily a strong reason, for doing X. But that reason is not always a good reason.

IV. CONCLUDING REMARKS

To show the invalidity of widely used arguments against a utilitarian account or defense of political obligation is not to show the validity of a utilitarian account or defense. A broadly utilitarian defense of the practice will be attempted in the next chapter. We will conclude the present chapter by emphasizing those points of a positive character that have emerged in the course of our attempt to refute or minimize the force of standard objections to utilitarianism.

The cardinal attractions of a consent theory of political obligation are twofold. First, such a theory puts political obligation in the realm of action rather than behavior. Second, it appears to emphasize, to place a high value upon, what might be called voluntarism or perhaps individualism. The individual largely determines his own political relationships and especially his political obligations, and political society assumes the characteristics of a voluntary association.

The first point is valid in the sense that obligations undertaken by consent are clearly in the realm of action. Insofar as it could be shown that political obligations are undertaken through genuine consent (express or tacit), some of the prominent but mistaken theories of obligation we have considered would be undercut. Our main point in this connection is that it is not necessary to show that an obligation was undertaken by consent in order to put it in the realm of human action. Accepting and acting upon a rule because one thinks it is a good rule is just as much a case of action (and much more common in human affairs) as is consenting to a claim or request. This is not a point against consent, but it is a point against stretching "consent" to "show" that consent theory does account for a respectable quantum of political practice. It is not a point against consent but it is a point against most consent theories.

The second point of attraction of consent theory is a much more problematical matter. A large part of the difficulty is indicated by the reluctance of the consent theorists themselves to accept fully the voluntaristic implications of a genuine or thoroughgoing consent theory of political obligation. Such a theory would give each individual a veto power concerning his political obligations. In fact we all have such a veto power in the sense that each of us can choose not to discharge his obligations. But to recognize this fact is not to concede that our choices will always be right and it is certainly not to concede that our choices are right because they are our choices. Thus all of the major consent theorists establish criteria of and constraints on "consent" that are not a part of the concept outside of the confines of their theory.

A consent theory of political obligation that did not place limits and constraints on consent would put forward a highly objectionable picture of political society as an ideal. As a member of the society in which A lives, B . . . N often have a very definite interest in what A does, hence in the factors that influence what A does, and hence in the obligations that A has and/or thinks he has. It may be attractive to A to be in a position to define his own political obligations, but it is not likely to be attractive to B . . . N that A be in such a position. Moreover, it is not likely to be attractive to A to have B . . . N each in a position to define his or her own political obligations. The very factors that lend significance to the notion and the practice of political obligation in a society militate against giving individual members of society complete control over their obligations. If the character of the members or the condition of the society was such as to make unqualified individual control over obligations workable and attractive, obligation itself would be superfluous. A theory urging the development of a society consisting of such human beings might put forward an attractive ideal but it would not put forward an ideal practice of political obligation. This argument, of course, by no means implies that the individual members should not participate in the social and political processes through which obligations are defined, assigned, and accepted.

One final point. Earlier we drew on the reflections of Hobbes in arguing the politically objectionable character of the thesis that authority based on consent is always a good reason for obedience, always a sufficient condition of an actual obligation to obey. We have now argued that it would also be objectionable to treat consent as a necessary condition of political obligation. Once again our argument has a Hobbesian flavor. In both cases the argument stressed the need to consider the ends or purposes of the practice of political obligation, a point that Hobbes makes in what, given the apparent formalism of his consent theory, is a remarkably powerful manner. But Hobbes thought that there is one overriding end or purpose to be served by political obligation and political society generally, namely making it possible for the individual members to avoid violent or premature death. We do not want to deny that he identified what is and should be a primary end or purpose of authority, law, and political obligation. But by excluding or undervaluing other ends or purposes he departed from practice and narrowed excessively the grounds on which to base both obedience and disobedience. Thus we must find ways to retain his salutary emphasis on ends and purposes while at the same time giving greater heed to the diversity of ends and purposes that are and/or should be served by authority, law, obligation, and political society generally. The often criticized capaciousness of the concept of utility will be an asset in this endeavor.

(8)

The Utility of Obligation

T HE QUESTION most prominently associated with the topic of political obligation is "Should I obey the law?". If this question arises in a practical manner, that is, in a particular time and place and with a particular law or other authoritative command at issue, we are very often able to answer it to our satisfaction. But the answer to it, while certainly making at least tacit use of considerations of general applicability, will always depend in critical ways upon characteristics of the situation at hand—e.g., the characteristics of the particular law in question, the consequences of obeying it in the time and place. Thus it will be valid or justified only for that situation and others that happen to be relevantly similar to it. Since there is no way of knowing for certain whether all or any future situations will be relevantly similar, there is no valid way of moving from the answer in the particular case to a general answer to the question; there is no way to move to an answer that will settle the practical question whether to obey or disobey whenever and wherever the question arises.

Political philosophers who have discussed political obligation have been accused of ignoring or failing to understand the foregoing point; they have been accused of trying to state conditions of obedience that are necessary, sufficient and entirely general.[1] Whatever the justice of this charge as applied to this philosopher or that, numerous philosophical discussions can be interpreted as attempting the entirely sensible enterprise of identifying the *kinds* or *types* of considerations that are relevant to deciding whether to obey or disobey. Philosophers have urged that citizens consider the will of God, the traditions of the society, self-interest, the characteristics of the regime or of those in authority in the regime, the justice of the law or code of laws, the social utility of obedience or disobedience, the benefits generated by the regime, the real good of the citizenry, and what has been consented to and not. To be told that one or more of these considerations is relevant to decisions about obedience is not to be told that one should obey or not in this case or that. The agent must determine what the will of God is concerning the case at hand, what tradition teaches or intimates, whether his interests would be served, etc.; and if more than one kind of consideration is relevant he must combine and weigh them as they apply in the circumstances. But he will not make these judgments if it does not occur to him to give consideration to the will of God, tradition, etc.

A more plausible charge against political philosophers is that they have excessively limited the kinds of consideration to be weighed. The will of God, consent, the full development of the personality—an entity like one of these is the only thing to be considered. But, while it is no doubt overdone in many cases, the tendency to reduce the range of considerations is not without justification. The question "(Why) should I obey the law?" arises only under certain quite definite circumstances. There must be authority, law, the notion of obligation or some equivalent, a notion that law is at once binding and yet subject to question, and other features of the practice of political obligation. The question of obedience to law could not arise (except

1. See for example Margaret MacDonald, "The Language of Political Theory," in Antony Flew, ed., *Logic and Language*, First Series (Oxford: Basil Blackwell, 1951).

for a person reflecting about the practices of other societies) in a society in which there were no laws and it could not arise (except for a person who stepped outside of the practice) in a society in which it was settled that whatever is called law in that society is always or never to be obeyed. Owing to the fact that the question arises only out of or as a part of such a practice, there are limitations on what will count as an answer to the question. For example reasoning that ignores or is based on ignorance of the relationships among "authority," "law," and "obligation" will not be relevant to answering the question. To take a more substantive example, in sixteenth- and early seventeenth-century England and France the notion of God's will played a crucial role in the practice of political obligation. A person who did not understand the significance of this notion in the practice would not have known how to deal with questions that arose within it. By contrast, in Soviet Russia the notion plays no part in the practice, and arguments for obedience or disobedience that made use of it would be out of place. In both cases, of course, a man might question the practice and argue that the notion of God's will should not, or should, be considered. But until he had succeeded in bringing about a change in the practice his arguments would be irrelevant to those thinking and acting within the practice.

In arguing that we ought to pay attention to certain considerations and not to others political philosophers may have been explicating the logic of the practice as they were familiar with it (or urging changes in that practice). To object categorically to this enterprise is to argue that the practice has no logical shape or character, that anything whatever is relevant to deciding questions that arise within it. Which is of course equivalent to arguing that nothing whatever is relevant to answering such questions. Particular political philosophers may have conducted this enterprise badly, but there is nothing wrong with the enterprise.

In the previous chapters we have explored characteristics of the practice of political obligation as it is disclosed by the rules governing the use of "obligation" and related concepts. We have suggested from time to time that our findings rule out or limit the significance of (except as recommendations for changing the practice) prominent attempts to answer the question "Why should I obey the law?". We will review a few of these suggestions to prepare the way for the main arguments of the chapter.

We have argued that "obligation" is used where there are precept- and regulation-type rules that are widely accepted in the society. We have also argued that guiding or being guided by such rules requires that the agent accept the rules because he thinks that there are good reasons for them. Thus the practice of political obligation is in that realm of human interaction that involves doing X or Y for reasons, not behaving in manner X or Y as the result of (sufficient) causes. In summary terms, political obligation is in the realm of human action, not in the realm of behavior. If this analysis is correct, theories that interpret the practice of political obligation as consisting exclusively or even primarily of behavior caused by force, fear, or habit are based on a misunderstanding of the concepts involved in the practice. Insofar as answers to questions about obedience are influenced by this misunderstanding, they are irrelevant to judgments made within the practice. Thus the view, argued by some anarchists, that law should never be obeyed because it is based on force is irrelevant insofar as the practice of political obligation as we have charted it is operative. Again, some writers have argued that men obey law out of fear or habit and that this is a good thing which ought to be continued. Such arguments are mistaken as analyses and irrelevant as prescriptions concerning steps that should be taken to assure that the discharge of political obligations continues.

Our thesis concerning good reasons for accepting obligation rules also suggests limits on various formalist theories of which consent theories are the most prominent example. Having consented to a rule is reason for accepting and obeying that rule; but having done so is not a necessary condition of accepting the rule and it is not always a good reason for obeying it in any particular case. (Nor is not having consented to a political obligation rule always a good reason for not accepting it or for disobeying it.) Consent theories call attention to a relevant consideration but they are mistaken insofar as they suggest that they have identified the only relevant consideration or a consideration that is always conclusive. We will suggest below that the same argument holds for a number of other prominent theories, for example the theories according to which having accepted or received benefits from a regime or having participated in the decision-making processes of a regime is a reason for obeying the rules promulgated by that regime. We have already argued this point concerning the view that the fact that a rule is authoritative is always a reason for accepting and obeying it. In the latter connection we have also suggested that to dismiss as irrelevant the fact that a rule is authoritative would be to recommend a change in the practice. This is also true of consent, and it may be true of benefits received, of participation, and of arguments based on the traditions of the society as well.

Thirdly, we have argued that there are a number of respects in which the practice of political obligation is intrinsically social. It depends upon language, it involves role concepts, and the notion of obligation requires second parties who can hold the agent to his obligations. Moreover, obligation rules are typically concerned with acts that not only have interpersonal consequences but also have consequences for institutions and arrangements shared among persons and for goals and objectives of societies and groups of persons as distinct from individuals taken alone. (Full employment or maintaining the rule of law would be examples of the latter.) The argument that the practice is intrinsically social does not exclude personal or individual considerations but it suggests definite limitations on them especially on radically individualistic theories which argue that the consequences of obedience or disobedience for the individual are the decisive criterion. The fact that obeying (or disobeying) a law will disserve my personal interests is a relevant consideration in deciding whether to do so. But it is a conceptual point that there is no valid inference from "Obeying this law is contrary to my interests" to "I have no obligation to obey this law" or from "It is in my interest to obey this law" to "I have an obligation to obey this law." Such reasoning would be no better than the argument of the judge who said: "My personal interest will be served by finding for the plaintiff; therefore I have an obligation to do so." The criteria of justified obedience or disobedience must take account of the social character of the practice of political obligation. All of these points hold for attempts to assess the merits and demerits of the practice qua practice as well as for reasoning about obedience and disobedience within the practice.

Reasoning concerning obedience and disobedience, in short, is not an unbounded enterprise in which anything goes. But neither is it narrowly limited to the practical application of one or two principles. The practice of political obligation has well-defined characteristics and dimensions that must be understood (though of course they can be called into question) and its characteristics are complex and many-faceted. Identifying, ordering, and defending them so as to facilitate reasoned judgments within and concerning the practice is a correspondingly complex task. The aim of this chapter is to take up this task. In doing so we will draw freely on previous efforts, especially the first systematic effort, namely that of Socrates in the *Crito*. We will try to show that, suitably interpreted and supplemented, Socrates identifies the kinds of considerations relevant to reflections about political obligation and orders and assesses them in a manner optimally conducive to effective reflection.

I. POLITICAL OBLIGATION AND SOCIAL UTILITY: SOCRATES' ARGUMENT IN THE *CRITO*

IN THE *Crito* Socrates is concerned with the problem of obedience in a form that has striking parallels with the problem as we know it in contemporary democracies. There is established authority and a presumption that there is an obligation to obey its legitimate commands. Socrates insists upon the importance of government and law, both for himself and all other citizens. Hence the problem of obedience is not assumed away by indulging anarchistic or hyperindividualistic simplifications. Further, Socrates finds much to respect in the polity that has condemned him to death, and he admits that he and the other citizens have greatly benefited from living within it.[2] As with all actual cities and governments, however, Athens has done injustice and other indefensible actions with regularity. Socrates will not be the first man who has been treated unjustly and he thinks it unlikely that he will be the last.[3] Nor is the injustice in the case at hand to be dismissed as trivial. The penalty in question is death, and the consequence for the city, and hence for its citizens, is the loss of an unusually valuable citizen and the gaining of a reputation destined to last through the centuries ahead.[4]

Faced with a decision as to how to conduct himself, Socrates can ignore neither the merits and importance of the city nor the injustice that it has done and is about to do. The conflict between them, scarcely an uncommon phenomenon in any politics, is commonplace in our time.[5]

Socrates states the issue before him as "[W]hether or not it

2. *Crito*, 506d, op. cit., p. 90. Unless otherwise indicated, all page references to Platonic dialogues are to this translation.

3. "They [a very large section of the people of Athens] have been fatal to a great many other innocent men, and I suppose they will continue to be so; there is no likelihood that they will stop at me" *Apology*, 28a-b, p. 59. See also ibid., 41a, p. 75.

4. See ibid., 30a, p. 62.

5. Our acquaintance with the substance of the problem examined in the *Crito* is complemented by the familiarity we perceive in Socrates' discourse concerning that problem. With the possible exception of the "blame not praise" rule, all of the features of discourse about obligation we have discussed above are present in the *Crito*. There is authority, but this is not taken to be a sufficient ground for obedience; Socrates is able to obey or not; there is a rule ("Judgments once pronounced shall be binding," *Crito*, 50b, p. 90) that is widely accepted and thought to be essential to the continued existence of the polity; disinclination to obey is evidenced (Socrates himself never evidences disinclination to obey, but Crito urges that he should not obey, and Socrates considers the argument important enough to counter it); most generally, Socrates thinks the question is to be decided by reasoned reflection and deliberation.

is right for me to try to get away without an official discharge." [6] But for us the significance of the immediate issue derives from the more general questions that lie behind it. To escape without official permission would be to disobey commands of the political authorities in Athens, to disobey Athenian law, and to refuse to submit to the penalties that Athens assigns for one or both of the former. Can we say, then, that Socrates' decision not to escape is a decision that it would always be wrong to disobey the commands of the Athenian authorities (and wrong to disobey authorities relevantly comparable to the Athenian authorities), that it would always be wrong to disobey the Athenian law, that it would always be wrong to refuse to submit to the penalties Athens assigned for disobedience?

In the *Apology* Socrates says flatly that he "would never submit wrongly to any authority, . . . but would refuse even at the cost of my life." [7] He cites two autobiographical "facts" ("What you can appreciate better" as he says contemptuously) to show that this is no mere theory but the creed by which he lived. The first was his refusal, as a member of the council, to acquiesce in a trial *en bloc* of Athenian naval commanders who had failed to rescue men captured in a battle at Arginusae. Such a trial, as everyone "recognized later," was illegal, and Socrates insisted, in the face of a threat of imprisonment and death, that the council not act "unconstitutionally." [8] Evidently, then, Socrates' principles did not require conformity to the commands of the constituted authorities under all circumstances. The incident, of course, tells us nothing about obedience to legitimate commands. And it is hardly conclusive concerning submission to penalty or rebellion. Socrates opposed the action despite his expectations of imprisonment and death, and it would appear that he did not contemplate resisting the latter.

The second incident occurred under the government of the Oligarchy, and it involved a command that Socrates "fetch

6. Ibid., 48c, p. 87.   7. *Apology*, 32z, p. 64.
8. Ibid., 32b–c, p. 64.

Leon of Salamis from his home for execution." Socrates believed that the object of the thirty commissioners in issuing the command was "to implicate as many people as possible in their wickedness." Socrates does not say explicitly that the action was illegal or unconstitutional. Perhaps such a statement was unnecessary given the general reputation of the Oligarchy. But this does not dispose of the problem. Although the Oligarchy ruled without a constitution, it was nevertheless recognized as an authoritative government, its commands were law, and to disobey them was to disobey law. Hence the incident provides some suggestion, though hardly conclusive evidence, that Socrates would disobey law. There is, however, no suggestion that Socrates would resist the authorities if they sought to punish him, and no suggestion that he would attempt to destroy their authority.

The most important passage on these points is Socrates' speculation that the charges against him in the *Apology* might be dismissed on the condition that Socrates "give up spending your time on this quest [for knowledge] and stop philosophizing." [9] Were such an offer tendered, Socrates vows, his reply would be: "[S]o long as I draw breath and have my faculties, I shall never stop practicing philosophy and exhorting you and elucidating the truth for everyone that I meet." [10] This categorical statement shows that Socrates would not always regard himself bound by the "law which enacts that judgments once pronounced shall be binding," [11] that there is at least one penalty to which he would not submit. It is explicit, however, that death is not such a penalty. If the state chose to "enforce" the first penalty by executing Socrates, he would not resist.

The *Apology* indicates, then, that Socrates would sometimes refuse to comply with the Athenian authorities, that he would sometimes disobey law, and that he would refuse to submit to certain penalties assigned by the authorities. Unless there is an inconsistency between the *Apology* and the *Crito*, the argu-

9. Ibid., 29b–d, p. 61. 10. Ibid. 11. *Crito*, 50b, p. 90.

ments of the latter must be interpreted as arguments for obedience and submission under certain conditions, not unconditionally. They must provide instruction as to how to decide when to obey and submit and when to refuse to do so.

Barely seven pages of *Crito* are explicitly and directly concerned with the question of obedience. But those seven pages contain discussion of a surprising number of the plausible arguments that have been advanced on the subject in more than 2,000 years. Simply taking the arguments in the order in which they appear, we read that the citizen should obey laws and other authoritative commands: (1) because he has agreed to do so, (2) because law and political society would be impossible without general obedience, (3) out of gratitude for benefits received from the political society, (4) because the particular regime in question is worthy of respect by the citizens, (5) because political society is extremely valuable, indeed "sacred" and "precious," (6) because the citizen has the opportunity to participate in the decision-making process and to bring about, through reasoned persuasion, changes in laws and commands that he dislikes, (7) because the citizen is free to emigrate if he cannot bring about the changes in the laws or commands that he desires, and (8) because the citizen, and his family, friends, and fellow citizens will be injured, both in this world and beyond, if he disobeys.

At first glance this extraordinary array of arguments, none of which is developed at any length, seems to be without order or structure. It is as though Socrates hoped that the very undifferentiated, unselective character of his attack would assure that no argument for disobedience would go unrefuted. But this is a most improbable hypothesis. In general distinction and discrimination are the essence of Socrates' philosophic method; and Socrates does discriminate among the various arguments in various indirect and subtle ways, showing that they play different roles in intelligent thinking about obedience and disobedience.

In sorting out Socrates' arguments we will employ the categories that Howard Warrender developed in analyzing

Hobbes's theory of obligation. Warrender distinguishes among the *ground* on which the argument for an obligation to obey rests, the conditions under which the argument is *validated* or *invalidated* in the case of particular laws or commands of a particular regime, and the *instrument* or instruments by which obligations may be assigned to or undertaken by individual members of a regime. Roughly, the ground refers to the reasons for the obligation, to the answer to the question "Why should there be an obligation to obey?" or "Why should I (ever) obey?". Validating conditions identify classes of cases in which a well-grounded obligation holds or not. To use Warrender's example, in most ethical systems the usual range of obligations do not hold for the insane and for young children. This does not mean that those who have obligations have them because they are sane or adult. "Nevertheless, the individual cannot be obliged if he is insane or a child. Sanity or maturity . . . operate . . . as validating conditions for obligations deriving from another source; or, to convert to the negative form, insanity or immaturity operate as invalidating principles for such obligations." [12] Instruments refer to how, to the means by which particular individuals sometimes acquire particular obligations. For example B, a sane adult, may acquire an obligation to do X by agreeing or contracting to do X. The obligation to keep agreements may be grounded in, say, social utility, nothing about B or his circumstances invalidates the obligation in his case, and *he* acquires the obligation to do X by agreeing to do so. None of Warrender's categories concern *what* the citizen or subject has an obligation to do. Given the characteristics of the theory that he is explicating, this is appropriate. Since we will continue to concentrate, as Socrates does, on obligations defined by law or other authoritative command, the categories will better display our discussion if we add one to Warrender's list, namely the "content" of the citizen's obligations.

12. Howard Warrender, *The Political Philosophy of Hobbes*, pp. 14–15 (London: Oxford University Press, 1957).

If the argument of the last chapter is correct there are many obligations to which the category "instrument" has no application and we will say little about it. The availability of a satisfactory ground, by contrast, is a necessary (but not a sufficient) condition of there being an obligation. (Belief that there is a satisfactory ground is a necessary condition of accepting an obligation.) Validating conditions clearly cannot be a sufficient condition of there being an obligation.

We will argue that for Socrates the ground of the obligation to obey is the argument that the state or political society is potentially of great value (argument [5]) supplemented by the instruction-type rule (which gives the content of most political obligations) that political societies would be impossible without general obedience to law and other authoritative commands (argument [2]). The argument concerning agreement (argument [1]) must be classed as identifying an instrument by which obligations can be undertaken. Since we have discussed the question of agreement at length we will say little more about it here. The arguments concerning benefits received, the general quality of the Athenian regime, the right to participate through reasoned discourse, and the right of free emigration (arguments [3], [4], [6], and [7]) are clearly validating conditions. Argument (8), that Socrates and his family and personal friends will be injured if he disobeys, is put forward primarily by Crito and is not effectively explored in the dialogue. Since it is an influential argument we will treat it as a separate category and examine the much more detailed presentation of it by Thomas Hobbes. We will argue that the foregoing summary is not only the proper interpretation of Socrates' argument but is the arrangement most conducive to intelligent thinking about obedience and disobedience.

A. *The Individual and the Well-Ordered State: The Ground of the Obligation to Obey*

Socrates says that for him to escape would not be merely to do an injury, but to do an injury "in a quarter where it is least justifiable." [13] When Crito says that he is not "clear in his mind" about this, Socrates entrusts the task of explanation to the Laws and Constitution of Athens who argue that in escaping Socrates will, insofar as it is in his power, overturn the Laws and the whole state as well. Evidently, then, the "least justifiable quarter" is the state. This point is reinforced later when the Laws contend that "violence is a sin even against your parents, and it is a far greater sin against your country." [14] The most general expression of the position is in the statements: "[C]ompared with your mothers and fathers and all the rest of your ancestors, your country is something far more precious, more venerable, more sacred, and held in greater honour both among the gods and among all reasonable men. . . ."; [15] "goodness and integrity, institutions and laws, are the most precious possessions of mankind. . . ." [16]

Why is the state of such extraordinary value? Socrates does not defend his contentions systematically or at length in the *Crito*. But we recall his belief that he owes his birth and above all his physical and cultural education to the Laws. Since he views such education, especially education concerning right and wrong, as necessary to the good life, he thinks that the state is of great value because it is in it and as a result of the value derived directly from its existence that numerous other values can be realized. Damage to the state is least justifiable because in damaging it one damages or endangers so much that is important to man.

It must be stressed that this argument does not support the charge that Socrates is what we might call a statist, that he views the state as a good in itself to which all other goods are to be subordinated. [17] There are states, for example Thessaly,

13. *Crito*, 49d, p. 89. 14. Ibid., 51d, p. 91.
15. Ibid., 50e–51a, p. 91.
16. Ibid., 53c, p. 94. The last two passages quoted are extracted from sentences that are interrogatives. It is clear from the context, however, that the clauses we have quoted are intended to be declarative of Socrates' view.
17. We take the liberty of using the anachronistic term "state" in discussing Socrates in part for brevity of expression, in part to emphasize

that are the home of "indiscipline and laxity," that do not provide the education, training, and other conditions that make a good life possible. So far from regarding such states as sacred or precious, Socrates prefers death to life within them.

The state in itself, then, is not a good. There are states that are precious and sacred, but they are precious and sacred because they are well-formed states that make possible "higher forms of human society." [18] We might say that the value of the state is instrumental, that its value derives from the fact that certain goods are attainable only where the state exists. This would be closer to the truth than a statist interpretation but it would be misleading because there are some goods that are simply a part of, simply come along with, a well-formed state. Since they are attainable only through the existence of the state, their value is identified with the state and the state is valuable because of them. Since the two are inseparable, it is misleading to think of the state in purely instrumental terms.

Argument (5), then, is that the state is important because it is at least a necessary condition of the attainment of higher forms of human society. But this argument provides a ground for obedience only if the state in question is a well-ordered state. Later we will try to show that arguments (3), (4), (6), and (7) validate argument (5) in the case of Athens (and validate it for any state that meets the criteria established in [3], [4], [6], and [7]). Argument (5) is the ground because it provides a reason for thinking that it is valuable to have a state that meets the criteria of (3), (4), (6), and (7); (3), (4), (6), and (7) are validating conditions because without argument (5) we would have no reason to think that the values discussed in (3), (4), (6), and (7) would be available only, or best, where there is a state.

---

that for all of the differences between the political society Socrates knew and the modern state, Socrates' views concerning obedience are relevant in our time, and in part to facilitate access to the significance of differences between his thinking about political society and later conceptions of it.

18. *Crito*, 53c, p. 94.

Socrates' willingness to talk of the state as precious and even sacred is likely to offend or at least disquiet the modern reader. Although we recognize that he is not a rabid statist on the model of, say, Treitschke or worse, the fact remains that we have been taught by a whole tradition to think of the state not as precious but as at best a necessary evil, and even as an alien force that must be checked and controlled lest it wreak destruction upon us. Nor can this tradition be dismissed as a record of the thought of small-minded men. It grew out of and is supported by a considerable part of man's experience with the state.

Despite this tradition, the state has become an ever more salient part of our lives. If we do not speak of it as "precious" or "sacred" we nevertheless look to it for solutions to a positively immense array of problems—by no means excluding the problem of achieving what Socrates spoke of as a "higher form" of human society. Our rhetoric and no doubt the bases of much of our thinking remains different from Socrates' but our actions betoken the conviction that our goals and purposes as individuals and as a society are indeed dependent upon the workings of a well-ordered state. Thus a challenge to Socrates' estimate of the importance of a well-ordered state would be credible only if it was also a challenge to a very wide range of the values, goals, and much of the organization of our society. Short of such a challenge, if it is true that the practice of political obligation is an integral part of the state it would follow that the practice contributes in important ways to the achievement of our goals and purposes as individuals and as a society. It would follow that the practice has considerable social utility.

But our discussion of the matter has subtly conceded far too much to the very way of thinking about the state and politics which makes it difficult to appreciate the force of Socrates' argument (5). Thinkers in the tradition of political thought to which we alluded earlier, roughly the Anglo-American liberal tradition, never doubted the importance of what they called the state. But they tended to view it as an entity discrete from the society in which it operated, an entity which was to be thought of less as an integral part of the society than as standing apart from and acting upon, for good or ill, the society with which it was connected. Thus they developed a distinction that has no place in the *Crito* or in Greek political philosophy generally, the distinction between state and society. Of course this distinction was drawn in part in order to facilitate presentation of their conception of the *proper* or *desirable* role or place of the state. The particular manner in which the distinction was drawn varied with the particulars of each theorist's conception of that role. For the moment, however, their views concerning the role of the state are of less interest than the analytic questions that are raised by the distinction they employed in presenting those views.

As is explicit in Locke—and the more emphatically so in Tom Paine—the view that the state is discrete from the society in which it operates was taken to support the belief that the state might undergo radical change and even disappear without changing the society except in the sense that the state would no longer be doing the things that it had been doing for or to the society. The state not only consists of institutions and arrangements that are distinct and discrete, it receives its support and sustenance from beliefs, attitudes, and commitments that are largely independent of the larger pattern of social beliefs, attitudes, etc., that obtain in the society.[19]

In rejecting this view (to speak anachronistically once again) Socrates presents in nonconceptual terms some of the important implications of the analysis we have developed in previous chapters. When Socrates says that he and his fellow citizens have benefited from life in the Athenian regime he is commending not just the laws or the governmental institutions in the narrow sense, he is arguing that the polis or city or political society, of which the governmental institutions and

19. For a detailed discussion of these ideas see Sheldon S. Wolin, *Politics and Vision* (Boston: Little, Brown, 1960), Chaps. 9 and 10.

laws are an integral part, is such that men can live a life of excellence within it. Particular laws and orders depend upon, reflect, and are otherwise influenced by other features and characteristics of the society and cannot be understood or assessed apart from them; and the decision to obey or disobey laws and orders should take these relationships into account.

We have in effect been detailing respects in which Socrates' view is correct. The heart of our analysis of "obligation" is the notion that the concept is used, and the practice operates, where there are rules that are widely accepted and thought essential to the basic goals and objectives of the society. Obligation rules presuppose language that is shared among men and they require second parties who know what B's obligations are and who can hold him to their discharge. Some of this language, and some of these relationships, can appropriately be described as political in character in the sense in which that term has been used in drawing the distinction between state and society or between social and political aspects of human interaction. But in this sense of "political" and "state" the generic phenomena of language and interpersonal relationships hardly deserve these labels and it is obvious that specifically political examples of them presuppose the existence of the generic phenomena. Again, in the case of regulation-type rules the content of the rules is largely determined by individuals in positions of authority and thus in positions distinguishable in important respects from other positions in society. But such positions of authority exist only where there are rules not promulgated by authority, rules that develop and attain standing in a manner common to numerous rules that we would not think of as political. Thirdly, we tried to show that regulation-type rules share with precepts a dependency upon shared experience that supports a judgment that particular ways of acting will in fact have certain predictable and desirable effects. Here again features of society that, as such, we would not call political are an essential part of political rules and the process that leads to their passage. In Chapter Five we suggested that the acceptance of obligation rules, whether regulation- or practice-type, and whether political in content in the narrow sense of having specifically to do with government or the state, integrates or binds together groups of men into the sorts of collectivities that we call societies and/or political societies. This might be taken to support the Lockean view that societies could exist without political arrangements and processes. It is better taken as evidence that both social and political relationships involve the evolution and acceptance of rules of conduct and ways of doing things concerning which the distinction between social and political is extremely difficult to draw. Finally and most generally, we have emphasized the intimate connections between rules and rule-guided conduct on the one hand and reasons and reasoned discourse on the other. Particular reasons, reasoning, and examples of reasoned discourse may have a political content; they may presuppose political arrangements and relationships in the narrow sense. But reasons, reasoning, and reasoned discourse are neither political nor nonpolitical phenomena; they are human processes and phenomena and there can be political reasoning or reasons only because this is so.

It does not follow from these remarks that the distinctions between social and political or between state and society are meaningless or necessarily misleading. Nor does it follow that it is never possible to single out laws or political institutions for criticism or attack. Socrates' respect for Athens did not prevent him from objecting to particular laws or from attacking the Oligarchy as a corrupt government. But when an unjust legal order prompted him to think systematically about obedience he moved swiftly from a consideration of the particular order to the more general and more fundamental characteristics of the regime from which that order emanated. To think about political obligation apart from obligation in general, and to think about obligation apart from the larger pattern of rules and rule-governed conduct of which it is a part, is to think of them in partial, incomplete terms. In this sense at least it is to distort them. Finally, it does not follow that politics and the state are simply derivative of other features of human interaction. For reasons stated most explicitly by Aristotle, the ancient Greeks thought of man as a political being and thought of the political aspects of his existence as primary. But whatever labels we choose to use, the point that needs emphasis is the need to understand the manifold interconnections and interrelationships among those aspects of human life and association which, for various purposes, we distinguish one from the other.

Viewed from this perspective Socrates' argument (5) is not merely an argument for the value of the state or government in the narrow sense of particular institutional arrangements, particular laws, or even the processes of interaction most immediately and specifically connected with government and laws. It is an argument for the value of living in an association in which the state and its laws, in integrated and mutually supportive combination with numerous other practices, arrangements, and ways of doing things, together provide a context in which men can aspire to "higher forms of human existence." We have tried to show that the practice of political obligation is integrated in a larger pattern of practices, arrangements, and ways of doing things and hence that Socrates is correct in his view that general assessments of its utility as a practice must be based on an understanding of its place in a larger pattern of things. Stated in the terms used above, to be credible a general challenge to the practice would have to involve not only a challenge to particular goals, objectives, and values of the society, it would have to involve a challenge to the principles of association and interaction out of which those goals, objectives, and values evolve and win acceptance.

B. The Well-Ordered State and Obedience to Law: The Content of Political Obligation

There is nothing in argument (5) that shows that *obedience* is essential to realizing the values that the well-ordered political society can make available. Disobedience is as much a part of the practice of political obligation as obedience, and there is nothing in the argument to indicate that disobedience damages the state or the larger association. Socrates attempts to show that obedience is important through argument (2). The Laws ask: "Can you deny that by this act [escape] . . . you intend, so far as you have the power, to destroy us the Laws, and the whole State as well? Do you imagine that a city can continue to exist and not be turned upside down, if the legal judgments which are pronounced in it have no force but are nullified and destroyed by private persons?"[20] Socrates asks Crito whether their reply to the Laws should be: "Yes, I do intend to destroy the laws, because the State wronged me by passing a faulty judgment at my trial." Crito accepts the reply without question. Socrates intends, of course, to criticize and reject the reply. But none of his criticisms question the statement that to escape would upset the Laws and the State.[21] Rather, he assumes that it would do so and argues that to injure the State in this way is ordinarily wrong.

If accepted, argument (2) would supply a case for obedience. Actions that contribute to higher forms of human society are right actions, actions that interfere with the development of such higher forms are wrong; a well-ordered State is a necessary condition of the achievement of higher forms of human society; law is necessary to a well-ordered State; disobedience makes law and a well-ordered State impossible; hence disobedience to a well-ordered State makes a higher form of human society impossible; hence disobedience is wrong. Since Athens is a well-ordered State, to disobey it is wrong. Hence for Socrates to escape is wrong.

Argument (2) raises anew questions concerning the relationship between the general rule "Obey the law" and the particular rules enunciated by any law, legal order, or other authorita-

20. *Crito*, 50a–b, pp. 89–90.
21. In keeping with the practice of the translator we will hereafter capitalize "State" when using it in the inclusive sense that Socrates has in mind and that we have discussed above.

tive command. When we discussed this question earlier we stressed the importance of being able to defend the particular rule in question, of not relying entirely on the case for the general rule to bring about or to justify obedience. We urged that obedience could best be achieved and most easily justified where the particular rules can be and are defended. We did not argue, however, that it is unimportant to defend the general rule, either in its application to a particular law, in the political society in question, or yet more generally. To have done so would have been to suggest that it is always wrong to obey particular rules that cannot themselves be defended—or perhaps that there is no point in or no possibility of meaningful thought about whether to obey such rules. Granting Socrates' view that the particular order addressed to him was indefensible, it would suggest either that it was (and is) obvious that Socrates should not obey the order or that there is no point in thinking about the question of obedience. By advancing argument (2) Socrates indicates that he does not take either of these views. By taking the hemlock he indicates that he thinks that there are cases in which arguments for the general rule provide good reasons for obeying particular rules that in themselves are indefensible.

But why should we accept argument (2)? What is there to make us think that refusal to obey a legal order will upset "the Laws and the whole State as well"? The Laws adduce no evidence to justify a prediction that Socrates' escape will cause turmoil or upset. Nor do they make any use of the now familiar "contagion" argument, the argument that disobedience by one person somehow prompts or encourages disobedience by others. Indeed, they simply make *no* predictions as to the effects of Socrates' escape.

If Socrates escapes, they argue, he "intends" "so far as" he has the "power," to destroy the Laws and the State. Since the consequences of Socrates' disobedience depend upon his "powers," it would seem that we would have to assess those powers in order to determine the consequences of his disobedience. But the Laws make no attempt to assess his powers. "So far as" is compatible with any amount of power (including none) and nothing more is said on the subject.

These considerations suggest that the rule announced by the Laws is more a logical or conceptual rule than an empirically based generalization. The reasoning is not spelled out, but it might be along the following lines. A legal judgment properly settles the question to which it is addressed. If it is nullified by private persons, in the sense in which Socrates' escape would nullify the judgment in his case, those persons do not treat it as a legal judgment and it does not have this effect. Hence *any* refusal to obey legal judgments, in and of itself and without considering any further consequences, serves to some degree to destroy the law. A judgment that is not taken as binding does not do what a legal judgment is defined as doing. Judgments that do not settle the issues to which they are addressed are not legal judgments in the full sense. Hence refusal to obey "destroys" the judgment that is disobeyed. If a well-ordered State is one that is governed by law, refusals to obey legal judgments upset such a State; they mean that matters are settled by non-legal means where this should not be the case.

The force and implications of this argument depend in large part on the concepts used in making it. Socrates speaks of law, the city and the State. As we noted in Chapters Two and Three, given that it is appropriate for him to use these terms in the circumstances at hand, it is also appropriate to use the concept "authority." There is no law or State, and no city in the sense in which Socrates uses the concept, without authority. We noted above that to say that a command is authoritative is to say that there is an obligation to obey it unless the case falls under a recognized exception, disobedience is excusable in the circumstances, or a justification can be given that meets the arguments for obedience. Putting the same point another way, to say that a command is authoritative is to say that issuing the command will ordinarily settle the question of *proper* action in the situation which the command concerns; the fact that the command has been issued provides the agents involved with reasons for acting in the manner required by the command. To deny this, to deny that the command affects the situation in this way, is either to deny that the command is authoritative or to urge a change in the use of "authoritative." Thus in using the concepts he does Socrates is reminding Crito (and anyone else who accepts the Athenian regime and the language as it is in the respect in question) that there are reasons for accepting the general rule.

But he is also doing more. He does not simply describe Athens as a State or city with laws and hence as an institution with authority; he extols this institution as sacred and precious. Since it is a matter of definition that there is no State or law without authority he also extols authority as one source of those values available to men where there is a well-ordered State. The man who denies that there is reason for accepting and obeying the general rule also denies that there is reason for having an institution to which the concepts "authority," "State," and "law" are applicable. Thus strictly speaking argument (2) is redundant given argument (5). Argument (2) serves only to remind Crito of some of the implications of accepting argument (5). But the entire argument is more than a reminder of conceptual facts because it depends upon an affirmation of the value of the State. It is this affirmation that gives cogency to the argument that in diminishing the effective operation of authority disobedience "damages" the State and hence is wrong.

Interpreted in this way, it would be difficult to reject argument (2) altogether. But the interpretation also reduces the conduct-guiding significance of the rule, reduces the degree to which it is clear from the rule itself that violations are undesirable and to be avoided. In Socrates' case, for example, where the penalty is both unjust and severe, if the consequences of disobedience are restricted to the nullification of a single legal judgment it is less than obvious from that fact alone that he should submit to the penalty (or that any similar person in a similar situation should do so). Disobedience might damage the State in one respect, but it might support or contribute to it in others—e.g., minimizing the injustice done by it. Socrates, of course, does not draw this conclusion. Perhaps this is because *he* had reason to expect more than the minimal upset required by argument (2); perhaps because he did not view the penalty as severe or because escape was distasteful on other grounds; perhaps he was, on this point, a rigid formalist who insisted upon obeying a rule despite the consequences; perhaps because he felt that the rule was extremely important owing to the volatile and often irrational populace of Athens and wanted to set a dramatic example that would help buttress the regime. All of these points can be read into the dialogue but Socrates does not reveal his thinking concerning them or their relative importance. Thus Socrates gives us little guidance in identifying considerations relevant to deciding how to assess argument (2).

Many of the attempts to take this matter further than Socrates did involve the notion that disobedience is "contagious." The immediate or direct consequences of A's disobeying a law or legal order may be insignificant or perhaps even beneficial. But A's disobedience sets an example or otherwise influences B . . . N in a manner that makes it more likely that they too will disobey laws or legal orders. If this happens the resulting upset and damage will be much more substantial than that resulting directly from A's disobedience taken alone. Whether because of the numbers involved, or because of the differences between A and B . . . N or their circumstances, what might otherwise have been defensible disobedience is rendered unjustified.

The contagion argument is based on, largely consists of, the empirical, causal generalization that one act of disobedience causes, brings about, contributes to, or otherwise influences the likelihood of other acts of disobedience. Very little attention has been paid to clarifying the formulation of the generalization such that the evidence requisite to support, refute, or determine the limits of its veracity can be gathered, and very little attempt has been made to gather such evidence. In periods of widespread disobedience (for example the late 1960's in the United States) the generalization is widely encountered as an explanation for the incidence of disobedience and as an argument against further disobedience.[22] Of course it should hardly need saying that a high incidence of disobedience does nothing *to establish* that disobedience has been contagious. It is always possible that the same considerations or forces that led or caused A to disobey also led or caused B . . . N to disobey. Not being in a position to verify the suggestion that disobedience was contagious in any particular case we must proceed hypothetically as regards the empirical questions. Our purpose will be to clarify the logic of the generalization and to explore the question of the conditions under which arguments based on it are of practical value in deciding whether to obey.

The argument is, as a practical matter, useless if A (a person considering or otherwise displaying an inclination to disobedience) is: (1) not acting rationally in the sense of deliberating about what to do and attempting to make his decision on the best evidence and reasoning available to him, or (2) is acting rationally but is convinced that it would be desirable for him to disobey *and* desirable for others to follow his example and disobey as well. An example of case (1) would be a man committing a "crime of passion." The knowledge that others might imitate his crime will not influence him not to commit it. We should note that this is a type of case in which something that might be called a contagion effect can sometimes be established quite conclusively. A commits a crime, often a "horrible crime," and soon thereafter B commits a very similar crime. When B

22. For examples of this use of the argument see the remarks of Mr. Justice Whittaker in Charles E. Whittaker and William Sloane Coffin, Jr., *Law, Order and Civil Disobedience* (Washington: American Enterprise Institute for Public Policy Research, 1967). See also Lewis H. Van Dusen, Jr., "Civil Disobedience: Destroyer of Democracy," *American Bar Association Journal*, Vol. 55 (February 1969): 123–26. Morris I. Liebman, "Civil Disobedience—A Threat to Our Law Society," *American Law Quarterly*, Vol. 3, (1964): 21–26.

is apprehended we learn that he knew of and was excited or otherwise influenced by A's crime. An example of case (2) would be the actions of a revolutionary. Revolutionaries fully intend to influence others to disobey. Telling them that others will follow their example will positively encourage them to disobey. Here again A's influence on B can sometimes be firmly established.

The second point about A calls attention to the fact that the applicability of the argument also depends on the characteristics of B (the person or persons who might be caused or otherwise influenced to disobey by A's disobedience). It is a general difficulty with the argument that it is cast in terms which suggest that A's disobedience is a necessary and perhaps even the necessary and sufficient condition of B's disobeying. The metaphor encourages us to think of B's disobedience on the model of his having caught the measles or the flu. It results from his having been "exposed" to a "virus." We should note that we do not ordinarily criticize people for catching the measles. On this way of thinking about disobedience the most we could say in criticism of B is that he had not maintained the sort of moral regimen that would keep up his resistance to the "germs" spread by A. (Or perhaps we could say that he had recklessly exposed himself when he could, and should, have remained in a more antiseptic environment.) The blame or the credit for B's disobedience goes primarily to A.

Perhaps we aren't expected to take the contagion metaphor quite so literally. Perhaps it is intended to exaggerate A's influence or causal efficacy in order to make him more cautious about disobeying. Yet there are cases which the metaphor fits tolerably well. B might be in a psychological state such that he will respond directly and positively to A's example. He would not have thought to disobey if A hadn't done so and A's disobedience uniformly, and without evidence of any reflection or deliberation on B's part, is followed by the latter's disobedience and by testimony such that it is clear that B was following, even imitating, A's example. If so, and if A knew it to be so, the contagion argument would certainly be a relevant consideration as A reflected on whether to disobey. Indeed this is the kind of case in which the argument is most obviously relevant to A's deliberations.

Whether it counted for or against disobedience, of course, would depend on whether A thought B's disobedience desirable or undesirable. Moreover, even assuming that A thought B's disobedience undesirable, it wouldn't follow that the contagion argument ought to be conclusive against his disobedience. A might reflect that other influences in the society could and should be brought to bear on B to prevent him from responding inappropriately to the stimulus supplied by A's disobedience. Short of there being a relationship between A and B such that A had a special responsibility for B's behavior, A might reflect that he should not be held responsible, or not peculiarly responsible, for the misuses to which other members of the society put his ideas or the example set by his conduct. This position would be especially cogent if B generally displayed the characteristics we have assigned him in the above example. We ordinarily expect society to take special precautions with people who respond unreflectively to such stimuli.

It is a point about the concepts involved, however, that if any very substantial part of a society behaved in the manner we have assigned to B there would be no practice of political obligation as we know it. That practice is in the realm of human action, and in that realm A's doing X cannot be a necessary and sufficient condition of B's doing X. B must *decide* to do X. It follows that in the realm of human action A cannot know with the certainty we have been discussing that his disobedience will be followed by B's disobedience. Of course A's disobedience can influence B in various ways and experience to this effect will sometimes warrant an expectation that A's disobedience will be followed by B's disobedience. But even if this expectation is very well supported by experience, the fact that B *decides* to disobey allows A to respond to C's use of the contagion argument against his (A's) disobedience in the following manner: "I am not going to *make* B disobey. He is a free agent who obeys or disobeys as he sees fit. I think that my disobedience is justified and I am prepared to defend it to you or anyone else. If you think B's disobedience would be unjustified go talk to him and persuade him to obey."

This response has a good deal of force and cogency. To dismiss it completely would be to take a very condescending attitude toward B and to place potentially very narrow limitations on A's activity. The only reason that it is not entirely conclusive is that it might be impractical for C to talk to B—to talk to all of the potential B's. In a society of any size C cannot hope to reach all those persons who might be influenced by A's disobedience. Just as it is sometimes thought necessary to silence a speaker rather than to persuade (or otherwise influence) the crowd responding to the speech to conduct itself in a civil manner, so it may be thought necessary to forego the initial, influential act of disobedience rather than to deal with the response to that act by the large number of people who might be influenced by it.

But these are no more the only alternatives in the case of disobedience than they are in the case of the speaker and the crowd. The speaker who does not want the crowd to riot can sometimes influence them not to riot and yet convey the message he had come to communicate. Similarly, A might take steps to influence B's response to his disobedience. For example he might indicate why he thinks his disobedience is justified and urge those not in a similar situation to obey. Or he might, as civil disobedients often do, attempt to communicate his general understanding that disobedience is a serious step that involves consequences which the disobedient must accept. Doing so might prompt B to reflect about the larger issues involved. His doing so will not necessarily prevent B from disobeying but it will certainly make it hard to argue that A caused B to disobey.

In the case of controlling crowds the policeman and the society on behalf of which the policeman is supposed to act are not limited to responding to the particulars of each situation that arises. If they limit themselves in this way they will not be very successful. They can, and they should, develop and seek to convey a more general understanding of the purposes and significance of speech and assembly in the society so that the response of audiences to speakers is influenced by that understanding as well as the particulars of the speech, the speaker, or the circumstances in which the speech is made. The case is the same with disobedience. If C is concerned about the contagious effects of disobedience his efforts to control and prevent them need not be restricted to advising A not to disobey or advising B not to imitate A's disobedience in this particular case. C can work toward the sort of society in which, as we tried to suggest in Chapter Two, "epidemics" of disobedience would be unlikely. (Recall in this connection our argument that those who obey uncritically or habitually bear some responsibility for widespread disobedience among those who have become dissatisfied with the obligation rules in the society and the manner in which they are developed and sustained.) If he and others would do so society might develop to the point that the case for "silencing" the disobedient on grounds of the contagion argument—and hence doing without the sometimes valuable results of disobedience—would diminish or even disappear.

Since there are few if any such societies, and since disobedience is often harmful (a point to which we return immediately below), the contagion argument cannot be entirely dismissed. But some people in some societies do act in the manner just sketched some of the time. Thus there are circumstances in which A can justifiably reject the contagion argument despite agreeing that it would be undesirable if many people followed the example of his disobedience. Which in the end is the main point to be made about the contagion argument. The contention, *simpliciter*, that disobedience is contagious is of value only as propaganda. When the available distinctions have been drawn it is clear that our knowledge about B's response to A's disobedience allows of few if any reliable generalizations. Knowing what he does about the society in which he lives, if A thinks that his disobedience would be justified he must make the best judgments he can in the circumstances in which the decision to obey or not arises. Of course the fact that he does not know how B will respond can be used as a ground for caution concerning disobedience. On the other hand he could argue that it is insulting to B to assume that he (they) will disobey when doing so would be unjustified. More important, it could be argued that acting on the opposite assumption might itself contribute to making that assumption true; that if the members of a society treat one another as rational men until they have specific evidence to the contrary, their mutual capacities to be rational will be stimulated and developed.

The contagion argument must be regarded as a problematical consideration in reflection about obedience and disobedience. Its conceptualization is misleading, the empirical generalizations on which it depends are not well established, its practical applicability is limited, and the assumptions on which its normative force depends are subject to serious question. Certainly it does not provide anything like a generally conclusive argument against disobedience which, aside from its allegedly contagious character, would be justified.

It does not follow that the only general argument against disobedience (as opposed to arguments based on the merits of particular laws or legal orders) is Socrates' highly formal argument (2). Part of the difficulty with the contagion argument is that it urges A not to disobey on the ground that the consequences of B's disobedience will be bad. A less problematic argument concerns the consequences of A's own disobedience and particularly the difficulty A is likely to have in anticipating those consequences adequately. In a tolerably stable political society the existence of a law regulating X brings about uniform conduct on the part of large numbers of people. It also leads them to expect that the other members of the society will conduct themselves in the manner required by the law and to count on their doing so in the sense of making commitments, arrangements, etc., based on that expectation. When A disobeys the law this expectation is upset. The arrangements based on it may then be rendered inappropriate with resulting inconvenience and/or injury to the persons who made them or are affected by them. If B adjusts his conduct to A's disobedience he may inconvenience C, etc., and a sequence or chain of consequences may ensue. Whether the sequence goes far enough to be called political upset, it may do serious injury to individuals. Of course it is always A's responsibility to try to anticipate the consequences of his actions and to be sure that he can justify them in the light of those consequences. In this respect the act of disobedience is not different in kind from any other action that has or might be expected to have other regarding effects. But the difficulties involved in anticipating consequences are compounded when A's action involves or affects an arrangement or institution shared and depended upon by large numbers of people—the vast majority of which A does not know at all.

It might be objected that this argument shares with the contagion argument the vice of asking A to base his decisions on consequences about which he does not and perhaps even cannot know. This *is* a difficulty with the argument and it is one of the reasons why it does not provide a general and conclusive argument against disobedience. But it does not follow that the argument should be dismissed as irrelevant to deciding to obey or disobey. Although A does not know exactly what the consequences of his disobedience will be, experience can teach him that disobedience often brings about unintended and undesirable consequences for others. If the benefits he hopes to generate by disobeying are modest, and/or if there is reason to doubt the efficacy of disobeying in bringing those benefits about, this knowledge might properly decide him against disobedience.

This argument can be extended somewhat when dealing with a society in which the political institutions, processes, and leadership have and deserve respect and confidence. The political institutions and arrangements are designed to facilitate gathering the information and acquiring the perspective and understanding necessary to defensible judgments. They are also designed to facilitate the selection of leaders responsive and responsible to the people. If they in fact do so with any regularity, the basis is laid for a presumption in favor of the decisions and judgments made by the political leadership acting through the political institutions. Put another way, a presumption is created that the political leadership had reason to believe that the members of the society would benefit if the law in question was passed and if the members of the society obeyed that law. When A finds himself in disagreement with a law or for other reasons inclined to disobey it, it is appropriate for him to raise the question whether his information and perspective are sufficient to challenge the judgment of the leadership. He should ask whether he can be confident that his acting in a manner prohibited by the law will not have injurious consequences for others, consequences of the sort that the leadership had anticipated and that had led them to pass the law, consequences which he, lacking their information and perspective, is unable to foresee.

This argument or consideration by no means constitutes, in general, a conclusive reason against disobedience. Ideally it should always be buttressed or even rendered superfluous by more particular arguments in support of the law or order in question. Moreover, good information and perspective do not guarantee good judgment and the political leadership has no monopoly on information, perspective, or judgment. But to dismiss the argument altogether might imply that there is no need for political institutions, leadership, and law. At best it would suggest that they are valuable only because it is sometimes better to have a common rule of conduct—however poorly devised—than no common rule at all.[23]

23. For further examination of the idea that laws are valuable chiefly because they provide a common rule to settle disagreement, see the discussion of the views of John Rawls below, pp. 286–290.

C. The Validating Conditions of the Argument for an Obligation to Obey

The last argument for obedience that we considered would carry little if any weight for, say, a Benthamite utilitarian in Calvinist Geneva. His experience with the political process and the political leadership would create a presumption *against* the laws of the regime. Assuming that he accepted Socrates' argument (5) he would be thrown back on the argument concerning the difficulty of assessing the consequences of his disobedience or on the formal argument advanced by Socrates' argument (2). But even these arguments would properly carry little weight with him if he believed that the regime failed to meet the criteria of what Socrates calls a well-ordered State, if his attitude toward the regime was like Socrates' attitude toward the regime in Thessaly. In such a circumstance he might obey a particular law because it chanced to be a law as well as a good rule or he might obey laws out of fear that disobeying them would weaken the regime and lead to yet a worse one. (For example a man might have obeyed the Rumanian government in the 1930's out of fear that weakening it would contribute to takeover by the German Nazis.) [24] But the decision to obey in such cases would not be grounded in Socrates' argument (5) or supported by argument (2). The latter apply, are validated, only when there is reason to believe that the continued existence of the regime in question will contribute to "higher forms of human life." There may be occasions on which it would be proper to obey regimes that debase the lives of their populace, but the considerations relevant to deciding to do so are distinct from, and much more ad hoc than, Socrates' general argument for obedience. Thus we must examine the conditions that validate argument (5).

1. THE WORTHINESS OF THE ATHENIAN REGIME

The most general formulation of the validating conditions of

24. Socrates' contention that it would be better to die than to live in Thessaly suggests that he rejected this line of thinking as regards regimes that are "the home of indiscipline and laxity." See *Crito*, esp. 52–53, pp. 94–95.

argument (5) is argument (4), namely that the Athenian regime, although imperfect, is worthy of respect. The very generality of the argument limits its utility; we must know why the regime is worthy of respect, what the criteria of "worthy of respect" are in this kind of case. For this reason it is tempting to interpret (4) as a summary statement indicating that the more specific criteria Socrates mentions are satisfied by Athens, not as a criterion with significance independent of the others.

It would be a mistake, however, to view (4) exclusively in this light. While we would always want to know why a particular regime was worthy of respect, it might be impossible to formulate the reasons for our respect in terms appropriate to a general argument. For example Socrates says that he approves of the Athenian laws concerning education. He could no doubt say what it is that he approves about those laws. But it would not follow that he would approve only laws on education that had the characteristics of the Athenian laws or that he could usefully abstract from the characteristics of the Athenian laws general criteria that should be satisfied by any such laws. Moreover, some other regime might have unsatisfactory laws on education but have other features that would make it worthy of respect. In other words, argument (4) indicates that it is impossible to state the necessary and sufficient conditions of a regime being worthy of respect. Socrates tries to identify types of features or characteristics that are especially significant and of general relevance, but each regime must be evaluated on its own merits in important respects. This point is important in itself and because of the perspective in which it places the more specific criteria-cum-arguments for obeying Athens that Socrates puts forward.

2. BENEFITS RECEIVED

Turning to the more specific criteria, we will begin with the argument that Socrates has an obligation to obey because he has received important benefits from the Athenian regime.

The Laws contend that "we have brought you [Socrates] into the world and reared you and educated you, and given you and all your fellow-citizens a share in all the good things at our disposal. . . ." [25] Socrates agrees that the Laws have done so and says that he is grateful.

It would be difficult to argue that Socrates should not be grateful. The question is whether his receipt of these benefits provides good reasons to accept an obligation to obey the laws and commands of Athens. Despite the fact that he values the benefits highly, we know from the *Apology* that Socrates did not think that they bound him to obedience in all cases. Past benefits could not put him under an obligation to do a seriously wrong act. It is difficult to quarrel with this position. If past benefits constituted a sufficient condition of obligation any citizen who had received benefits from, say, the Nazi regime would have an obligation to obey the commands of that regime. It might be argued that the citizen who intended to continue to accept benefits from that regime, even after learning of the bestial policies of the regime, would be obligated to obey its commands. But this too, while no doubt accepted by the regime in question, is an offensive doctrine. It is a perversion, though not an uncommon one, of gratitude to treat it as a basis for requiring wrongdoing. True gratitude sometimes requires a refusal to cooperate in the hope of preventing the agent or agency to whom gratitude is owed from doing wrong. Or to put the point another way, true gratitude requires acting so as to prevent the political society from deteriorating to the point that it cannot benefit other members of the community as well as the agent himself. In a political society that benefits its members as substantially as Athens had (by his testimony) benefited Socrates, this requirement will often, indeed most of the time, be best satisfied by obedience. But situations may arise in which disobedience would be the appropriate way to meet it.

But perhaps past benefits would make obligatory an action that is wrong but not seriously so, undesirable but still right

25. Ibid., 51c–d, pp. 91–92.

(the best thing in the circumstances), or right but distasteful to the individual. But we must ask whether having received benefits should be decisive. Let us assume that Socrates had been born and reared elsewhere, only recently emigrated to Athens, and was arrested and tried before he had enjoyed an opportunity to partake of the benefits generated by Athens. His disobedience could nevertheless have either desirable or undesirable consequences—for example leading to changes in an injust law or subverting the authority of the law. If so the fact that he had not received benefits would hardly be decisive as to whether he should disobey.

These arguments do not prove that the question of benefits is irrelevant to the question of obligation. Whether Socrates had personally received benefits is not a sufficient basis for decision. But the fact that the regime generates benefits may be of considerable importance. If the regime benefited no one, or benefited only a few at great cost to others, it might be right to undermine it.[26] By emphasizing the benefits that he and "all his fellow-citizens" had received, Socrates indicates that there is at least this reason to think the Athenian regime worth preserving. When combined with the argument that escape would undermine the regime and hence make further benefits impossible, this fact leads him to conclude that it would be wrong to escape. Benefits received, by Socrates and "all his fellow-citizens," contributes to validating the general argument against undermining governments in its application to the Athenian regime. Taken alone, past benefits are not a sufficient ground of obligation. When generalized so as to consider benefits to the community, and when combined with assumptions concerning the effects of disobedience, they contribute to the validation of an obligation to obey.

To assess these points further let us think of them in connection with urgent practical issues of our own day. Consider

26. We must say "might be" only because once again one would have to know something about the probable consequences of undermining the regime.

the question whether black Americans have an obligation to obey the law. Black Americans have undoubtedly benefited less (and suffered more) at the hands of the American regime than other segments of the population. If obligation is grounded in benefits received there is a strong case that these citizens are not obligated to obey, or not obligated to obey in many instances in which other Americans would be obligated. Socrates' argument, however, suggests that the dismal performance of the American regime in this respect is relevant to questions of obligation, but not peculiarly to the obligations of blacks or any other segment of the American population. The failure of the regime indicates flaws in it and raises questions concerning the degree to which it is deserving of obedience. If the distribution of benefits is wrong, and if (or to the extent that) disobedience (under various conditions) is the only or the best way to right that wrong, then it will, in principle, be good or right for *all* citizens to disobey. Conversely, if the distribution was not wrong, or if disobedience (or disobedience of a particular kind under particular circumstances) would make impossible the distribution of benefits to the community in general, it would be wrong for blacks or for anyone else to engage in disobedience because of the distribution of benefits. The question, in other words, turns upon judgments concerning the regime and its impact on the entire community. The distribution of benefits to individuals or groups is evidence relevant to those judgments.

Socrates' argument about benefits received calls attention to normative dimensions and implications of themes that have recurred throughout our analysis. "Obligation" is used to guide conduct where there are rules that are widely accepted in the regime or group and where it is widely thought that conformity to the rules in question is essential to the continued existence or at least to achieving the minimum objectives of the regime. If discharging obligations is a virtue it is a social virtue par excellence. Acceptance of such rules binds the members of the regime into a collectivity such that the crucial question in deciding what to do in a particular case is the consequences of the available options for the collectivity. It does not follow that the consequences for individuals are irrelevant. The collectivity has no existence apart from individual members and the objectives of the community will have to do with the character and quality of the lives of those members. Thus it does not follow that questions of distributive justice are irrelevant. But it does follow that consequences of actions for individuals are not properly relevant only or even primarily to those individuals. If the action of the regime affects A in a manner contrary to the regime's conception of the manner in which its members should be treated, his treatment is properly of concern to all members. Of course just as society may largely delegate the task of enforcing obligation rules to police and other specialists, so it may, in more informal ways, in effect leave the task of disobeying unjust rules to particular groups. But such practices do not alter, indeed they reinforce, the significance of the fact that the rules are addressed to and concerned to maintain characteristics of the collectivity. The most salient evidence for the fact that this view is widely accepted is that members of the collectivity respond—and think they should respond—very differently to what happens to members of other collectivities than to what happens to members of their own.

From the standpoint of the benefits-received argument then, the question of whether the argument for obedience has valid application to black Americans is no different from the question of whether any other member of the society has a valid obligation to obey. The question turns, at least in the first instance, on whether the treatment accorded black Americans, whether viewed absolutely or comparatively, violates the rules designed to assure that the regime maintain itself and achieve at least its minimal goals as a regime. Insofar as the question of validation turns on benefits received or not, and insofar as black Americans have not been treated in a manner that accords with the minimum objectives of the regime, the regime has failed to achieve its objectives in this respect and the argument for obligation grounded in Socrates' argument (5) and validated or not according to argument (3), is not only invalidated for blacks but for all members of the regime.

To decide the practical question under the rubric of obligation, then, one would have first to know about the situation of black Americans and about the obligation rules of the regime and the conception of its minimum goals that they reflect and embody. Both are in large part a matter of public record that is quite accessible. (This, of course, is why so many people have concluded that in respect to the situation of its black citizens—to mention only the most salient case—America stands condemned by its own criteria.) It requires no esoteric research to discover that the rules of the United States Constitution are thought to embody minimum objectives of the regime and that insofar as the rules are violated without redress the regime has failed to achieve those objectives. Nor is it difficult to establish that these conditions have often not been satisfied as regards black Americans—to take again, only the most salient case. And the notion of constitutional rules and of laws passed under the authority of the constitution presupposes the notion of the rule of law. Here again the record is anything but satisfactory.

We could go on at great length detailing respects in which black Americans have not been treated according to the principles on which the American regime itself is based. For present purposes the important question is the significance of dismal facts such as these for thinking about political obligation. The first point to notice is that a showing that the argument for an obligation to obey is invalidated is not a showing that there is an obligation to disobey or even that it would be right or good to disobey.[27] More than one conduct-guiding concept can

27. The notion of an obligation to disobey was employed by idealist political philosophers such as Green and Bosanquet but it is only recently that it has come to have currency in nonphilosophical discourse. Although the idea that disobedience is sometimes justified is widely accepted, few regimes have developed the sort of rules concerning disobedience

apply to a particular action. The very fact that the concepts differ shows that invalidating the argument for the application of "obligation" leaves open the question of the applicability of other concepts. As closely related as they are, the decision that there is no obligation to obey is not the same as the decision to disobey. To decide to disobey one would have to have good reasons for thinking that the consequences of disobedience would be desirable. If a regime was officially and publicly committed to worthy objectives, and if it achieved them some of the time, there might be grounds for thinking that it would be good to obey, or to restrict disobedience narrowly, in order to maintain the regime so that its performance could be improved. As already noted, even a regime with few redeeming features might be obeyed if doing so was necessary to avoiding a worse one. Thus a showing that the argument for an obligation to obey is invalidated eliminates what is ordinarily a good reason for obedience. It does not do more than that.

Secondly, as Socrates uses the notion of benefits, the fact that a regime does or does not benefit its citizens is only one of several criteria by which it should be judged and in terms of which the argument for an obligation to obey can be validated or invalidated. Socrates never says that satisfaction of any of the criteria, or any combination of them, is a necessary or a sufficient condition of validating the argument for obedience. Thus a showing that one criterion is satisfied or not cannot be

---

that would give the notion of an obligation to disobey established standing. Germany amended its constitution so as to allow disobedience under certain circumstances, but it is a right of disobedience not an obligation to disobey. See Article 20, Section 4 of *The Basic Law of the Federal Republic of Germany*. International tribunals came close to the notion of an obligation to disobey in trying cases arising out of the Second World War, but these decisions apply to only a few countries and their present standing in those countries is problematical. It is worth noting that if such rules were established they would define the conditions under which there is such an obligation and thus have the effect of increasing the extent to which the practice of obligation was tied to characteristics internal to the regime in question. Where there are no such rules the person who speaks of an obligation to disobey is either speaking loosely or metaphorically or trying to win acceptance of a rule.

more than a weighty consideration for or against obedience. We might consider the argument validated in the case of a regime which generated few benefits but encouraged active political participation among its citizens and allowed free emigration on the part of those who are dissatisfied. Socrates tells us only that these are factors we should consider. How to weight them must depend on the details of the circumstances at hand and the argument that can be built out of them.

The third point concerns our emphasis on the conception of the minimal goals of the regime embodied in the obligation rules or otherwise manifested from within the regime. Concern with standards and norms internal to the society in which the question of proper conduct has arisen is always an appropriate first step in thinking about such questions. Because of the rule-dependent character of "obligation" it is especially so as regards questions that arise under that concept. But it does not follow that those standards and norms cannot be questioned or that we cannot make use of standards, norms, or arguments not accepted in a regime in judging the worth of that regime. Conflict among standards widely accepted or among members of the society as regards which standards should be accepted will often require that we do so. But even where such conflicts do not obtain, we may, whether outsiders or insiders, find the regime worthy or not according to criteria that have no standing within it. Thus we might judge the Nazi regime unworthy on the grounds that it regarded members of certain racial or ethnic groups as intrinsically inferior. Until such time as this criticism was accepted within the regime it would not affect the question of the obligations assigned to its members and it would not alter the fact that, according to the norms of the regime, there are good reasons for accepting and discharging those obligations. A person who rejected the obligations that were assigned him on the basis of a principle that had no standing in the regime would be engaged in a radical enterprise: the enterprise of challenging not merely the decisions and judgments of the regime but the basis on which its judgments and decisions are made. That this enterprise is possible and very important does not alter the fact that it is difficult and often costly to the person or persons who engage in it.

a. Addendum: Hart and Rawls on benefits received as a basis of obligation   In Socrates' theory benefits received figures as one important argument for obedience. In influential articles H. L. A. Hart and John Rawls have developed versions of the benefits-received argument and have assigned it a more important place in thinking about obligation than Socrates accords it.[28] Readers familiar with their articles will recognize important similarities between them and the adapted version of the Socratic position developed here. There are also important differences, however, and some of these should be noted. Since Hart's discussion is a very brief aside in an article on rights, we will concentrate on Rawls's more developed version.

Both Hart and Rawls stress that it is not individual receipt of benefits, *simpliciter*, which creates political obligations. It is receiving benefits generated by a cooperative practice which involves rules that restrict individual action. Also, they both wish to distinguish their arguments from consent theories of obligation. Their position nevertheless involves a difficulty familiar from consent theories. On their argument, having benefited from a cooperative practice is a necessary condition of having obligations under it. Indeed Rawls enlarges the importance of the condition by saying that the individual must intend to continue to accept benefits. In his words: "[I]f the constitution is just, and if one has accepted the benefits of its working and intends to continue doing so, and if the rule is enacted within certain limits, then one has an obligation . . . to obey it when it comes one's turn." [29] Because it also requires

28. See H. L. A. Hart, "Are There Any Natural Rights," *Philosophical Review* 64 (1955): 175–91, reprinted in Anthony Quinton, ed., *Political Philosophy* (London: Oxford University Press, 1969). John Rawls, "Legal Obligation and the Duty of Fair Play," *Law and Philosophy*, ed. Sidney Hook (New York: New York University Press, 1964).

29. Rawls, loc. cit., p. 9.

a just constitution and laws "within certain limits," this formulation allows a number of ways out of obligations incurred by accepting benefits. Hence the argument as a whole does not create the problem we illustrated with the example of Nazism, namely that having accepted benefits obligates one to obey a regime that does evil. (In short, having accepted benefits under a cooperative practice is not a sufficient condition of having an obligation to obey.) But it does seem that a person who consistently refused to accept any benefits, or even who decided not to accept any further benefits, would thereby exempt himself from the obligation to obey. Thus if B decides to emigrate from the United States, Rawls's language suggests that he thereby nullifies his obligation to pay his income tax for the last year of his residence, to pay parking tickets he had incurred prior to his departure, and to discharge any other legal obligations which did not involve acts that are *malum in se*. If so it is difficult to see how a government could justify compelling him to pay his taxes, etc., or to urge his new government to compel him to do so.

Interpreted in this way, the benefits-received argument seems to give B a veto power over his obligation. He can nullify his obligations by deciding not to accept benefits. He does not have to show that the law in question is unjust or otherwise make reasoned arguments against it. To use one of Rawls's criteria for the sake of brevity, this conclusion seems to us to be "counter to our intuitive judgments." [30]

Of course Rawls might argue that the decision to emigrate exempts B from future obligations, not from those already incurred. If he takes this view, the only case in which the benefits-received argument would itself serve to exempt B from legal obligations would be if B had never received benefits from the practice. Thinking about this kind of case calls attention to the problem of deciding what counts as having received benefits. Leaving aside the uninteresting case of B's having only

30. Ibid., p. 18.

just arrived, B might refuse welfare payments, not use parks, highways, and other public facilities, not call the fire department if his house is burning down, etc.—that is, he might refuse a large number of the particularized benefits generated by the cooperative practice. In our time this is to say that he could live as a recluse or hermit. But even the recluse benefits in important ways from the fact that there are laws that others obey. As a practical matter "receiving benefits" and "living in a political society" (especially one with a just constitution) are one and the same thing (are extensionally equivalent). No one who lived in a society would be exempted from political obligations by the benefits-received doctrine.

When given the importance Rawls and Hart assign to it, the benefits-received argument creates the same problem that arises in consent theory. Depending on the interpretation given crucial but ambiguous terms, obligations are *either* justified *or* nullified much too readily. Taken as *the* principle underlying and justifying political obligation, benefits received is simply not very helpful in thinking about how the practice does or how it should work.

As noted, Rawls says that accepting benefits creates an obligation only in a just constitution. In this respect he builds into his theory many if not all of the other validating conditions Socrates stresses. And since he obviously thinks it is desirable to live under a just constitution, it may be that he is also assuming a version of what we have called the ground of obligation in Socrates' theory. (It seems to be a Humean or even Hobbesian version. Note his quasi-utilitarian remark: "Unless one obeys the laws enacted under [a just constitution], the proper equilibrium, or balance, between competing claims defined by the constitution will not be maintained.") [31] In this perspective our disagreement is simply that he places more weight on one aspect of his argument than it will bear. We suggest that it is the combination of principles or arguments

31. Ibid., pp. 10–11. See also p. 17.

that does the work of supporting the argument that one has an obligation to obey.

But Rawls's emphasis on a just constitution and the benefits it generates calls attention to a second difficulty with his argument. In order to solve the apparent paradox involved in obeying an unjust law passed under a just constitution, Rawls treats the constitutional procedures through which legal rules are promulgated as "a process of social decision that does not produce a statement to be believed (that B is the best policy) but a rule to be followed. Such a procedure, say involving some form of majority rule, is necessary because it is certain that there will be disagreement on which is the best policy. . . . The acceptance of a constitutional procedure is, then, a necessary political device to decide between conflicting legislative proposals. If one thinks of the constitution as a fundamental part of the scheme of social cooperation, then one can say that if the constitution is just, and if one has accepted the benefits of its working and intends to continue doing so, and if the rule enacted is within certain limits, then one has an obligation, based on the principle of fair play, to obey it when it comes one's turn." [32] Aside from the phrase "if the rule enacted is within certain limits" (at least some of which would presumably be identical to the requirements of the just constitution), this formulation directs attention, so far as obedience and disobedience are concerned, away from the quality of the particular legal rule and to the constitution under which it is passed. In the terms we have been using it directs attention away from the particular rule and to the general rule and a particular kind of defense for the latter.

Readers of earlier chapters will not accuse us of denying that the general rule is relevant or important to questions of obedience. But we have argued throughout that the question of whether good reasons can be given for particular rules is a vital question *from the standpoint of political obligation*. The crux of the matter is in Rawls's statement that constitutional

32. Ibid., p. 9.

procedures (for example those governing the legislative process) produce not "a statement to be believed" but a "rule to be followed." If "a statement to be believed" means "a rule of conduct that one accepts because there are good reasons for it," Rawls's contrast between such statements and "rules to be followed" is not coherent. B *cannot* be said to be following a rule unless he thinks there are good reasons for it. He may do what the rule requires because he accepts some other rule which, in the circumstance, requires the same action, because he is coerced, or for some other reason. He does not follow the rule. Rawls in effect urges him to do what the particular rule requires *because* there is another rule or rules, in this case the rules of the just constitution and the rule of fair play, which, in the circumstance, also require him to do what the particular rule requires. The reasons to be considered and given for his obedience concern the constitutional rules and the rule of fair play, not the content of the particular rule. Thus his argument has a consequence we have been contending against throughout this essay, namely taking reflection and discourse about the content of particular legal rules all but out of the practice of political obligation. If our earlier arguments are correct, this position is mistaken as an analysis of the practice and unfortunate as a recommendation about how the practice should operate.

3. Reasoned participation

Although Socrates does not explicitly rank the validating conditions that he discusses, there are indications that he regards number (6) as most important. According to (6) Athenian citizens have the opportunity to participate in the lawmaking process and to bring about, through reasoned argument, changes in the laws they dislike. The Laws say: "[O]ur orders are in the form of proposals, not of savage commands, and we give him [Socrates and all citizens] the chance of either persuading us [in accordance with universal justice] or doing what we say." [33] Despite his harsh strictures against the Athenian

33. *Crito*, 52a, p. 92.

populace,[34] Socrates believes that the foundations of the regime facilitate and encourage reasoned discourse about issues of public concern. Apparently he also believes that some group of men, presumably those responsible for establishing and maintaining the foundations of the regime, are capable of and not indifferent to such discourse. Socrates claims that it is always his aim to discover "the best course that reason offers," [35] that this is best done through serious conversation or dialogue, and that it is impossible to hold a serious conversation with people who do not have this aim.[36] Hence these facts are obviously of cardinal importance to him (and to anyone with similar views). If the Laws did not have these characteristics, and if there were not some men capable of making appropriate use of them, examination of the question of the obligation to obey would be a waste of time if not impossible in the regime.

We must remind ourselves again that Socrates disobeyed or said he would disobey despite these facts. It was not his view that disobedience is never justified in a regime with these characteristics. Reasoned argumentation does not guarantee defensible conclusions. And it hardly needs to be said that regimes that generally display the characteristics the Laws claim for Athens sometimes take on a very different character in particular circumstances or on certain issues or questions. The possibility that disobedience would be the only effective counter to or remedy for such eventualities cannot be dismissed. It is nevertheless very important that the citizen can hope to influence the conduct of the regime in a manner less erratic and unpredictable than disobedience. We suggested earlier that where the methods of decision-making which the Laws claim to use are characteristic of a regime, a presumption is created in favor of its laws and commands. This is because a presumption is created that there are reasons for the law in question (even though an individual citizen may not know what they are) and that the law will be changed if the reasons

34. They "put people to death, and would bring them back to life if they could, with equal indifference to reason" ibid., 48c, p. 87.
35. Ibid., 46b, p. 84.   36. Ibid., 49b–d, p. 89.

for it can be shown to be bad reasons. Given this presumption (and assuming there is no evidence that the presumption doesn't hold in the circumstances at hand), a person who accepts argument (5) and either (2) or the extensions of (2) we proposed above will disobey only if he believes that the evil of the law or command in question is both pressing and severe.

It is important to stress in this connection that Socrates is not advancing the now familiar argument that the possibility of participation as such is an important validating condition. If the laws are passed by holding political shoving matches with the wishes of the winners of the matches becoming law, the fact that I participate in the matches (whether I win or lose) adds not one whit to the case for obeying the resultant laws. Such a process of "passing" laws, including my participation in it, gives me no reason for thinking that the laws are good laws and/or that my obeying them will have good consequences for those affected. If the laws are passed by such a method I may want to participate in the hope of protecting what I conceive to be my interests. But participating in a shoving match won't help me to determine whether my conception of my interests is correct and it certainly won't help me to determine whether any of the proposed laws would be in the public interest. The possibility of reasoned participation in the law-making process is important largely because it is through reasoned discourse that my best interests and the public interest are best determined.[37]

4. RIGHT OF EMIGRATION

The Laws "openly proclaim this principle: that any Athe-

37. The fact that the laws are open to persuasion by reasoned discourse is also important in connection with the question of "freedom not to do" discussed in Chapter Five. To begin with, it makes it more likely that I will find reasons to accept the laws as good or at least defensible. And even if I find a particular law bad or indefensible the fact that it is not a "savage command" might encourage me to accept the general rule "Obey the law" as it applies to the particular law in question. If I find even this impossible the fact that the regime proceeds by the method of reasoned discourse might give me a reason to abstain from resisting the penalty I incur by disobeying the law. Argument (6) plays the third of these roles in the specific case under discussion in the *Crito*.

nian, on attaining to manhood and seeing for himself the political organization of the State and its Laws, is permitted, if he is not satisfied with us, to take his property and go away wherever he likes. . . . [N]ot one of us Laws hinders or prevents him from going . . . without any loss of property." [38] If a person remains in Athens under these circumstances he signifies his approval of the regime and undertakes "under no compulsion or misunderstanding" [39] to live his life "as a citizen in obedience to us." [40]

The policy of allowing unpenalized emigration is certainly admirable in itself and it may speak well of a regime in more general ways as well. It suggests that the regime is confident that it provides an attractive setting for human life and that men will choose to remain in it and even to enter it because of the desirability of doing so. Membership in the regime is based on choice, can be based on reasoned choice, not on "compulsion or misunderstanding." Thus taken as an indicator that the regime is "well-ordered" and deserving of respect this feature of Athens is certainly relevant to validating the argument for obedience grounded in Socrates' argument (5). The relevance of the consideration is particularly striking in an age in which many of the regimes of the world conduct themselves in a manner more analogous to prison camps than on the principle which the Athenian Laws enunciate.

The Laws, however, suggest that there are tighter connections between the right of emigration and the obligation to obey than the foregoing remarks suggest. They argue that the citizen has an obligation to obey *because* he is free to leave and has chosen not to do so. The right of emigration, together with the decision not to exercise that right, is the *ground* of the obligation to obey not a mere validating condition of the argument for such an obligation. Commonly employed in our own day, this argument is unacceptable.

The Laws take the view that a man who, upon "attaining to

38. Ibid., 51d–e, p. 92.   39. Ibid., 52d, p. 93.   40. Ibid.

manhood," chooses to remain in Athens, thereby commits himself to strict obedience. In this respect the argument is a version of the consent or agreement argument and it has the same shortcomings as the latter. The fact of agreement or commitment to stay rather than the continued quality of the regime is treated as the basis of the obligation to obey. In fact, the decision to remain should be treated as an indication that the person in question judges the regime to be a good one that merits his respect.

What follows from that judgment is neither obedience or disobedience as such, but such conduct as will contribute to the regime continuing to deserve respect: obedience where it is appropriate, etc. The regime should want of the citizen critical, reflective conduct, not a commitment to undeviating obedience.

Leaving aside the contractarian aspects of the argument, the use the Laws make of the right of emigration encourages the citizen to leave the regime if he objects to a law or set of laws so strongly that he cannot obey them. From the standpoint of the conduct of the regime (as opposed to that of the individual) this policy smacks all too much of an attempt to deal with dissent and conflict in a superficial, ad hominem manner, that is, without getting at the difficulties that prompted the dissent and conflict. Although generally an obedient citizen, Socrates had objected to and sought to change a number of the characteristics and practices of Athens. To banish him would not eliminate those characteristics and practices and would not answer his objections to them. It would only eliminate an important source of questioning and criticism and a force for change.[41]

---

41. Socrates' penalty was of course death not banishment. That death would also have the effect of silencing Socrates' dissent and criticism is a point to which Socrates himself gives too little attention. But there are indications that the Athenians hoped that Socrates would in effect transform his penalty from death to a kind of banishment or ostracism by escaping. Crito not only urges that it would be right for Socrates to escape, he makes it quite clear that Socrates could easily escape if he decided to do so. (See esp. Crito, 44b–d).

Of course the Laws might respond that they do not want dissenting citizens to leave, only to obey. They are welcome to remain and criticize so long as they do so within the established procedures of the regime—which of course they are also free to try to change so long as they do so by lawful means. If, however, they are unwilling to use the methods of dissent and criticism allowed by the law they ought to leave. As an argument to justify penalizing a disobedient citizen this view seems altogether unobjectionable. The regime cannot be expected to abandon the enforcement of the law because some citizens object to a particular law or some other characteristic of the regime. It is also unobjectionable as a general argument for obedience. But when tied to the right of emigration it takes on the objectionable connotation of (the now highly familiar) "If you don't like it here, go somewhere else." To insist that disobedience, even justified disobedience, will be punished need be to insist on no more than that the regime will not sacrifice the rule of law in order to remedy some other difficulty or evil in its operation. It need not be to insist that disobedience can never be justifiable and even important. And to make a general argument against disobedience is not necessarily to take the view that disobedience can never be justified. But to argue that any person who is unwilling to obey the law (for whatever reason) should leave is precisely to take the view that the regime can never benefit from disobedience, that its members can never be so blind to its evils, that its procedures can never become so clogged or distorted, as to benefit from the sometimes dramatic and forceful method of political action known as disobedience. We know of no regimes that would be (or would have been) warranted in taking this view.[42]

The argument is also objectionable if it is used by the in-

42. Although account would have to be taken of the differences between political and educational communities, the above remarks are relevant to current discussions of how educational institutions should come to terms with disruptive activities on the part of students and others. They raise questions about the policy most analogous to banishment or ostracism, namely expulsion.

dividual as a basis for choosing to leave the regime rather than making an effort to remedy it. Of course this is sometimes the only effective, even the only possible, course of action. But where this has been the case it has usually also been true that the regime in question did not allow free emigration anyway and was an extremely bad regime in other respects as well. The argument put forward by the Laws has objectionable effects when a member of a generally good regime, who objects to particular laws or policies, leaves the regime on the ground that one should either "live in obedience" or leave. If the regime is good, if he has good reasons for thinking that the law or policy has seriously undesirable consequences, and if he has good reasons for thinking that disobedience is the only effective way to bring about a change in the policy or law, then his commitment to the regime and the principles on which it is built urges him to remain and disobey, not to emigrate.[43]

43. As we noted in Chapter Seven, insofar as the argument based on free emigration involves the notion of agreement, Socrates clearly rejects it. Since he was willing to disobey Athens he also rejects the view that one ought either always to obey or leave. His decision to take the hemlock, however, suggests that he believed that this and the other arguments he uses require the conclusion that one should never resist the punishment assigned for disobedience. One can attempt to persuade the state that certain punishments ought never to be used or ought not to be used in a particular case (as Socrates does, albeit in a somewhat contemptuous manner, in the *Apology*), but if unsuccessful he must submit. To resist the punishment is to forego the method of reasoned discourse on which the regime generally, including the right of emigration, is based and hence to violate the very principle that must be appealed to in justifying disobedience. Even for Socrates, of course, the prohibition against resistance applies only in good regimes. The *Crito* is not to be interpreted as a condemnation of all resistance to penalties or all rebellion. But it is difficult to accept the almost unqualified condemnation of resistance in well-ordered regimes. Violence is not itself a rational instrument or method, but there are times when its use can be defended on rational grounds. Socrates seems to accept this as regards the state (the hemlock is scarcely a rational instrument), but to reject it for the citizen. There is much to be said for his view as the basis of a general rule of conduct. Violence harms other persons in ways reasoned argument and even disobedience to most laws (laws against violence would be an exception) cannot do and resistance to penalties upsets the state in ways that mere disobedience to law does not. Thus (as civil disobedients have always recognized) there are circumstances in which disobedience is justified but resistance to penalties is not. The latter has consequences beyond the

II. POLITICAL OBLIGATION AND PERSONAL
INTEREST: THE ARGUMENT OF HOBBES

THE FINAL ARGUMENT that Socrates considers is that he should obey because it is in his personal interest to do so. Crito urges Socrates to refuse to submit to the hemlock on the ground that it would harm Socrates, his family, and his closest friends. Socrates first dismisses this sort of consideration as irrelevant.[44] Later, however, he troubles to argue that it would be personally advantageous as well as right to submit.[45] Crito's view seems to be that personal interest is a decisive validating or invalidating condition and perhaps even the ground of obedience and disobedience. Since it is contrary to Socrates' interest to submit, he ought not to do so. In Socrates' argument personal interest is certainly not the ground and may be a validating condition only in a derivative sense. One must do what is right, and the

consequences of disobedience and justifications for it must take account of those consequences. But we could accept an unqualified condemnation of resistance to penalties in well-ordered states only if we could know for certain that the consequences, for the regime, of resistance will always be worse than submission. It is a logical point that such certainty is not available to us, and more than a little experience testifies that resistance to penalties is sometimes beneficial. Thus the general rule must be regarded as defeasible. (Socrates does make one exception to this rule, namely his insistence that he would never submit if his penalty was that he cease to philosophize. If we read "philosophize" to mean "think and discourse critically" we could take it to be a potentially large and important exception. Since Socrates is convinced that very few people are capable of philosophizing—in the sense just stated or any other—it is not a very large exception in his mind. Also, since Socrates does accept a penalty, death, that has the effect of causing him to cease philosophizing, the practical importance of the exception is diminished in his own case. And the fact that he has elevated, or at least uncommon, views about living and dying does not alter the fact that his death deprives Athens of an extremely valuable citizen. The fact that he gives no explicit attention to this point is the single greatest deficiency in the argument of the *Crito*.)

44. "If it becomes clear that such conduct [escape] is wrong, I cannot help thinking that the question whether we are sure to die, or to suffer any other ill effects . . . ought not to weigh with us at all in comparison with the risk of doing wrong." *Crito*, 48b–e, p. 87.

45. *Crito*, 53a–54b, pp. 94–95.

question of personal interest is not relevant to determining what is right. But it is a fact that doing what is right is personally advantageous at least in the long run. In other dialogues Socrates argues that doing the right or acting justly is, in point of fact, *always* personally advantageous. Thus on Socrates' use of the argument it has no independent significance in his decision as to what to do.

Crito's position also suggests that discharging one's obligations and acting to serve one's interests are, existentially, one and the same thing, but in his case "interest" is the operative concept not "obligation" or "right." Thus discharging one's obligations is not, or is not very often, something that one must or ought to do despite the fact that he does not want to do it. This would be the case only if a person did not want to act so as to serve his own interests. As we said at the outset of the chapter, this is not a very plausible account of the way the concept of "obligation" and the practice of obligation work. But it can be formulated, was formulated by Hobbes, so as to appear to be a plausible account. Moreover it has proven to be perennially attractive as a view of how the concept and the practice ought to work. Thus it deserves examination. Unfortunately Crito proves to be a very undetermined advocate of his own position, giving way to Socrates when the latter has done little more than employ a more high-toned vocabulary. In order to examine the position in a developed form we will turn to the more articulate and systematic formulation of Hobbes. We will then be in a position to summarize Socrates' argument and make some broader comparisons between Socrates and Hobbes, comparisons that will bring us back to the question of ideals and obligations with which we began and provide an appropriate note on which to conclude.

We have noted a number of reasons why it is not cogent to say: "It is in my personal interest to do X and therefore I have an obligation to do X" or "It is contrary to my personal interest to do X and therefore I have no obligation to do X." Hobbes nevertheless makes a sustained and not obviously unsuccessful effort to defend exactly these propositions. He defends them not only as cogent but as the only defensible foundation for political and all other kinds of obligation. The crucial moves in his argument are two: first he transforms "interest" into a purely objective concept such that "in the interest of B" is synonymous with "good for B" and such that B's understanding of or testimony concerning what is in his interest is in no way privileged, has no more authority than A's understanding of B's interest.[46] Secondly, he asserts that it is a scientifically established fact that the interests of all men, or at least the most basic or fundamental interests of all members of the same political orders, are identical. If X is in the interest of B it is also in the interest of all other members of B's political order.

Owing to his transformation of "interest" into a completely objective concept Hobbes is able, despite his acceptance of something very close to psychological egoism, to provide an internally valid and even persuasive argument for many of the demands that he thinks a proper political order must make of its subjects.[47] He is able to show that accepting these demands is in the interest of the subjects. But his theory also displays the weaknesses of arguments that rely entirely on appeals to self-interest, even true or objective self-interest.

We can best explore the strengths and weaknesses of the

46. This use of "interest" is one of its established uses in present-day English. If this was also the case in seventeenth-century English we should say that Hobbes restricts the concept to one of its uses, not that he transforms its use. On uses of "interest" see Flathman, op. cit., Chap. 2.

47. Hobbes sometimes writes as though he accepts the position that all human action is self-interested, that there is no such thing as altruistic or benevolent action. For example he says that "of the voluntary acts of every man, the object is *some good to himself*," *Leviathan*, Chap. 14, par. 8. In other places, however, he concedes that men sometimes act from altruistic or benevolent motives. For example in *Leviathan* he recognizes benevolence as a motive for action and accounts for it in non-egoistic terms. What Hobbes thinks is that most men act from self-interested motives most of the time and that a realistic political philosophy and a realistic political order must accept this fact and adapt to it. For an excellent discussion of Hobbes's alleged egoism and of egoism generally see Bernard Gert, "Hobbes and Psychological Egoism," *Journal of the History of Ideas* 286, No. 4 (October–December 1967).

theory by considering the case of the obligation to perform "dangerous and dishonourable offices." The case is crucial to Hobbes's argument because it goes to the heart of the main purpose of his theory of obligation, namely to provide a basis for accepting and justifying the obligations Hobbes thinks essential to a stable political order. If a stable political order requires that men sometimes execute dangerous and (aside from the justification the theory provides) dishonorable offices, and if Hobbes's theory of obligation cannot, consistent with his basic premises, provide a justification for the obligation to execute such offices, then the theory is inadequate by his own criteria. Since most of us would probably agree that a political order does sometimes require the execution of dangerous and otherwise dishonorable offices, the case is also crucial to our estimate of the helpfulness of Hobbes's answer to some of our problems. Conveniently this case is also well suited to discussion of metaethical questions of concern here.

Hobbes can make a plausible, even a strong, argument that it is in every man's interest that all men be under obligation to do those actions necessary to sustain the conditions or institutions from which each man benefits. The difficulty arises in applying this general argument so as to select particular men to do a potentially self-damaging or self-destructive act in particular circumstances. Each man's self-interest will be best served if other men are selected to do the act. Accordingly, Hobbes goes very far in allowing men to evade the more disagreeable burdens of the political order. Of military service, for example, he says:

> . . . a man that is commanded as a soldier to fight against the enemy, though his sovereign have right enough to punish his refusal with death, he may nevertheless in many cases refuse without injustice; as when he substituteth a sufficient soldier in his place: for in this case he deserteth not the service of the commonwealth. And there is allowance to be made for natural timorousness; not

only to women, of whom no such dangerous duty is expected, but also of men of feminine courage. When armies fight, there is on one side, or both, a running away; yet when they do it not out of treachery, but fear, they are not esteemed to do it unjustly, but dishonourably.[48]

But Hobbes's own analysis of the sources of conflict and disorder in human affairs forced him to recognize that there would be situations in which preserving the political order would require the services of men unwilling to provide them. It is at this point that his reliance upon appeal to self-interest is most severely strained. Following Hobbes's example, let us consider the case of recruiting men for military service, a dangerous office that many men will want to avoid.

Even here Hobbes's argument allows him to deal effectively with at least two of the familiar types of situations that develop as regards military service. The first is covered in the passage just quoted. If enough men are willing to fight to preserve the sovereignty, those who do not wish to do so can be excused or given some other duty. Their interest in maintaining the sovereignty will be served without their having to perform dangerous offices against their will. We should remember that this arrangement proved sufficient to meet the needs of western nation-states in Hobbes's day and for a considerable period afterwards. Some of its attractions are obvious, and it has been advocated with renewed vigor as large-scale conscription has become an established feature of some of the states of the twentieth century. It comes as no surprise that some of its leading advocates are men whose thought often follows paths trod by Hobbes.

48. *Leviathan*, Chap. 14, par. 6, p. 165. It is not to be thought that Hobbes approves of these men. They act "dishonourably" and out of "cowardice," not words of praise even in Hobbes's lexicon. But he cannot judge them guilty of "injustice" in the technical sense in which he uses it in his theory, namely violation of a contract or agreement. This is a striking example of Hobbes's insistence upon adapting his theory to the lowest common denominator in human nature—not because he admires the qualities he thinks he has discovered, but because sound political philosophy requires it.

But Hobbes foresaw that the type of nation-state for which he was arguing might not be able to make do with voluntary or mercenary armies. If preservation of the sovereignty required "at once the help of all that are able to bear arms, every one is obliged." [49] Given Hobbes's account of man, indeed almost any account of man, we can expect that some men will not voluntarily overcome their disinclination to perform this obligation and will have to be compelled. The case at hand, however, i.e., when the services of *all* men are required, is the second type of case which Hobbes can handle in a manner consistent with his reliance upon self-interest as he has interpreted it. If the sovereignty is really threatened, and if Hobbes is right in his assessment of the dire consequences of the dissolution of the sovereignty, the rationally self-interested man will fight to preserve the sovereignty.

The difficult case is where not all men are required but more are required than are willing to serve. Although each man has an interest in the preservation of the sovereignty, each man can hope that this interest will be served without his undergoing the risks of military service. If the sovereign nevertheless commands B to serve, B will regard doing so as contrary to his most fundamental interests. Pointing out that *his* service is not essential and hence that he cannot be interpreted to have covenanted to provide it, he will refuse to do so.

It might be argued that B's interest in the preservation of the sovereignty gives him an interest in the sovereign's recruiting sufficient men to protect it, that is in a recruitment *policy* that will meet the sovereign's needs. Whereas B might be tempted to think that the ideal arrangement would be one that excluded him (or the ideal argument one that justified his noncooperation), he must realize that such an arrangement, altered only to exclude C or D instead of B, would be ideal for all those who wished to be excluded. To adopt it for B would hardly solve the sovereign's problem. He would still have to compel others contrary to their objective interests and hence in a manner that

49. Ibid.

they could justly—in Hobbes's sense—resist. His need to use force or threats of force to obtain their services could weaken the sovereignty and hence damage B's most fundamental interests. Therefore B's interest in preserving the sovereignty gives him an interest in serving in situations of this kind.

The foregoing arguments overlook the possibility that B might understand them fully and yet calculate correctly that the sovereignty could be maintained despite his being excused or his refusal to cooperate. It is true that B's refusal to serve leaves the sovereign with the problem of conscripting C and D. And it is true that (assuming B to be relevantly similar to C and D) the sovereign can make no better case for conscripting C and D than for conscripting B. But B knows that *his* absence as such will not be decisive in the war. Given this knowledge, why should B, the calculating egoist, be disturbed if C and D are conscripted? Because they too will refuse to cooperate, this will weaken the sovereignty and hence damage B. Perhaps. But perhaps C and D will not know about B's case and will calculate that for them to refuse to serve would weaken the sovereignty contrary to their most fundamental interests. If so, the sovereign will get his soldiers, and both of B's interests will be served. *If* the evidence shows that B's noncooperation is having a seriously detrimental effect, that his service really is necessary, B will alter his conduct in the appropriate manner. (It should be made explicit that Hobbes's view cannot be saved by use of the [we are assuming] contrafactual conditional "question" "What if everybody did that?" If *in fact* everybody would refuse to serve, the general rule would hold and the parasite's position would be irrational. But if B has evidence to suggest that everybody will not, that evidence has to be rebutted by other evidence, not merely by reciting sloganary questions.)

Hobbes anticipates this objection and his answer is that the calculations required by B's contemplated parasitic conduct are too risky or dangerous to be thought rational: ". . . [W]hen a man doth a thing, which notwithstanding any thing can be forseen, and reckoned on, tendeth to his own destruction, howsoever some accident which he could not expect, arriving it may turn it to his benefit; yet such events do not make it reasonably or wisely done." [50] The force of Hobbes's argument here stems from the cogency of his version of Socrates' arguments (5) and (2), that is, his case that political society is essential to human well-being, and that obedience to the sovereign is essential to political society. If accepted, this argument establishes a presumption that actions contrary to the rule will produce an ill result. Having accepted the argument, B can rationally do X only if that presumption is rebutted by reliable evidence or persuasive considerations concerning the case at hand. But accepting a general argument or rule, however well-grounded it may be, does not settle the rational course of action in all cases that fall under that rule. Hobbes relies upon the strength of his general argument to carry him past the objection that it might not hold in particular cases in the future. But there might be cases in which the argument would not hold for the rational egoist.

It should be added that when we begin to think about parasitic conduct in modern societies we are reminded that from the standpoint of a rational egoist the argument for it extends to many matters other than military service. Almost all of us (revolutionaries and anarchists excepted perhaps) recognize that we have an interest in having taxes paid, laws obeyed, and votes cast in elections. But my interests as a rational egoist are best served if I cheat on my taxes without detection, disobey laws when unobserved, and fail to vote on rainy days, all in the confidence that sufficient people will discharge their obligations to maintain the cooperative practice and its benefits to me.

If the foregoing arguments are cogent there are likely to be cases in which parasitical conduct will be rational for the egoist, in which the parasite not only violates no obligation rule that is consistent with Hobbes's argument but in fact does what he must do, namely maximize the service of his own interest. To attack the parasite's position it would be necessary to go beyond

50. Ibid., Chap. 15, par. 5, p. 115.

arguments based purely on self-interest and appeal to concern for the welfare of other men or the society as such, to fairness, or to some other nonegoistic consideration as a basis for holding the individual obligated to sacrifice his personal interests. If we regard parasitical conduct as undesirable and wish to be able to present arguments to support our disapproval of it, we will regard the fact that Hobbes has deprived himself of such an appeal as a weakness in his theory.

This criticism, however, at least as we have stated it thus far, does not show that Hobbes's system cannot perform the task he assigns it. From a strictly Hobbesian point of view parasitical conduct of the type we have described is of little significance. It remains rational only so long as most men do not engage in it, so long as "What if everybody did that?" (or even "What if very many people did that?") can be dismissed with "They won't." This concedes that parasitical conduct is rational only so long as the political order—or whatever cooperative arrangement is involved—continues to meet the human needs that it is intended to meet. Even if Hobbes granted all that we have said, he could justly retort: "If my arguments provide a basis for achieving all of the human benefits of a stable and secure political order, is it rational to be disturbed by the possibility that a few men might be benefited more than others?" Within the framework of Hobbes's thought it would be difficult to answer affirmatively.

Secondly, even if deficient from certain perspectives, Hobbes's argument is impressive in its capacity to handle important types of cases. The argument shows that there is probably less distance and certainly less conflict between rational self-interest and morality than has sometimes been thought. Since it is desirable that men think it in their interest to do the actions necessary to maintain cooperative practices, this is an understanding of no small importance.[51] We should add that the type of case that

---

51. The last point is one of the main themes of a provocative book by Robert G. Olson, *The Morality of Self Interest* (New York: Harcourt, Brace and World, 1965).

is most difficult for Hobbes has proved to be very troubling for other theories as well.

If the first point can be used to defend Hobbes, it is also grist for the mill of the ethical formalist in his debate with utilitarianism. "If Hobbes's system leaves parasitical conduct beyond criticism, it may be admirable as an example of prudential calculation or instrumental rationality, but it has little to do with morality. What is more, it cannot deal with parasitical conduct because it is concerned exclusively with ends and ignores the importance of motives in morality."

It is true that concern with other-regarding motives plays an important part in the way most systems of morality deal with parasitical conduct. To this degree the formalist's criticisms of Hobbes are justified. But the centrality of ends and purposes in Hobbes's theory does not fully account for his inability to deal with the parasite. The difficulty traces at least in part to his unduly narrow conception of the ends worthy of concern. We can see the basic difficulty with Hobbes and one of the difficulties with formalist theories by carrying our discussion of conscription somewhat further.

Not all noncooperation is parasitical. Consider the case of civil disobedience—in a number of respects similar to parasitical conduct. The civil disobedient grants that he (and other men) benefit from an orderly society governed by law, and he claims that he would not disobey if it could be shown that his disobedience would make such a society impossible. He grants that his disobedience is defensible only when there is a general pattern of obedience—if not to the particular laws that he disobeys at least to law generally. Given Hobbes's theory, however, the only explanation for the civil disobedient's conduct that would be credible would be that he personally stood to gain by it. We noted earlier that Hobbes can be interpreted as a defender of a kind of civil disobedience, but that it is precisely on the ground of the self-interest of the disobedient that he condones it.

We do not want to say that the disobedient's action must be contrary to his personal interest in order to be acceptable. But the civil disobedient is distinguished from the parasite exactly by the fact that he thinks it important to be able to show that his conduct benefits the entire society or very large segments of it as well as himself. It is this fact that explains and (in our judgment) justifies our willingness to give a hearing to his claim that his conduct is acceptable. (It is also true, though very difficult to justify, that the disobedient's willingness to suffer personal deprivation and injury makes his position more attractive to society generally.) If a man claimed the right to engage in a damaging form of conduct in order to serve a purely personal interest his claim would properly be dismissed out of hand.[52]

But why exactly is the civil disobedient's conduct preferable to that of the parasite? The formalist answers that it is better, or that conventional morality judges it to be better, because the motive is better. It is better to act from the other-regarding motive of benefiting other men or society than from the self-regarding motive of benefiting oneself. This position is of course difficult to generalize; it is not the case that other-regarding motives are always preferable to self-regarding motives. Some kinds of self-regarding motives, for example selfishness, are, as a matter of convention, condemned. If we can describe a person's conduct as selfish we have thereby condemned it. The ordinary use of "selfish" is to condemn or criticize, and it can be used without condemning only if its ordinary force is explicitly avoided by showing that in the circumstances selfishness was not wrong.

But notice that a showing that a man's motive is bad is not always sufficient to condemn his conduct or the conduct he pro-

52. Sometimes other people must find general interests in claims that are expressed in purely self-interested terms. Indeed, in a politics such as ours in which blatant assertion of self-interest (or group interests) is a standard form of political behavior, this is a major task. And societies sometimes rightly decide that there is a general interest to be served despite considerable upset and inconvenience for society generally. Exempting conscientious objectors from military service might be justified in this way (or perhaps simply as an act of generosity).

poses. For example: a man seeks deferment from military service out of what we know to be purely selfish motives. But the man possesses unusual skills that are urgently needed by society and cannot be effectively used in the military. We condemn his selfish attitude but we grant the deferment. Or a man seeks deferment for altruistic reasons, say to continue to work, at great self-sacrifice, among indigents and derelicts, but we decide that the national interest requires that he do military service.

These examples show no more than that motive is not always decisive in our judgments of conduct or proposed forms of conduct. But if motive is not always decisive we require criteria to decide when it is and when it is not. And the search for such criteria prompts us to ask why motive is thought important and why some motives are approved and others disapproved, questions that we have little reason to ask in our day-to-day use of the vocabulary by which we assess particular motives. These questions have of course been answered in many ways: motives are known to be important and particular motives are known to be good or bad by intuition, by revelation from a divine being, by pure reason, by a study of the patterns of history, and in other ways. Without entering in detail into the merits of these alternatives, it is not implausible that motives have come to be thought important because they bring about conduct that affects other men, and that particular motives have come to be approved or disapproved according to the types of conduct they usually lead to and the effects that those types of conduct usually have on other men. (If it would be difficult to prove that motives have "come to be" evaluated in certain ways for these reasons, it is surely the case that they *are* important for these reasons.) The utilitarian moralist, in other words, can recognize and account for the importance of motives without giving up the essential features of his theory. Motives are important, but their importance is not independent of ends, purposes, and consequences.

The example of civil disobedience also indicates a part of the reason that the substance of Hobbes's teleological theory is inadequate. Insofar as rationally egoistic disobedience would benefit society *as* it benefits the individual, a Hobbist society could reap the benefits that might flow from disobedience. If, for example, a sovereign was considering what would almost certainly be a disastrous war, and if a number of men refused to do military service on self-interested grounds, their refusal might deter the sovereign from the war and thereby benefit society. Of course the more effective the sovereign is in bringing about effective punishment of disobedience the less rational disobedience would be and the less likely it would be that society would benefit from it. The modern totalitarian state, which is uniquely in need of disobedience, would be least likely to benefit from it. In general, to the degree that the benefits of disobedience depend upon genuinely altruistic or benevolent behavior, they are unavailable in Hobbes's system. If it is true that these motives are valued because experience has shown them to be the source of benefits to man, Hobbes's egoism is unsatisfactory. It is unsatisfactory less in its inability to condemn parasitical behavior than in its inability to account for an important aspect of the conceptual apparatus of morality and an important source of human benefits. There are acts that we would sometimes want to approve or praise that we could not approve or praise on Hobbes's theory. To the extent that justifying disobedience is an important part of a theory of political obligation, Hobbes's theory is unsatisfactory.

But this difficulty traces as much to Hobbes's narrow conception of the ends and purposes of political society as to his egoism. If Hobbes remained an egoist but broadened his conception of the purpose of political society beyond contributing to self-preservation (beyond the maintenance of peace and defense), the possibilities of the individual acting to benefit society—and hence in his own long-term interest—would be enlarged. Hobbes would still be unable to satisfy the strict formalist's criteria of a moral system, but he could achieve a larger number of the substantive benefits that action from other-regarding motives can make possible. Similarly, if Hobbes abandoned his egoism but retained his narrow conception of the ends of political society, the range of individual acts that would be thought to benefit other men would not enlarge substantially.

Now of course the egoism and the conception of the benefits to be hoped for from society are not unrelated. Hobbes's conception of the ends of political society was influenced by his understanding of what could and what could not be reasonably expected from men. And there is an appearance of compatibility between his psychology and an overweening concern with self-preservation, an appearance that Hobbes seeks to enhance by arguing that self-preservation is essential to all other rational objectives. But self-preservation is not essential to all other objectives. Self-destruction may itself be an objective and an entirely rational one—to mention only the most obvious objection. More important, concern with self-preservation is compatible with having other concerns as well. Because Hobbes reasoned from the extreme case of the war of all against all, in which concern with self-preservation must be constant and all but exclusive, he gives the impression that any diversion of energy to lesser objectives would necessarily endanger the one greatest objective. But it is the very sign of a society successful by Hobbes's own criteria that it has the problem of preservation sufficiently under control to allow attention to be given to more elevated matters. One could agree that self-preservation must, as a general rule, come first, without accepting the view that it exhausts the list of legitimate ends.

Hobbes's argument depends heavily on his view that the basic interests of all of the members of a political society are the same; if properly understood there is no conflict among them and what benefits or injures one benefits or injures all. His treatment of disobedience exemplifies this view. He would say that even if A were able to subject himself to the risk of punishment in order to benefit others, his sacrifice would stem from a mistaken understanding and would be in vain if not worse. His disobedience would benefit neither himself nor the other members of the political society. The basic interest of all members is peace and order, peace and order require a stable authority, and disobedience is destructive of a stable authority. A harms others as he harms himself.

We can readily agree that the interests of the members of a political society often coincide—and this is sometimes simply because they are members of the same society. Indeed Hobbes tends to underestimate the range and significance of the shared interests that develop when political and related arrangements are shared. Hence he fails to make the fullest possible use of appeal to self-interest as a means of inducing men to accept political obligations. It is nevertheless one of the obvious and elementary facts about politics that there is often conflict among interests, whether objectively or subjectively defined, and that in fact some interests are and probably will always have to be sacrificed to others. Much of the importance of political obligation lies in the fact that such situations arise. It is an equally obvious fact that it is sometimes possible for one man to benefit others by sacrificing himself or his interests. The premise of an identity of basic interests may solve some of the problems of theory of obligation grounded exclusively in self-interest, but it will do so only at the price of creating an enormous gulf between the theory and elementary aspects of politics.

It would be ridiculous to suggest that Hobbes was unaware of the existence of diversity and conflict of interest in human affairs. He wanted to show that when properly understood the most basic interests can be seen to be compatible if not identical and that identity of basic interests provides a basis on which to resolve more superficial differences. But there are two aspects of his theory in which he admits, if only tacitly, that there are and will continue to be genuine and deep-going conflicts that must be dealt with.

The first is his treatment of cases in which it *is* right to disobey and resist authoritative commands. This right is necessary in Hobbes's theory only on the assumption that there can be conflicts between the most basic interest or need of one individual, self-preservation, and the basic interest or need of the members of political society qua members, the maintenance of an authority structure that can preserve peace and order. Hobbes says that the individual can not only disobey but resist if his life is threatened. In this respect he seems willing to sacrifice community interest to the interest of the individual. But he also says that the individual's right to disobey and resist holds only as long as resistance is certain to be unsuccessful. In this respect he seems willing to sacrifice the individual to the community. In fact his theory does not deal very satisfactorily with either the individual or the community. At most the individual has the right to commit a last desperate act, to inflict minor and probably gratuitous damage on those acting for the community that is putting him to death. The community is given the right to put the individual to death, but its task will be dangerous and costly because the individual will be emboldened by the view that it is proper for him to resist. What is more, the community is denied the comfort of thinking that in putting down the resistance it is putting down injustice or some other improper conduct.

The second is an extension of the first to situations in which the individual's life is not directly threatened. Hobbes knows about taxation, punishment, and other practices in which the community demands that individual interests be subordinated if not sacrificed. He believes that this is necessary and he supports it, thereby seeming to support the sacrifice of individual interest. But his position is that, short of threats to life itself, the individual's true or real interests are always served by obeying the command of the state.

Part of the problem here is whether it is helpful to say that the individual's *interests* are always served by such policies or at least by obeying the commands connected with them. Hobbes seems to sense that it is not helpful to say that it is in a man's interest to swing from the gallows or to be decapitated in a muddy trench in a distant land. But is it any more helpful to say that it is in a man's interest to be taxed at ninety percent, to have the home which has been his life's work destroyed to build a highway or an airport, or to be jailed for a lengthy period because he has been detected in an attempt to obtain a profitable monopoly? Of course it may be in his interest that *policies* of capital punishment for certain crimes, conscription for military service, high income tax on high incomes, etc., be adopted by his government. But it will often be in his interest to avoid having these policies applied to him—which is presumably one of the factors that produces disinclination to accept such policies and unwillingness to obey the commands that are connected with them.

If we understand Hobbes's use of "interest" the linguistic question per se is perhaps of little importance. But the linguistic difficulty is symptomatic of the deeper difficulty that runs through his theory of obedience and disobedience. Owing to his psychology, it is *impossible* for Hobbes to appeal to anything other than self-interest as a ground or as a motive for political conduct on the part of any substantial number of people. This is part of the reason why his treatment of disobedience and resistance is unsatisfactory. A cannot justify the pain, possibly even death that he might cause when he resists the hangman in terms of any good or benefit that it produces for anyone else. He could not, for example, claim that his resistance would be justified because it would dramatize the evil of capital punishment or the horror and cruelty of the mode of execution in question, or because it would call attention to his innocence and lead to improvements in judicial procedure. He can act only to satisfy his own interests, and his own interests will no longer be engaged in these matters. If he injures or kills the warden or the guards the most he can say in his defense is that he has obtained psychological or other personal satisfaction from his action. Genuine concern for other men qua other men is impossible for him. But we want to say, I want to say, that personal satisfaction is not an adequate reason for causing upset, injury, and death. However much we may understand and even sympathize with the action, it cannot be approved. And of course the same point applies to disobedience in less dramatic circumstances. A man with Hobbes's psychology but with a less circumscribed view of the ends of political society than Hobbes might encourage a wider range of disobedience than Hobbes would condone; but he could not provide an acceptable justification for it.

Neither could he provide a satisfactory justification for holding men obligated to obey when they are, rationally or not, disinclined to do so. Since the laws and commands do not come from God, they are made by men for whom self-interest must be assumed to be the motive of action. Of course the fact that the law is made by A to serve A's interests does not necessarily prove that it is contrary to B's interests or that it would be contrary to B's interest to obey it. But if B thinks that it is contrary to his interest to obey, it is A's duty as sovereign to hold B obligated to obey and to try to induce him to discharge that obligation. Since A can only act to serve his own interest, the only accurate explanation he can give for holding B obligated and for his use of various inducements is that doing so serves his (A's) interests. But B can hardly be expected to regard this explanation as a justification. Why should A's interests be preferred to B's? Unless B has accepted Hobbes's suggestion that it is *always* in B's interests to obey A (save when A commands B to give up his life), he will properly regard the obligation and the compulsion as an attempt to impose A's interests on him. If A succeeds in compelling B to obey, both B and A will properly regard the event, can only regard the event, as a victory of A over B.

In short, in Hobbes's theory the only principle out of which a believable justification could be constructed is the principle of self-interest. But this principle can serve as a justification for acts that affect other men only where all of the interests that are affected by the action are either identical or compatible. When conflicts of interest develop, use of interest as "justification" leaves nothing further to which to appeal—save, of course, force. In this respect the leviathan Hobbes sought to raise, and every theory that relies on this principle, is built ultimately on force, not on obligation. It is relevant to the theory of political obligation primarily in that it shows us some of the missteps which such a theory must avoid. Assuming that Crito's arguments were based on this principle, Socrates did well to treat them as he did.

III. SUMMARY AND CONCLUDING REMARKS

THE STRUCTURE of Socrates' argument is as follows: The practice of political obligation is an integral and important part of the State or political society, of the form of human association that, if well ordered, enables men to work towards higher forms of human life. The utility of the practice results from the fact that it is an integral and important part of the State, and the argument for accepting the rules of which the practice consists is grounded in the value of the State and the importance of the practice in the workings of the State. The State is valuable only if or insofar as it is well ordered. Accordingly Socrates considers a number of criteria by which to judge whether any particular State is well ordered, including criteria by which to judge that aspect of the State that we have called the practice of political obligation. He does not claim to have identified all of the relevant criteria and he does not rank the criteria he does discuss. But his judgment of and conduct vis-à-vis Athens shows that he thought that States satisfying those criteria are of sufficient value to man to warrant substantial sacrifices to sustain and otherwise contribute to them. In such States the argument for accepting the practice of political obligation is validated. Obedience to the law and authoritative commands is a form of support for the State, and hence there are reasons for obedience, including obedience to laws and orders that are seriously objectionable. But obedience can sometimes harm the State and disobedience can contribute to it. Thus there is no generally conclusive inference from the ground and the validating conditions to the obligation to obey or disobey any particular law or order in any particular circumstance. The ground and validating conditions supply considerations relevant to this judgment; a man who is not aware of them and who has not reflected concerning them is in a poor position to make the practical judgments that particular laws and particular circumstances require of him. We have amended and added to Socrates' argument on various points, but we have tried to suggest respects in which it is superior to the prominent alternatives both as a guide to thinking about the practice of political obligation and to the questions of conduct that arise within that practice. In the hope of integrating this judgment with our larger analysis of political obligation we will now conclude with a more general comparison of the theories of Socrates and Hobbes.

One of the most pronounced features of Hobbes's theory is his insistence that the problem of political obligation is the problem of every man, and that an adequate theory of political obligation must take account of and must be adapted to the conditions and the needs of every man. Hobbes knows that some men are more intelligent, more virtuous, and more proud than others, and he knows that these differences affect the way men perceive and think about politics and the way they act politically. Casting diverse men into a single political society does not do away with these differences. It does make the men involved dependent on one another and on shared conditions and arrangements, and hence it does put them all on the same ground in important respects. This means that certain benefits might become available to all—benefits that Hobbes judges to be of the greatest possible value. But shared arrangements impose heavy demands as well as confer great benefits, and the benefits continue to be available only as long as the demands are met. Because men differ from one another they respond differently to demands, even to identical demands, and the diversity in response complicates the workings of the shared arrangements and threatens the loss of the shared benefits. Hence a diversity of men and of conduct constitutes a problem that a political society must resolve or at least bring under control. In part for these reasons Hobbes thinks that States should institute uniform obligation rules for all of their members. Since "obligation" implies ability, uniformity of rules can be achieved only by adapting the rules to a common denominator of politically relevant capacities and by demanding that men above that level as it were "live down" to it. This will be distasteful for some—which is a part of the reason that the "superior man" often has difficulty in adapting to life in political society—but it is not impossible. Because it is necessary to political society, and because political society is essential to man, political society is justified in making the demand. Because the superior man benefits enormously from political society, it is in his interest to submit to the demand despite his distaste for it.[53]

The practice of most modern western nation-states corresponds substantially to Hobbes's views. There are obligation rules that apply to all citizens. Men who stand apart from and question what are thought to be the basic obligation rules are often viewed, as Hobbes viewed them, with suspicion and even hostility. This is scarcely surprising. If obligation rules must be widely accepted to be effective and if acceptance means that they are thought to delineate right and wrong in fundamental matters, we would expect strong support for the rules. In this respect Hobbes's theory helps us to understand salient aspects of political practice.

Socrates knew about uniform obligation rules and he did not doubt that they should be obeyed in well-ordered States. But whereas Hobbes thought that all members of the State should commit themselves to strict obedience in all but a very special class of cases, Socrates thought that at least some men—certainly philosophers such as himself and perhaps all those not "indifferent to reason"—should adopt a more critical stance.

53. On Hobbes's analysis superior men can be said to benefit most from political society despite the restrictions it places upon them. Political society provides the conditions under which men can effectively use their abilities to satisfy their passions. The superior man has the most ability and hence benefits most from conditions under which abilities can be put to effective use.

Had Socrates taken the attitude toward the rule "Obey the law" that Hobbes urges (and that Socrates probably thought appropriate for the bulk of the members of Athens), it would have been impossible for him to have taken the position that he would not give up philosophy if the law commanded him to do so.[54] Had he given up philosophy, he could not have done that service for the State that he believed to be his unique calling, the service of subjecting the laws and other features of the State to constant critical scrutiny. And if that service was not performed the State might survive as a human institution (as Thessaly had survived) but it would not aid its members in achieving that "higher form of life" of which they are capable.

One way to describe the differences between Hobbes and Socrates would be to say that only the latter hoped to combine a morality of obligation with a morality of ideals and aspirations. The morality of obligation provides or contributes to stability and order, the morality of ideals and aspirations directs the State toward higher achievements.

There is a good deal to be said for this way of characterizing the differences between the two theorists. Hobbes was so insistent that peace and order are the main ends of political society, and he was so conscious of the multitudinous threats to peace and order, that he was prepared to sacrifice almost everything else to them. He would have been profoundly suspicious of the notion that there is a group of men, however small, that is justified in adopting a special set of attitudes toward the obligation rules or that has a special responsibility to evaluate those rules critically. He would fear that Socrates' position would diminish the supremacy of the sovereign and would threaten to reduce the uniformity of the obligation rules. Thus we find not the slightest hint of sympathy for the Socratic position in Hobbes's theory of obligation.

It would be a mistake to suggest that Hobbes was entirely

54. Consider Hobbes's remark, perhaps made with Socrates in mind, that "disobedience may lawfully be punished in them, that against the laws teach even true philosophy," *Leviathan*, Chap. 46, last par.

unaware of the differences between obligation and ideals or entirely indifferent to the latter. Perhaps he thought that politics was not the proper realm for the expression of the differences among men and not the arena in which ideals should be pursued. But in the sort of society Hobbes had in mind, achieving peace and order would be the fundamental problem, and it would be difficult to solve because the threats to peace and order would be various and difficult to combat. In such a society there would be a great deal to be said for the view that basic political obligations should be as uniform and as stable as possible, and that all members should commit themselves to strict conformity to them. The problem would not be avoiding a condition of stasis, but achieving some modicum of stability.

Hobbes seems to have had very little hope that societies, even societies founded on his principles, would settle down to the point that peace and order would no longer be a continuously urgent and pressing problem. Given his lack of attention to decentralized social process and historical development, it would have been difficult for him to have entertained such a hope. In societies that have brought the problem of order under considerable control the case for Hobbes's position is weaker. A body of obligation rules develops that is widely accepted and generally acted upon as a matter of course. These rules are deeply ingrained in the life of the society, in its language, in its moral, legal, religious, and other beliefs, arrangements, and practices. These beliefs, arrangements, etc., can be questioned, criticized, and defended in particular contexts, and over time they can undergo significant alterations. But it is impossible to change, criticize, or even to evaluate them all at one time. In criticizing a legal rule we typically make use of, and hence hold constant, moral rules and principles. New legal or political arrangements develop and when they have become established they provide a stable point against the backdrop of which attitudes toward moral rules and beliefs can be discussed and altered. (An example would be changes in attitudes regarding the moral obligations of the now adult children to their parents. At a time when many people were unable to care for their aged parents effectively, there developed strong agitation for the state to initiate programs of old-age assistance. This was a case of evaluation and criticism of political and legal practice on the basis of a widely accepted moral rule. When old-age assistance programs had developed to a reasonably effective level, the context of the moral rule that one should care for his parents was altered. In the new context it became possible to think it unnecessary to care for one's parents [or to plan to do so when the time came] because the government would do so. It is plausible to think that this is one reason that the moral rule has been noticeably weakened in recent generations.) More important perhaps, thought and discourse concerning these rules are carried on in the language shared by the members of the society. This language is overwhelmingly a product of the past, a result of the attempt of men to think and communicate about their mode of life and the problems it has cast up for them. Hence the language reflects, indeed incorporates, in a myriad of subtle ways, the rules that obtained in the mode of life (or succession of modes of life) out of which it emerged. In using language to evaluate, defend, criticize, and change particular arrangements, we use a vehicle that must itself be marked by great constancy if we are to communicate through it. In such a society the collapse into disorder that Hobbes feared, while by no means impossible, is unlikely. Or rather, it is more likely to result from a lack of critical discussion of arrangements and rules than from an excess of the latter.

Socrates suggests that in such a society (which, without specifying its features systematically, he clearly has in mind) the most desirable state of affairs is one in which the obligation rules are accepted and the acceptance is supported by good reasons. There will be good arguments for conforming to the rules, many citizens will be aware of those arguments, and they will be able to perceive and communicate about situations in which those arguments are not convincing and in which criticism, disobedience, and perhaps even resistance might be justified. Or better, the citizens will be able to perceive that such situations are likely to develop if certain policies are adopted or certain laws passed, and they will act to halt the development. Criticism and critical reflection will contribute to peace and order rather than endanger them. (And of course critical reflection is a good in itself for Socrates.)

Thus Socrates' understanding of obligations and ideals in a well-ordered State is quite different from that which we have attributed to Hobbes.[55] He lays great stress on the importance of obligation rules and of not disobeying them in the absence of a powerful justification for doing so. Indeed he goes beyond Hobbes in this respect in that he is willing to lay down his life rather than disobey when he thinks it is not justified. Moreover he agrees with Hobbes in thinking that there are likely to be large numbers of citizens in any political society who should commit themselves to strict obedience to those rules. But this is because these citizens are not capable of critical thought about the rules and their relationship to the objectives of the society, not because he thinks that critical thought, including critical

---

55. For his use of the distinction see especially the *Phaedo* where Socrates develops an elaborate "tale" concerning the fate that is in store, after death, for people who have, respectively (1) done surpassing evil, (2) committed lesser crimes, (3) "cultivated the goodness of the ordinary citizen . . . which is acquired by habit and practice, without the help of philosophy and reason," and (4) "lived a life of surpassing holiness" and "purified themselves . . . by philosophy." The first are "hurled . . . into Tartarus, from whence they emerge no more" (*Phaedo*, 113b–114a, pp. 177–78); the second undergo a painful but limited period of purification (Ibid.); the third "will probably pass into some other kind of social and disciplined creatures like bees, wasps, and ants; or even back into the human race again, becoming decent citizens," (*Phaedo*, 82b–e, pp. 134–35); and the fourth pass upward "to their pure abode," to "habitations even more beautiful" than those in group three (*Phaedo*, 114b–d, p. 178). In the terms we have used, those in group (1) have violated the most fundamental obligation rules. The members of group (2) may have broken lesser laws or failed to keep promises when there was no adequate justification for doing so but when no serious harm resulted. Group (3) consists perhaps of loyal followers of Hobbes, living their lives in quiet obedience to the laws and other obligation rules of their societies, that is according to the canons of the morality of obligation. Group (4) clearly consists of those who transcend obligation and not only aspire to but in some measure achieve the highest ideals.

thought that sometimes leads to disobedience, is inappropriate or damaging.[56] If the objectives of the State are defensible and if the rules are good rules such that obeying them in fact contributes to achieving those objectives, then critical thought will strengthen commitment to them.[57] If they are not good rules in at least this sense the very purposes that led Hobbes to urge strict obedience in fact counsel criticism and sometimes disobedience. In this respect, while accepting a distinction between obligation and ideals, Socrates does not accept the view that critical reflection and deliberation is appropriate only in the realm of the latter. He also insists on a further connection between the two, namely that achieving the fundamental but minimal objectives served directly by obligation rules is not a sufficient reason for obeying them; they must be such that obeying them will also facilitate, if only indirectly, working toward the higher objectives that are the characteristics of the well-ordered State. If the obligation rules are such that maintaining peace and order renders the pursuit of higher ideals impossible, then the case for obeying them loses its force. It follows that the obligation rules must be scrutinized not only in terms of whether obeying them contributes to the objectives peculiar to them, but also in terms of the consequences of doing so for the possibility of pursuing the higher ideals of the State.

Throughout this essay we have tried to show that the practice of political obligation (as distinct from various other phenom-

56. Thus the limitation is entirely dependent upon the contingent fact of the number of men who lack the capacity or the willingness to engage in critical reflection. Since it is a contingent fact it can be changed and it is possible to work to change it. Thus if critical scrutiny of obligation rules is not only appropriate but desirable, every effort should be made to develop and encourage the use of the capacity to engage in this activity. The most objectionable feature of Socrates' stance in the *Crito*, to say nothing of Plato's stance in the *Republic*, is that he accepts as a largely unchangeable given what he takes to be the fact that the great bulk of the Athenian citizenry are incapable of and indifferent to such activity and hence have to be gulled into obedience.

57. Socrates' critical examination of the rule "Judgments once pronounced must be binding" leads him to accept it and obey at great cost to himself; Crito and many other Athenians who had not thought critically about the rule urged him to disobey it.

ena with which it has been confused) is such that it is not only possible but appropriate to think about it as Socrates does. If it was not this way, and/or to the extent that it is corrupted into something else in any regime at any point in time, it would nevertheless be appropriate to use Socrates' way of thinking as a basis for criticizing and changing whatever practice or arrangement in fact obtained. It is because Socrates understands political obligation as he does that he is an excellent guide to thinking about it. It is because it is appropriate to think about the practice as Socrates does that it is a valuable part of the human condition.

Bibliography of Works Cited

Gabriel Almond and Sidney Verba, *The Civic Culture* (Boston: Little, Brown and Co., 1965).

G. E. M. Anscombe, *Intention*, 2nd Edition (Oxford: Basil Blackwell, 1963).

Aristotle, *Politics*, Ernest Barker, ed. and trans. (London: Oxford University Press, 1958).

Jane Austen, *Pride and Prejudice* (New York: The Pocket Library, 1940).

J. Austin, *The Province of Jurisprudence Determined, etc.* (London: Weidenfeld and Nicolson, 1954).

J. L. Austin, *Philosophical Papers*, J. O. Urmson and G. J. Warnock, eds. (London: Oxford University Press, 1961).

J. L. Austin, *Sense and Sensibilia*, G. J. Warnock, ed. (London: Oxford University Press, 1962).

Kurt Baier, *The Moral Point of View* (Ithaca: Cornell University Press, 1958).

Michael D. Bayles, ed., *Contemporary Utilitarianism* (Garden City: Doubleday and Company, 1968).

Hugo Bedau, ed., *Civil Disobedience* (New York: Pegasus, 1969).

Hugo Bedau, "On Civil Disobedience," *The Journal of Philosophy*, Vol. 58 (1961), pp. 653 ff.

Henri Bergson, *The Two Sources of Morality and Religion,* R. Ashley and Audrey and Cloudesley Brereton, trans., with assistance of W. H. Carter (Garden City: Doubleday and Company, 1935).

Max Black, *Models and Metaphors* (Ithaca: Cornell University Press, 1962).

Max Black, ed., *Philosophical Analysis* (Englewood Cliffs: Prentice-Hall, 1963).

Peter Blau, *Exchange and Power in Social Life* (New York: John Wiley and Sons, 1964).

Richard Brandt, "The Concepts of Obligation and Duty," *Mind,* Vol. 73 (1964), pp. 374–93.

David Braybrooke, ed., *Philosophical Problems of the Social Sciences* (New York: The Macmillan Company, 1955).

Keith Brown, ed., *Hobbes Studies* (Oxford: Basil Blackwell, 1965).

Norman S. Care and Charles Landesman, eds., *Readings in the Theory of Action* (Bloomington, Indiana: Indiana University Press, 1968).

V. C. Chappell, ed., *Ordinary Language* (Englewood Cliffs: Prentice-Hall, 1964).

Emile Durkheim, *Suicide,* George Simpson, ed., John A. Spaulding and George Simpson trans. (Glencoe, Ill.: The Free Press, 1951).

Richard Flathman, *The Public Interest* (New York: John Wiley, 1966).

J. A. Fodor and J. J. Katz, eds., *The Structure of Language* (Englewood Cliffs: Prentice-Hall, 1964).

Philippa Foot, "Goodness and Choice," *Proceedings of the Aristotelian Society* Supplementary, Vol. XXXV (1961).

Philippa Foot, "Moral Arguments," *Mind,* Vol. LXVII (1958), pp. 502–13.

Philippa Foot, "Moral Beliefs," *Proceedings of the Aristotelian Society,* Vol. 59 (1958–59), pp. 83–104.

Harrop A. Freeman et. al., *Civil Disobedience* (Santa Barbara: Center for the Study of Democratic Institutions, 1966).

Lon Fuller, *The Morality of Law* (New Haven: Yale University Press, 1964).

David Gauthier, *Practical Reasoning* (London: Oxford University Press, 1963).

Bernard Gert, "Hobbes and Psychological Egoism," *Journal of the History of Ideas,* Vol. 28 (1967), pp. 503–20.

M. Gandhi, *Non-Violent Resistance,* B. Kumarappa, ed. (New York: Schocken Books, 1961).

Robert A. Goldwin, ed., *On Civil Disobedience: Essays Old and New* (Chicago: Rand McNally, 1969).

Stuart Hampshire, *Thought and Action* (New York: The Viking Press, 1960).

R. M. Hare, "Descriptivism," *Proceedings of the British Academy*, Vol. XLIX (1963).

R. M. Hare, *Freedom and Reason* (London: Oxford University Press, 1963).

R. M. Hare, "The Lawful Government," in Peter Laslett and W. G. Runciman, eds. *Philosophy, Politics and Society*, 3rd Series (Oxford: Basil Blackwell, 1967).

H. L. A. Hart, "The Ascription of Responsibility and Rights," in A. G. N. Flew, ed., *Logic and Language*, 1st Series (Oxford: Basil Blackwell, 1963).

H. L. A. Hart, *The Concept of Law* (London: Oxford University Press, 1961).

H. L. A. Hart, "Are There Any Natural Rights," *Philosophical Review*, Vol. 64 (1955), pp. 175–91.

Thomas Hobbes, *Leviathan*, Michael Oakeshott, ed., Intro. by Richard S. Peters (New York: Collier Books, 1962).

David Hume, *Essays: Moral, Political, and Literary* (London: Oxford University Press, 1963).

David Hume, *Treatise of Human Nature* (London: Oxford University Press, 1888).

Norman Jacobson, *Law Enforcement and Racial and Cultural Tensions* (Berkeley: University of California Press, 1964).

Bertrand de Jouvenel, "On the Nature of Political Science," *The American Political Science Review*, Vol. LV (1961), pp. 773 ff.

Bertrand de Jouvenel, *Sovereignty*, J. F. Huntington, trans. (Chicago: University of Chicago Press, 1957).

Donald B. King and Charles W. Quick, eds., *Legal Aspects of the Civil Rights Movement* (Detroit: Wayne State University Press, 1965).

Martin Luther King, Jr., *Why We Can't Wait* (New York: Signet, 1964).

Julius Kovesi, *Moral Notions* (London: Routledge and Kegan Paul, 1967).

Irving Kristol and Robert Penn Warren, "On Civil Disobedience," *Yale Review*, Vol. 50 (1959), pp. 470 ff.

Morris I. Liebman, "Civil Disobedience—A Threat to Our Law Society," *American Law Quarterly*, Vol. 3 (1964), pp. 21 ff.

Lord Lindsay, *The Two Moralities* (London: Eyre and Spottiswoode, 1948).

A. R. Louch, *Explanation and Human Action* (Oxford: Basil Blackwell, 1966).

David Lyons, *Forms and Limits of Utilitarianism* (London: Oxford University Press, 1965).

Alasdair MacIntyre, "The Idea of a Social Science," *Proceedings of the Aristotelian Society*, Supplementary, Vol. XLI (1967).

Nancy McMillin, *Reconversion and Political Obligation Theory in Guinea and Senegal*, Masters Thesis, The University of Chicago, 1967.

Norman Malcolm, *Dreaming* (London: Routledge and Kegan Paul, 1958).

Marcell Mauss, *The Gift*, Ian Cunnison, trans. (Glencoe, Illinois: The Free Press, 1954).

A. I. Melden, ed., *Essays in Moral Philosophy* (Seattle: University of Washington Press, 1958).

T. R. Mischel, ed., *Human Action* (New York: Academic Press, 1969).

Franz Neumann, *The Democratic and the Authoritarian State* (Glencoe, Illinois: The Free Press, 1957).

P. H. Nowell-Smith, *Ethics* (Baltimore: Penguin Books, 1954).

Robert G. Olson, *The Morality of Self-Interest* (New York: Harcourt, Brace, and World, 1965).

Felix Oppenheim, *Dimensions of Freedom* (New York: St. Martin's Press, 1961).

J. R. Pennock and J. C. Chapman, eds., *Political and Legal Obligation* (New York: Atherton Press, 1970).

R. S. Peters, ed., *Thomas Hobbes, Body, Man, and Citizen* (New York: Collier Books, 1962).

R. S. Peters, ed., *The Concept of Education* (London: Routledge and Kegan Paul, 1967).

R. S. Peters, *The Concept of Motivation* (London: Routledge and Kegan Paul, 1964).

J. P. Plamenatz, *Consent, Freedom, and Political Obligation*, 2nd Edition (London: Oxford University Press, 1968).

Plato, *The Last Days of Socrates*, Hugh Tredennick, ed. and trans. (Baltimore: Penguin Books, 1959).

Hanna Pitkin, "Obligation and Consent—I," *American Political Science Review*, Vol. 59 (1965), pp. 990–99.

Hanna Pitkin, "Obligation and Consent—II," *American Political Science Review*, Vol. 60 (1966), pp. 39–52.

H. A. Prichard, *Moral Obligation* (London: Oxford University Press, 1949).

Lucian Pye and Sidney Verba, eds., *Political Culture and Political*

Development (Princeton, New Jersey: Princeton University Press, 1965).

Race Relations, Statement adopted by the Biennial Convention of the Lutheran Church in America, 1964. No date or place of publication.

John Rawls, "Legal Obligation and the Duty of Fair Play," in Sidney Hook, ed., *Law and Philosophy* (New York: New York University Press, 1964).

John Rawls, "The Sense of Justice," *Philosophical Review*, Vol. 72 (1963), pp. 281–305.

John Rawls, "Two Concepts of Rules," *Philosophical Review*, Vol. 64 (1955), pp. 1 ff.

Richard Rorty, ed., *The Linguistic Turn* (Princeton, New Jersey: Princeton University Press, 1967).

Jean Jacques Rousseau, *The Social Contract*. G. D. H. Cole, trans. (New York: E. P. Dutton and Co., 1950).

Bertrand Russell, "Civil Disobedience," *New Statesman*, Vol. 61 (1956), pp. 245 ff.

John Searle, "How to Derive 'Ought' from 'Is'," *Philosophical Review*, Vol. 73 (1964), pp. 43 ff.

John Searle, *Speach Acts* (Cambridge: Cambridge University Press, 1965).

Alexander Sesonske, *Value and Obligation* (New York: Oxford University Press, 1964).

John R. Silber, "Being and Doing," *The University of Chicago Law Review*, Vol. 35 (1967), pp. 47–91.

B. F. Skinner, *Science and Human Behavior* (New York: The Macmillan Co., 1953).

Peter Strawson, *Introduction to Logical Theory* (London: Methuen and Co., 1952).

Charles Taylor, *The Explanation of Behaviour* (London: Routledge and Kegan Paul, 1964).

Joseph Tussman, *Obligation and the Body Politic* (New York: Oxford University Press, 1960).

Lewis H. Van Dusen, Jr., "Civil Disobedience: Destroyer of Democracy," *American Bar Association Journal*, Vol. 55 (1969), pp. 123 ff.

Friedrich Waismann, *The Principles of Linguistic Philosophy* (London: Macmillan and Co., 1965).

Michael Walzer, *The Revolution of the Saints* (Cambridge: Harvard University Press, 1965).

Howard Warrender, *The Political Philosophy of Hobbes* (London: Oxford University Press, 1957).

Richard Wasserstrom, "The Obligation to Obey the Law," *University of California at Los Angeles Law Review*, Vol. 10 (1963), pp. 780–807.

Carlo Weber, "The Birth Control Controversy," *The New Republic*, Nov. 23, 1968.

A. R. White, ed., *The Philosophy of Action* (London: Oxford University Press, 1969).

Charles E. Whittaker and William Sloane Coffin, Jr., *Law, Order, and Civil Disobedience* (Washington: American Enterprise Institute for Public Policy Research, 1967).

Peter Winch, *The Idea of a Social Science* (London: Routledge and Kegan Paul, 1958).

Ludwig Wittgenstein, *The Blue and Brown Books* (Oxford: Basil Blackwell, 1960).

Ludwig Wittgenstein, *Philosophical Investigations*, G. E. M. Anscombe, trans. (London: The Macmillan Co., 1958).

Sheldon S. Wolin, *Politics and Vision* (Boston: Little, Brown, 1960).

Index

Richard E. Flathman

Richard E. Flathman is a Professor in the Department of Political Science at The College of the University of Chicago. Trained in political science and particularly the tradition of political philosophy, he has been interested in, and influenced by, developments in contemporary Anglo-American philosophy. He is one of a growing number of persons who address questions and issues traditionally of concern to both political science and philosophy, and who draw upon and attempt to develop ideas and approaches prominent in each. Professor Flathman previously taught political science and humanities at Reed College. He has enjoyed two years of study in England, and recently returned from a year in Paris, where he read contemporary French philosophy and political theory and began work on a study of the concept of rights.